English in Malaysia

Brill's Studies in Language, Cognition and Culture

Series Editors

Alexandra Y. Aikhenvald (*Cairns Institute, James Cook University*)
R. M. W. Dixon (*Cairns Institute, James Cook University*)
N. J. Enfield (*University of Sydney*)

VOLUME 14

The titles published in this series are listed at *brill.com/bslc*

English in Malaysia

Current Use and Status

Edited by

Toshiko Yamaguchi
David Deterding

BRILL

LEIDEN | BOSTON

Library of Congress Cataloging-in-Publication Data

Names: Yamaguchi, Toshiko. | Deterding, David.
Title: English in Malaysia : current use and status / edited by Toshiko
 Yamaguchi ; David Deterding.
Description: Leiden ; Boston : Brill, [2016] | Series: Brill's Studies in language, cognition and culture,
 14 | Includes bibliographical references and index.
Identifiers: LCCN 2016003770 (print) | LCCN 2016012257 (ebook) | ISBN 9789004314290 (hardback :
 alk. paper) | ISBN 9789004314306 (e-book) | ISBN 9789004314306 (E-book)
Subjects: LCSH: English language—Malaysia. | English language—Malaysia—History. | Malaysia—Language.
Classification: LCC PE3502.M3 E543 2016 (print) | LCC PE3502.M3 (ebook) | DDC 306.442/2109595—dc23
LC record available at http://lccn.loc.gov/2016003770

Want or need Open Access? Brill Open offers you the choice to make your research freely accessible online in exchange for a publication charge. Review your various options on brill.com/brill-open.

Typeface for the Latin, Greek, and Cyrillic scripts: "Brill". See and download: brill.com/brill-typeface.

ISSN 1879-5412
ISBN 978-90-04-31429-0 (hardback)
ISBN 978-90-04-31430-6 (e-book)

Copyright 2016 by Koninklijke Brill NV, Leiden, The Netherlands.
Koninklijke Brill NV incorporates the imprints Brill, Brill Hes & De Graaf, Brill Nijhoff, Brill Rodopi and Hotei Publishing.
All rights reserved. No part of this publication may be reproduced, translated, stored in a retrieval system, or transmitted in any form or by any means, electronic, mechanical, photocopying, recording or otherwise, without prior written permission from the publisher.
Authorization to photocopy items for internal or personal use is granted by Koninklijke Brill NV provided that the appropriate fees are paid directly to The Copyright Clearance Center, 222 Rosewood Drive, Suite 910, Danvers, MA 01923, USA. Fees are subject to change.

This book is printed on acid-free paper and produced in a sustainable manner.

Contents

Abbreviations VII
Preface IX

Introduction

1 English in Malaysia: Background, Status and Use 3
   Toshiko Yamaguchi and David Deterding

Linguistic Features

2 Malaysian English: Evidence of Contact with Classifier Languages 25
   Siew Imm Tan

3 The New [t] in Malaysian English 45
   Toshiko Yamaguchi and Magnús Pétursson

4 How do We Stress? Lexical Stress in Malaysian and British English 65
   Rachel Siew Kuang Tan

Language Attitudes

5 Attitudes towards Malay, English and Chinese among Malaysian Students: A Matched Guise Test 89
   Paolo Coluzzi

6 English for the Indigenous People of Sarawak: Focus on the Bidayuhs 102
   Patricia Nora Riget and Xiaomei Wang

Malaysian English Online

7 English and Other Languages in the Online Discourse of East Malaysians 125
   James McLellan

Malaysian English and Language Policies

8   Literacy Practices in English in Malaysian Educational Settings   147
    Ambigapathy Pandian

9   Impact of the English Language on University Policy in Malaysia and Japan   172
    Sachihiko Kondo

Afterword

10 A Prognosis for the Future   193
    David Deterding and Toshiko Yamaguchi

    Index   197

Abbreviations

1S	first person singular
3P	third person
ASEAN	Association of Southeast Asian Nations
AV	active verb
BE	British English
BM	Bahasa Malaysia 'Language of Malaysia'
BN	Barisan Nasional 'The ruling coalition'
CA	classified advertisement
CALL	Computer Assisted Language Learning
CD	compact disk
CL	classifier
DBNA	Dayak Bidayuh National Association
df	degrees of freedom
EF	Europeiska Ferieskolan in Swedish referring to 'Education First', now a company operating language schools worldwide
ELF	English as Lingua Franca
ELT	English Language Teaching
EMD	electronically-mediated discourse
Eng	English
ESL	English as a Second Language
Ex	experiment
Fo	fundamental frequency
FeliCa	blending of 'Felicity' and 'Card'
G30	Global 30
Gala-kei	blending of 'Galapagos' and 'keitai' (the latter meaning a mobile phone in Japanese)
GPA	Grade Point Average
GTP	Government Transformation Programme
HOTS	higher order thinking skills
IC	integrated circuits
ICT	Information and Communication Technology
IDG	indigenous speech community
JASSO	Japan Student Services Organisation
KBSR	Kurikulum Bersepadu Sekolah Rendah 'Integrated Primary School Curriculum'
KBSM	Kurikulum Bersepadu Sekolah Menengah 'Integrated Secondary School Curriculum'
KLF	Kadazandusun Language Foundation

KSSR	Kurikulum Standard Sekolah Rendah 'Standard Curriculum for Primary School'
KSSM	Kurikulum Standard Sekolah Menengah 'Standard Secondary School Curriculum'
LINUS	Literacy and Numeracy Screening
ME	Malaysian English
MEN Corpus	Malaysian English Newspaper Corpus
MEXT	Ministry of Education, Culture, Sports, Science and Technology
MOE	Ministry of Education, Malaysia
ms	millisecond
MUET	Malaysian University English Test
NTT	Nippon (Japan) Telegraph and Telephone
OECD	Organisation for Economic Co-operation and Development
PASS	passive
PISA	Programme for International Standard Assessment
PL	plural
Q	question
QS	Quacquarelli Symonds
R	respondent
REL	relative pronoun
S	speaker
SADIA	Sarawak Dayak Iban Association
SASA	Sabah and Sarawak
SAL	Self Access Learning
SE	Singapore English
SMK	Sekolah Menengah Kebangasaan 'National Secondary School'
SPM	Sijil Pelajaran Malaysia 'Malaysian Certificate of Education'
STL	settler speech community
STPM	Sijil Tinggi Persekolahan Malaysia 'Malaysian Higher School Certificate'
syl	syllable
TIMSS	Trends in International Mathematics and Science Study
UM	University of Malaya
VCD	video compact disk
VOT	voice onset time

Preface

The use of English in postcolonial countries such as Malaysia is a fascinating topic for scholars from diverse disciplines as well as for teachers and professionals with a keen interest in the English language. The main title of this book, *English in Malaysia*, reflects the pervasive role of English throughout Malaysian society. This is especially the case in urban areas, where the presence of English originated from the arrival of British administrators from the East India Company in the late 18th century, but in fact English is a second or foreign language for the majority of Malaysians. Indeed, the linguistic landscape of contemporary Malaysia cannot be fully described without substantial reference to the presence of English due to its sociohistorical, political, sociocultural and linguistic significance.

The subtitle of the book, *Current use and status*, signals that its main focus is on describing how the language is used in everyday life and also its status in present-day Malaysia. For this reason, no single theoretical framework has been adopted across the entire volume. After the introduction, which provides an overview of the status of English in Malaysia, the book is divided into four sections focusing on four central themes (linguistic features, language attitudes, Malaysian English online, and education); finally, an afterword offers a prognosis for the future of English in Malaysia. Overall, the eight main chapters seek to draw an accurate portrait of Malaysian English (ME), a non-native variety of English that is currently developing its own pronunciation, grammar and lexis but whose development is at the same time constantly subject to global influences.

We are grateful to the reviewers who have made valuable comments on earlier versions of the manuscript. This book could not have been completed without the professional support and advice of Brill, especially from Stephanie Paalvast and Irene van Rossum as well as Marjolein Schaake and her production team. And thanks to Jean Sévery for his support during the final stage of indexing.

Introduction

CHAPTER 1

English in Malaysia: Background, Status and Use

Toshiko Yamaguchi and David Deterding

Introduction

Malaysia is a multi-ethnic and multilingual country that has been independent from Britain since 1957. In 1963, two states in northern Borneo, Sabah and Sarawak, joined the states of the Malay Peninsula to create the new country of Malaysia, and henceforth the Peninsular States have been known as West Malaysia, while Sabah and Sarawak are referred to as East Malaysia. Figure 1.1 shows Malaysia together with its neighbouring countries.

The 2015 census puts the total population of Malaysia at 30,699,000 (Department of Statistics, 2015). The major ethnic groups are Malays, other

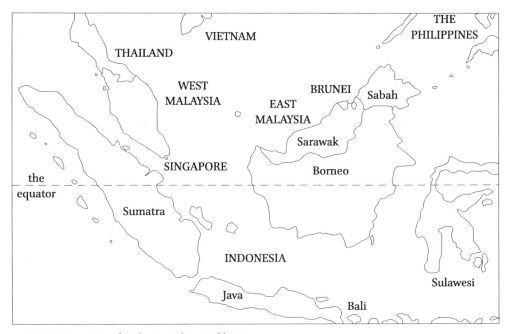

FIGURE 1.1 *Map of Malaysia and its neighbours.*

bumiputera (indigenous people, lit. 'sons of the land'), Chinese and Indians. Malaysia's multi-ethnicity is rooted in the three major waves of migration in its history. Malay migration from the Indonesian islands began definitively in the early 15th century, whereas although both Chinese and Indian people had settled in the region prior to this period, the large-scale migration of these ethnic groups, primarily to provide labour in a new world, took place during the 19th and 20th centuries (Saw, 2015, Chapter 2). Table 1.1 shows the population distribution in 1991, 2000 and 2010. We can see that although the number of Chinese increased from 4.6 million to 6.4 million between 1991 and 2010, they represented a decreasing proportion of the total population as the number of Malays and other bumiputera increased much more during that period.

TABLE 1.1   *Distribution of Population by Ethnic Group, 1991–2010 (from Saw, 2015, p. 64)*

Ethnic group	1991	2000	2010
Malay	8,521,900 (50.7%)	11,680,400 (53.4%)	14,191,700 (54.6%)
Other bumiputera	1,778,000 (10.6%)	2,567,800 (11.7%)	3,331,800 (12.8%)
Chinese	4,623,900 (27.5%)	5,691,900 (26.0%)	6,392,600 (24.6%)
Indian	1,316,100 (7.8%)	1,680,100 (7.7%)	1,907,800 (7.3%)
Others	572,400 (3.4%)	269,700 (1.2%)	189,400 (0.7%)
Total	16,812,300	21,889,700	26,013,300

Table 1.2 presents the distribution of the bumiputera groups in the two states constituting East Malaysia. It can be seen that no ethnic group represents the majority in either state, although the Iban are the largest group in Sarawak.

TABLE 1.2 *Distribution of Bumiputera Population in Sabah and Sarawak in 2010 (from Saw, 2015, p. 67)*

Sabah Group	Number	Sarawak Group	Number
Malay	184,197 (9.4%)	Malay	568,113 (32.3%)
Dusun	568,575 (28.9%)	Iban	713,421 (40.5%)
Bajau	450,279 (22.9%)	Bidayuh	198,473 (11.3%)
Murut	102,393 (5.2%)	Melanau	123,410 (7.0%)
Other bumiputera	659,865 (33.6%)	Other bumiputera	156,436 (8.9%)
Total	1,965,309	Total	1,759,853

Table 1.3 compares the populations of West Malaysia and the two East Malaysian states, illustrating how Malays are the majority in West Malaysia but not in Sabah or Sarawak, while there are substantial Chinese and Indian minorities throughout the country.

TABLE 1.3 *Percentage of Population by Ethnic Group and Region in 2010 (from Saw, 2015, p. 65)*

Region	Malay	Other bumiputera	Chinese	Indian	Other
West Malaysia	61.0	1.4	27.4	9.5	0.7
Sabah	9.0	75.8	12.8	0.3	2.1
Sarawak	24.1	50.7	24.5	0.3	0.4
Total	54.6	12.8	24.6	7.3	0.7

Table 1.4 shows that the majority of the Chinese and Indian population is concentrated in urban areas, constituting almost the same percentage (45.7%) of the population as the Malays (46.6%), while the Malays and other bumiputera people dominate in rural areas.

TABLE 1.4 *Percentage of Population by Ethnic Group and Area in 2010 (from Saw, 2015, p. 68)*

	Urban	Rural	Total
Malay	46.6	64.6	54.6
Other bumiputera	6.4	20.5	12.8
Chinese	35.9	9.7	24.6
Indian	9.8	4.1	7.3
Other	1.2	1.2	0.7

The languages spoken in Malaysia include Malay (standard and various dialects), which is the dominant tongue, Mandarin and other Chinese dialects (especially Hokkien and Cantonese), Indian languages (predominantly Tamil), a large number of non-Malay indigenous languages such as Iban and Bidayuh, and English. While almost all Chinese and Indians speak Malay, their level of proficiency depends largely on the type of primary and secondary schools they attended. In fact, the Malaysian educational system perpetuates ethnic segregation. While the majority of Malays are enrolled in national schools, in which Malay is the medium of instruction, at both primary and secondary levels, the majority of Chinese and Indian children are enrolled in Chinese and Tamil schools respectively. Malay-medium national schools do not attract many non-Malays, partly because the parents of Chinese and Indian children believe that retaining their heritage language assures the preservation of their ethnic identity. Among the 2,211,971 pupils enrolled in national primary schools in 2002, only 46,670 (2.1%) were Chinese and 95,180 (4.2%) were Indian (Tan & Santhiram, 2014, p. 114). At the secondary level, a large percentage of Chinese pupils choose either national-type Chinese schools (where Malay is the medium of instruction but some support is provided for the learning of Mandarin) or independent Chinese schools (where Chinese is the medium of instruction) rather than national schools (where Malay is the sole medium of instruction). There are no Tamil schools at the secondary level, and so Indian pupils are sent either to national or national-type schools. In all these schools, English is taught only as a subject in the curriculum.

Historically, English was first brought to Malaysia by the British colonial authorities in the late 18th century (Asmah, 2012, p. 155), but it only became firmly established a century later when in 1895, the British founded the Federated Malay States, comprising the four states of Selangor, Perak, Negeri Sembilan and Pahang (Saw, 2007, p. 3). English was initially used by a small number of the elite, but after the foundation of the Federation of Malaya in 1948, and then after full independence in 1957, English spread throughout the country by means of education (Schneider, 2007, p. 145). This historical presence of English went through various stages, mainly due to shifts in language policy which had substantial repercussions on the use and status of the language.

After the establishment of Malaysia in 1963, English continued to be used as an official language, and it was the medium of instruction in national-type English schools. However, this practice did not last long due to the implementation of the national education policy in 1967, which established Malay as the sole national and official language. This key event, the switch from English to Bahasa Malaysia (Malay, lit. 'the language of Malaysia'), marked the beginning of 'Malaysianisation' (Hajar & Shakila, 2014, pp. 16–17), for which Malay nationalism, which had intensified in the 1960s, was an important trigger (Pennycook, 1994). Thus, in 1970, Malay was introduced as the medium of instruction in all national schools, eventually including national-type schools aimed at Chinese and Indian pupils (Baskaran, 2005, pp. 8–9; Foo & Richards, 2004, p. 232). In subsequent years, particularly between 1970 and 1990, English was phased out in stages, with Malay becoming the medium of instruction in universities in 1983 (Baskaran, 2005, p. 9; Doshi, 2012, pp. 18–19). Consequently, English gradually lost much of its functional role in Malaysian society (Lee, 2011, Chapter 5; Tan, 2013, p. 3). Indeed, the status of English in Malaysia has inevitably been a complex issue, and Preshous (2001, p. 52) noted that 'there are political, social and economic implications' which are deeply ingrained in Malaysian language policy.

The Malaysianisation process has had the following consequences for contemporary Malaysia:

1. a perception that there is a decrease in the number of proficient English speakers (Doshi, 2012, pp. 15–16);
2. a shortage of qualified local English-language teachers (Tan & Santhiram, 2014, p. 146); and
3. a disparity in English usage between urban areas, such as Kuala Lumpur, and rural/suburban areas, where there is little need to use the language (Schneider, 2003, p. 53).

Looking closely at Malaysia today, English is emerging, especially in urban areas, as an independent variety detached from its historical origins as Malaysians use it in their daily life for various socioeconomic needs and institutional or private demands, and for a range of sociocultural motivations. Kaur's (1995) survey showed that 20 years ago, young Malaysians already strongly perceived the need for English in their personal, academic and career-related endeavours, and they considered it beneficial for the nation. One year later, a survey conducted among teachers and students by Crismore, Ngeow and Soo (1996) indicated that a majority of respondents regarded the English used in Malaysia as 'wrong' English, reflecting a desire to improve the standards taught in schools.

The fact that the various ethnic groups in Malaysia have mostly maintained their own languages (Gill, 2014, p. 2) does not necessarily diminish the overall status of English. In today's Malaysia, English has the following six features:

1. It is considered an international language promoted in business and commerce in alignment with the country's target for economic growth by 2020.
2. It serves as a lingua franca, facilitating communication between ethnic groups.
3. It is the first language for some Malaysians, particularly among ethnic Chinese and Indians, and a second language for others, notably in urban areas.
4. It is a foreign language for many Malaysians, particularly those residing in rural areas and those who use their own ethnic language for daily communication.
5. While English is taught in many national schools as a second or foreign language, it is the medium of instruction in many private institutes, including the off-shore campuses of overseas UK and Australian universities (see Chapter 9 in this volume).
6. Some young people, particularly ethnic non-Malays, tend to be more proficient in Malay than in English, while their own ethnic language is their first language.

The fourth and sixth of these features were not envisaged by Malaysian language policymakers, who intended to make English the second language after Malay for all Malaysians (Asmah, 1996). Indeed, Asmah (2012, p. 163) recalled an incident when she was contacted by then prime minister Dr Mahathir Mohamad, who wanted to know why graduates of the University of Malaya were not able to speak good English; recently, Dr Mahathir has noted that education producing proficient English speakers can only be found in private or international schools in the country and in schools overseas, so only privileged Malaysians like himself can afford to send their children to benefit from such an education (Bedi, 2014).

Despite its restricted official status in Malaysian society, most Malaysians see English as prestigious because of its international status. The majority are also aware that they speak a variety that is not the same as the British English (BE) from which it is historically descended, as will be seen later in this book (Chapters 5 and 6). Indeed, Görlach (2002, p. 10) observed that the English currently used in former colonies has become radically different from the postcolonial concept of English (see also Kirkpatrick, 2007, p. 179), and a tolerance of linguistic pluralism, which Quirk (1990, p. 10) condemned 25 years ago, is emerging in many countries, including Malaysia. Leimgruber (2014) noted the robust existence of such a local variety, known as Singlish, in neighbouring Singapore, and scholars in recent years have increasingly focused on the use of English in its local contexts (see Chapter 7 in this volume), in contrast with classical studies (e.g. Killingley, 1968; Tongue, 1974), in which 'Standard English' was often the point of departure. The current volume serves to contribute to this new research direction, investigating English in contemporary Malaysia by examining how people use it in different contexts, the status it has, and what issues arise from its use in different aspects of Malaysian life.

The notion of 'Malaysian English', abbreviated to ME throughout this volume, is an umbrella term that refers to the English currently used in Malaysia. It is an emerging 'non-native' variety for which the pronunciation, grammar, lexicon and discourse have not yet been fully described, and it is inevitably still evolving under the influence of the local culture and various indigenous languages. In Kachru's (1986) Three Circles model, ME is in the Outer Circle as it is a variety of English that originated from colonial roots and may typically still maintain some kind of official status. Schneider (2007) considered ME to be in the third phase of his five-phase Dynamic Model of postcolonial language development. The status of ME in Schneider's model will be discussed in greater depth in the final section of this introduction.

Here, we aim to describe the status of ME as a 'New English' variety. First, in the next section, we look briefly at how the public perceives the current use and status of English in Malaysia; our observations are based on four letters to the editors of local newspapers. Second, we introduce Platt, Weber and Ho's (1984) definition of a New English and draw attention to its resemblance to second language acquisition. Third, some aspects of past and current research on ME are introduced.

Voices From the Public

The reality of English in Malaysian schools is a hotly debated topic in local newspapers. Many writers express concern about the state of English in Malaysia today and call for a better implementation of English-language education. According to Schneider (2007, pp. 42–43), complaints such as these typically occur during phase three of his Dynamic Model, termed *nativisation*, in which conservatives often complain about incorrect usage, ultimately clashing with more progressive users of the nativised language. Those voicing complaints sometimes point out changes in the quality of the English taught at school, and a common suggestion is for the re-implementation of English-medium schools at national level.

In extract (1), the writer is concerned about the way English teaching has been conducted, believing that one problem is that many Malay-speaking teachers tend to use their first language in the classroom:

1. English has been taught in Bahasa Malaysia for some 40 years. But why is this happening? In the 70s, the Education Ministry decided that more Malays should be trained as English language teacher [sic].... In the 50s and 60s there were a few Malay teachers teaching English. They were good. They had a very good command of the language.... But the candidates taken in the 70s could hardly speak or write a sentence of English correctly. Overall entry requirements into teacher training colleges were lowered... (Ravinder Singh, *The Malay Mail*, 24 January 2013)

In extract (2), the writer refers to the lower performance of pupils in national English language exams, partly because of the shortage of proficient teachers:

2. The 2012 SPM [*Sijil Pelajaran Malaysia*, Malaysian Certificate of Education] and STPM [*Sijil Tinggi Persekolahan Malaysia*, Malaysian Higher School Certificate] results reveal that proficiency in English subject [sic] has deteriorated among young Malaysians, mainly due to inadequate teaching methods and curriculum, educator [sic] and parents said.... There is also a lack of teachers who are proficient in English. (Dorothy Cheng, *The Sun*, 28 March 2013)

In extract (3), the writer discusses the limitations of knowledge, maintaining that this has been caused by the elevation of Malay as the sole medium of instruction:

3. One of the main reasons why our progress is behind many developed nations is the literacy of its [sic] citizens.... The fact that Bahasa Malaysia is the medium of instruction in schools has limited access to knowledge. Let's be realistic, only a small percentage of books written in English are translated into Bahasa Malaysia. I have encountered many of my Malaysian peers pursuing studies in varsities abroad who had to drop out

because of their low proficiency in the English language... I think that importance should also be given to Bahasa Malaysia, Chinese and Tamil but English language must be made the medium of instruction in schools. (Mohamad Ridzuan Abdahir, *The Star*, 2 March 2014)

The author of extract (4) recalls the good old days when people were given more space to master three languages:

4. Most of us who are in our 50s now remember those days well. My parents sent me to an English-medium school so that it would be easier for me to get a government job later, they said. No [*sic*] wanting me to be too westernized and forget my roots, they also made me attend adult classes in Mandarin at night. So I ended up proficient in all three languages, English, Mandarin and Bahasa Malaysia, thanks to the far-sightedness of my parents.... Bring back the English-medium school, yes, and strengthen the national schools. (Foo Siew Ping, *The Star*, 23 April 2014)

These four extracts show that there is opposition to the use of nativised features of English. At the same time, it is evident that as a consequence of promoting Malay as the medium of instruction, there is no longer an urgent need to communicate in English, so the status of English may have diminished.

New Englishes and Second Language Acquisition

ME is a non-native variety, also known as a New English, a term introduced by Platt et al. (1984), who provide four criteria for it; ME fits these criteria neatly. The four criteria are as follows:
A New English is

1. taught as a subject in the education system;
2. not the language spoken by most of the population;
3. used for certain purposes and acts as a lingua franca in some domains; and
4. localised by adopting some language features of its own, affecting pronunciation, sentence structures, words and expressions.

New Englishes differ from so-called native varieties of English (such as American and Australian English) as the latter show continuity in the use of the language. Certainly, those varieties of English were once 'new', but they emerged in a different environment. Platt et al. explained the crucial difference:

> People came to these areas speaking English and remained speaking English. Other immigrant groups were absorbed into the main body of English speakers. It has been different with the New Englishes. English was, in most cases, at first a language learned at school. (1984, p. 10)

Some studies categorise New Englishes as second-language varieties of English (Mesthrie, 2008; Schreier, 2012; Schneider, 2014) rather than non-native varieties. In addition, there is a strong consensus among scholars that these varieties typically emerge from a wide range of contact situations, and it is axiomatic that they are typically spoken by bilingual or multilingual speakers (Schneider, 2013). In this volume, both terms, *non-native variety* and *second-language variety*, or something akin to them, are used interchangeably to refer to this emerging variety of English that is increasingly independent of the language of the former colonial power and has some features of second language acquisition (Mesthrie, 2008, p. 25).

Malaysian English at a Glance

The past few decades have witnessed an increasing number of publications on ME, many of which have described the language, particularly its structure and sociolinguistic patterns, with respect to the various domains in which it is used. This section will summarise how previous researchers have described ME and provide an overview of some of the notions that have been considered central in research on the language. The section focuses on three topics: (i) tendency to simplify, (ii) lectal variation and (iii) nativisation.

Tendency to Simplify
ME shares common features with other New Englishes (see Kachru & Nelson, 2006; Kirkpatrick, 2010; Mesthrie, 2008; Mesthrie & Bhatt, 2008; Schreier, 2012). Scholars have tended to identify features in New Englishes that are absent from standard Inner Circle varieties, and prominent in this respect are what one may call simplifying features in sound and grammar. Simplification is a process by which the structure of the target language is made less complex or shortened by the speakers of New Englishes (Kortmann & Szmrecsanyi, 2009).

In phonology, diphthongs tend to become monophthongs, stops may be used instead of dental fricatives as they are easier to articulate (see Chapter 3 in this volume) and final consonant clusters are often simplified (Baskaran, 2004a; Azirah & Tan, 2012). A tendency to stress the second syllable of a word may also be regarded as simplification as it involves regularisation (see Chapter 4 in this volume). Most of the pronunciation features shared by users of English as a lingua franca (ELF) in the ASEAN summarised by Kirkpatrick (2010, p. 80) can be understood as kinds of simplification.

In grammar, simplification can be found in the omission of articles or past tense markers. In addition, use of the tag *isn't it*, as in *She likes cooking, isn't it?* (Azirah & Tan, 2012, p. 64), regardless of the type of clause to which it is attached, can be regarded as simplification. The distinction between count and mass nouns is often blurred, so the use of *staffs, stationaries, accommodations* and *jewelleries* have been noted in Malaysia (Baskaran, 2004b, p. 1046), just as *equipments* and *furnitures* occur in many varieties of English around the world (Mesthrie & Bhatt, 2008, p. 53).

Why do people simplify? The simplification of pronunciation and grammar is often triggered by cross-linguistic influence, in which the source language does not have the same linguistic system as the target language (Kirkpatrick, 2010). A second answer derives from the perspective of the observer rather than the speaker. The fact that there are speakers who do not pronounce words in the manner characterised by the summary of Kirkpatrick (2010) implies that the change may not be 'the aggregate outcome of many individual decisions' (Ferguson, 2012, cited in Bolton, 2014, p. 62). The simplified features of a non-native variety can be striking, but we may have failed to detect the broader reality. Given that not all speakers produce non-native features, Kirkpatrick's (2010) 'multilingual model' aiming to 'teach English as it is used in social contexts within the region' (p. 177) may need further scrutiny.

Lectal Variation

Baskaran (2005) classified ME into acrolect, mesolect and basilect subvarieties, terms originally adopted in creole studies (Mesthrie, 2008). The acrolect is considered the educated norm appropriate for formal contexts such as official purposes or teaching. The basilect is a less-educated subvariety featuring highly informal usage, and in the context of Malaysia, it is often pejoratively called 'Manglish'. The mesolect stands between the two: It is a colloquial variety, but it mostly avoids the strong negative associations of the basilect. As the basilect may be highly variable and less stable, recent research has focused more on the acrolectal and mesolectal varieties in order to gain a systematic picture of ME.

It is generally stated that ME arose from a spoken style, or what Richards (1979, cited in Baskaran, 2005, p. 20) termed a 'communicative style'. This link to spoken language reminds us of the early study by Soo (1990), in which ME was judged to be more acceptable in spoken form than in written form, for which BE is often deemed more appropriate. This conclusion supports the idea that the mesolectal variety is the basis of ME.

In pursuit of a definition for 'Standard Malaysian English', ME has sometimes been identified with a level between the acrolect and mesolect because one cannot expect a 'pure' acrolect without some local features that are tolerated by educated speakers. Newbrook (2006 [1997]) studied printed English in Malaysian newspapers and found that an acrolectal variety, or what he dubbed 'a local endonormative standard variety', equates to a formal written language that is close to Standard English. Note that this type of acrolectal written English tolerates minor grammatical non-standard usage, such as use of the plural *staffs* in *How many staffs are on medical leave?* (Baskaran, 2004b, p. 1076). One may note that the acrolect and mesolect are not defined in the same way by all researchers and that the distinction may not always be systematically maintained.

An instrumental study on the pronunciation of three vowels (occurring in *north, wind* and *sun*) conducted by Pillai, Zuraidah and Knowles (2012) focused exclusively on acrolectal experienced teachers of English; they noted that one important criterion for speakers to be described as acrolectal was that they did not exhibit ethnic differences in the pronunciation of these vowels, suggesting that ethnic differences can only be found with mesolectal and basilectal speakers. Indeed, Newbrook (2006 [1997], pp. 414–415) stated that inter-ethnic variation may have already disappeared in ME unless the speakers are weak second-language users who rely heavily on their first language. The issue of the influence of ethnicity on lectal variation and how it affects the establishment of a standard model require further investigation.

Nativisation

Morais (2001, p. 36) recalled that some Malay students used to look down on English as *bahasa penjajah* (a colonial language), but this is no longer the case as the language has undergone nativisation, a process in which it has been assimilated in local contexts (Kachru, 1981, p. 18; Schneider, 2007). Speakers of New Englishes adopt local features of pronunciation, grammar and lexis which are largely absent from Inner Circle varieties, although some forms (such as the invariable *isn't it* tag and the plural *furnitures*) may also be shared by a wide range of Outer Circle varieties (Mesthrie & Bhatt, 2008), and Deterding and Kirkpatrick (2006) have suggested that some features, such as the use of [t] for the voiceless TH sound at the start of words such as *think* and *three* (see Chapter 3 in this volume) and the avoidance of reduced vowels, may constitute part of an emergent regional English occurring throughout South East Asia.

On the basis of a corpus of 183 tokens of misunderstanding, Deterding (2013) showed that some features of pronunciation, particularly the confusion between /l/ and /r/ and the simplification of initial consonant clusters, can cause problems in conversations in South East Asia between speakers from different countries, and Dumanig and David (2014) confirmed that some localised usage can result in a loss of intelligibility in spoken interactions. However, Smith (1982, p. 79) suggested that this issue of intelligibility may be reduced when the hearer has a good knowledge of different varieties of a language. Dumanig and David (2014) observed that the communicative strategies (e.g. asking questions) employed by hearers in discourse to repair miscommunication may signal one of the processes leading to familiarity with the varieties, as suggested by Smith (1982), and both Jenkins (2007) and Walker (2010) emphasised that accommodation strategies represent an essential tool in enhancing the success of international communication.

The study of nativisation attracts researchers on ME because it offers the opportunity to categorise and also explain some of the features that are found. Research on lexical borrowing is a case in point (e.g. Tan, 2013; Hajar, 2014) as it clearly stems from a contact situation between two languages. In the Malaysian context, this contact emerges from the fact that Malaysians are generally bilingual or trilingual (Tan, 2009, p. 454; Chapter 2 in this volume), and such contact situations flourish in specific domains such as family life and local festivals.

Note, however, that evidence for nativisation is absent from some studies, and the instrumental study of monophthongs by Tan and Low (2010) reported no acoustically significant difference between ME and Singapore English (SE). SE is in the fourth phase, termed the *endonormative stabilisation*, of Schneider's (2007) Dynamic Model and so is characterised by its greater linguistic stability, and one might have expected some distinct features of pronunciation between ME and SE, partly because native-like mastery of pronunciation is harder for an English as a second language (ESL) learner to achieve than native-like mastery of grammar and lexis. Furthermore, one would predict that some speakers of ME and SE would choose to maintain some aspects of a nativised accent.

Nativisation may also penetrate pedagogy. Although a certain degree of nativisation is perceived as positive in a descriptive writing exercise because it expresses Malaysian identity, teachers may not accept excessive use of a local variety in their classroom (see Chapter 8 in this volume). This seems ironic since Mukundan and Khojasteh's (2011) study on modal auxiliary verbs revealed that there is a discrepancy between the secondary school English textbooks used in Malaysia and the language usage found in the British National Corpus, which suggests that textbook writers already adopt local usage to a certain extent.

In conclusion, ME accommodates nativised pronunciation, grammar and lexis, but the exact details are still subject to investigation. The current volume aims to contribute to this research and thereby provide insights into the current state of the nativisation of ME.

Status of Malaysian English: Insights from the Research in this Volume

The varied material in this volume offers an opportunity to reflect on the status of ME as it evolves with its own identity but at the same time participates in the regional and worldwide development of English. Here, we briefly consider insights from the chapters in this book concerning the current status of ME from the perspective of the Dynamic Model proposed by Schneider (2007).

Schneider has proposed that ME is in the third phase of his model, termed nativisation, as it is in the process of developing its own distinctive style of usage, but for its norms, it still makes substantial reference to external varieties, particularly those of Britain and America. Furthermore, in Malaysia, there is limited official acceptance of an indigenous variety of English and, as noted above, there are regular complaints about falling standards of English in local newspapers, something that is also characteristic of the third phase of Schneider's model.

Although there is some evidence that ME may be moving towards phase four of the Dynamic Model, termed *endonormative stabilisation*, Schneider (2007, p. 152) concluded that traces of this progress remain tenuous, and he further noted that the evolution of ME has been 'marked by non-linear developments' (Schneider, 2007, p. 152) as use of English was for many years discouraged in efforts to promote Bahasa Malaysia (Malay) as the national language. This non-linear development of English is reflected in the decision taken in 2002 to teach mathematics and science in English, a policy which was subsequently revoked in 2009 (Kirkpatrick, 2010, p. 27).

Schneider (2014) recently updated his model to consider how some newly emergent styles of English usage relate to it, and he concluded that the colloquial mixed code found in Malaysia that is sometimes termed Manglish does not fit into the model very well. Although this informal code may be used by the urban elite to project a cherished multicultural identity, it is unlikely to ever be accepted by the authorities, adopted as a medium of education or used in formal contexts. But it seems that it is this informal style of usage, incorporating the widespread mixing of Malay words and phrases into English, that carries the pan-Malaysian identity and that the more formal variety that might be termed ME may continue, for some time at least, to retain its traditional exonormative orientation.

The fact that this formal variety is nowadays widely referred to as ME rather than English in Malaysia is an indicator that it may be moving towards phase four of the Dynamic Model (Schneider, 2007, p. 50). Moreover, the publication of academic papers such as the chapters in this book indicates that there is a certain degree of codification of ME, another of the features of phase four. This codification is particularly illustrated in the analysis of the structure of ME in chapters 2, 3 and 4.

Chapter 2 discusses a shift in the grammatical distinction between count and mass nouns, with logically plural things such as *furnitures* and *equipments* occurring as plurals. This feature has been reported for many varieties of World Englishes (Mesthrie & Bhatt, 2008), so in this respect, ME seems to be participating in an emergent trend found in new varieties of English throughout the world. However, the ME patterns may also reflect substantial influence from the classifiers of Malay and Chinese, particularly the use of *pieces of* together with count nouns, as in *400 pieces of mattress*, something that has been reported in other regional varieties of English (e.g. *12 pieces of $100 notes* in Brunei; Deterding & Salbrina, 2013, p. 55). In this respect, ME may be participating in the emergence of a regional style of English (Deterding & Kirkpatrick, 2006) rather than contributing to worldwide trends.

In Chapter 3, it is claimed that there is a new [t] sound in ME, and this offers evidence of a reanalysis of the sound system. In ME, the TH sounds are not simply realised as [t] or [d]; rather, they have their own acoustic identity, with less aspiration than that expected for ordinary [t], and this offers evidence about the nativisation of English taking place in Malaysia. Chapter 4 also deals with pronunciation, showing that while BE speakers have a different tonal contour on compound nouns such as *blackbird* compared with noun phrases such as *black bird*, Malaysians tend not to make this distinction. Just as with the evidence from Chapter 2, the two features of pronunciation analysed in chapters 3 and 4 suggest that ME may not just be forging its own identity, but rather might also be participating in the emergence of a regional variety of English. Deterding and Kirkpatrick (2006) have shown that the pronunciation of voiceless TH as [t] is widespread throughout South East Asia, although it remains uncertain whether the new [t] sound of ME is distinct from the sound found elsewhere in the region. Similarly, the research reported in Chapter 4 ties in with that of Low (2000), who analysed the lack of distinction between phrasal and compound nouns in SE.

One crucial indicator of the status of a language in forging its own identity and moving into phase four of the Dynamic Model is the attitude of its users, and chapters 5 and 6 report on this. Do listeners feel that people with a clear local accent are intelligent? And do they find them friendly? Chapter 5 provides insights into this facet of the status of ME based on a matched guise test, and a clear pattern that emerges is that the English spoken by local people is generally perceived as intelligent, confident and friendly, which confirms that ME is becoming a mature variety that is accepted by many of its speakers. However, Chapter 6 reports that there is a common perception among older respondents from the Bidayuh community living in the west of Sarawak that standards of English are falling, even though younger people acknowledge that learning English is important and many claim that their English is actually not bad. So it seems that not everyone is happy about recent developments with the language, and indeed there may be some entrenched resistance to the emergence of a nativised variety.

Chapter 7 deals with ME online, reminding us about the extent of code-mixing in on-line texts in newspaper advertisements and also in social networking sites, reflecting the widespread occurrence of mixing in informal Malaysian discourse and reflecting the observations of Schneider that some aspects of language use in Malaysia do not fit very well into his Dynamic Model.

Finally, chapters 8 and 9 deal with pedagogical issues. Education, of course, plays a key role in the development of a language, and Chapter 8 traces the somewhat tortuous route followed by policy towards English in Malaysian schools. The conflict between the demands of nationalism that insist on the promotion of Malay and the need for students to develop competency in English in order to compete in the global marketplace is, of course, found throughout South East Asia (Kirkpatrick, 2010), but some of the policies adopted in Malaysia are unique to the local context. Chapter 9 extends the discussion about education and considers how Malaysian universities deal with English-medium education, comparing the situation with what is happening in Japan. Malaysia has promoted itself as a regional hub for tertiary English education, encouraging foreign universities to establish campuses in the country, and this makes Malaysia quite distinct from Japan, where there has been a longer history of successful research in Japanese and where there is also pride in independent development in what has been termed the *Galapagos syndrome*.

In summary, this book provides valuable insights into the emergent status of ME in a wide range of domains, including its grammar and phonology, as well as in on-line discourse and in education. It therefore offers substantial evidence about how the language is developing its own distinct identity but at the same time is linked with other regional and worldwide varieties of English. Many of the features of ME that are documented in this book are consistent with it moving into the fourth phase of Schneider's model, even though some of the phenomena that are described may lie outside of the development of postcolonial Englishes as originally envisaged by Schneider. It is hoped that the chapters in this book provide valuable material that will help focus discussion about this issue and also stimulate further research into the nature and status of English in Malaysia.

References

Asmah, Haji O. (1996). Post-imperial English in Malaysia. In J. A. Fishman, A. W. Conrad, & A. Rubal-Lopez (Eds.), *Post-imperial English: Status change in former British and American colonies, 1940–1990* (pp. 513–533). Berlin: Mouton de Gruyter.

———. (2012). Pragmatics of maintaining English in Malaysia's education system. In E. L. Low & H. Azirah (Eds.), *English in Southeast Asia: Features, policy and language in use* (pp. 155–174). Amsterdam: John Benjamins.

Azirah, H., & Tan, R. (2012). Malaysian English. In E. L. Low & H. Azirah (Eds.), *English in Southeast Asia: Features, policy and language in use* (pp. 55–74). Amsterdam: John Benjamins.

Baskaran, L. (2004a). Malaysian English: Phonology. In E. W. Schneider, K. Burridge, B. Kortmann, R. Mesthrie, & C. Upton (Eds.), *A handbook of varieties of English, volume 1: Phonology* (pp. 1034–1046). Berlin: De Gruyter Mouton.

———. (2004b). Malaysian English: Morphology and syntax. In B. Kortmann, K. Burridge, R. Mesthrie, E. W. Schneider, & C. Upton (Eds.), *A handbook of varieties of English, volume 2: Morphology and syntax* (pp. 1073–1085). Berlin: De Gruyter Mouton.

———. (2005). *A Malaysian English primer: Aspects of Malaysian English features*. Kuala Lumpur: University of Malaya Press.

Bedi, R. S. (2014, 18 November). Dr M: Malaysian education policy creating rift between rich and poor. *The Star OnLine*. Retrieved from http://www1.thestar.com.my/News/Nation/2014/11/18/Dr-M-education-policy/.

Bolton, K. (2014). Language policies and English worldwide [Review of the book *The Cambridge handbook of language policies*, B. Spolsky (Ed.)]. *English Today, 30*(3), 61–63.

Crismore, A., Ngeow, K. Y.-H., & Soo, K.-S. (1996). Attitudes toward English in Malaysia. *World Englishes, 15*(3), 319–335.

Department of Statistics. (2015). Department of Statistics Official Portal. https://www.statistics.gov.my.

Deterding, D. (2013). *Misunderstandings in English as a lingua franca: An analysis of ELF interactions in South-East Asia*. Berlin: De Gruyter.

Deterding, D. & Kirkpatrick, A. (2006). Emerging South-East Asian Englishes and intelligibility. *World Englishes*, 25(3/4), 391–409.

Deterding, D. & Salbrina, S. (2013). *Brunei English: A new variety in a multilingual society*. Dordrecht: Springer.

Doshi, A. (2012). Changing tides: The story of the English language in Malaysia. In M. D. Zuraidah (Ed.), *English in multicultural Malaysia: Pedagogy and applied research* (pp. 15–30). Kuala Lumpur: University of Malaya Press.

Dumanig, F. P., & David, M. K. (2014). Miscommunication in Filipino-Malaysian interactions: Intercultural discourse in English. In A. R. Hajar & A. M. Shakila (Eds.), *English in Malaysia: Postcolonial and beyond* (pp. 253–278). Bern: Peter Lang.

Ferguson, G. (2012). English in language policy and management. In B. Spolsky (Ed.), *The Cambridge handbook of language policy* (pp. 475–498). Cambridge: Cambridge University Press.

Foo, B., & Richards, C. (2004). English in Malaysia. *RELC Journal*, 35(2), 229–240.

Gill, S. K. (2014). *Language policy challenges in multi-ethnic Malaysia*. Dordrecht: Springer.

Görlach, M. (2002). *Still more Englishes*. Amsterdam: John Benjamins.

Hajar, A. R. (2014). Malaysian English lexis: Postcolonial and beyond. In A. R. Hajar & A. M. Shakila (Eds.), *English in Malaysia: Postcolonial and beyond* (pp. 35–53). Bern: Peter Lang.

Hajar, A. R. & Shakila, A. M. (2014). Postcolonial Malaysian English: Realities and prospects. In A. R. Hajar & A. M. Shakila (Eds.), *English in Malaysia: Postcolonial and beyond* (pp. 9–33). Bern: Peter Lang.

Jenkins, J. (2007). *English as a lingua franca: Attitude and identity*. Oxford: Oxford University Press.

Kachru, B. B. (1981). The pragmatics of non-native varieties of English. In L. Smith (Ed.), *English for cross-cultural communication* (pp. 15–39). New York: St. Martin's Press.

———. (1986). *The alchemy of English: The spread, functions, and models of non-native Englishes*. Urbana, IL: University of Illinois Press.

Kachru, Y., & Nelson, C. (2006). *World Englishes in Asian contexts*. Hong Kong: Hong Kong University Press.

Kaur, K. (1995). Why they need English in Malaysia: A survey. *World Englishes*, 14(2), 223–230.

Killingley, S. Y. (1968). The phonology of Malayan English. *Orbis*, 17(1), 57–87.

Kirkpatrick, A. (2007). *World Englishes: Implications for international communication and English language teaching.* Cambridge: Cambridge University Press.

———. (2010). *English as a lingua franca in ASEAN: A multilingual model.* Singapore: NUS Press.

Kortmann, B., & Szmrecsanyi, B. (2009). World Englishes between simplification and complexification. In T. Hoffman & L. Siebers (Eds.), *World Englishes—Problems, properties and prospects: Selected papers from the 13th IAWE conference* (pp. 265–285). Amsterdam: John Benjamins.

Lee, T. H. (2011). *Chinese schools in Peninsular Malaysia: The struggle for survival.* Singapore: ISEAS Publishing.

Leimgruber, J. R. E. (2014). Singlish as defined by young educated Chinese Singaporeans. *International Journal of the Sociology of Language, 230,* 45–63.

Low, E. L. (2000). Is lexical stress placement different in Singapore English and British English? In A. Brown, D. Deterding, & E. L. Low (Eds.), *The English language in Singapore: Research on pronunciation* (pp. 22–34). Singapore: Singapore Association for Applied Linguistics.

Mesthrie, R. (2008). Introduction: Varieties of English in Africa and South and Southeast Asia. In R. Mesthrie (Ed.), *Varieties of English 4: Africa, South and Southeast Asia* (pp. 23–31). Berlin: Mouton de Gruyter.

Mesthrie, R. & Bhatt, R. M. (2008). *World Englishes: The study of new linguistic varieties.* Cambridge: Cambridge University Press.

Morais, E. (2001). Lectal varieties of Malaysian English. In V. B. Y. Ooi (Ed.), *Evolving identities: The English language in Singapore and Malaysia* (pp. 33–52). Singapore: Times Academic Press.

Mukundan, J., & Khojasteh, L. (2011). Modal auxiliary verbs in prescribed Malaysian English textbooks. *English Language Teaching, 4*(1), 79–89.

Newbrook, M. (2006 [1997]). Malaysian English: Status, norms, some grammatical and lexical features. In B. Kingsley & B. B. Kachru (Eds.), *World Englishes: Critical concepts in linguistics* (Vol. 2) (pp. 390–417). London: Routledge.

Pennycook, A. (1994). *The cultural politics of English as an international language.* Harlow: Pearson.

Pillai, S., Zuraidah, M. D., & Knowles, G. (2012). Towards building a model of standard Malaysian English pronunciation. In M. D. Zuraidah (Ed.), *English in multicultural Malaysia: Pedagogy and applied research* (pp. 195–211). Kuala Lumpur: University of Malaya Press.

Platt, J., Weber, H., & Ho, M. L. (1984). *The New Englishes.* London: Routledge & Kegan Paul.

Preshous, A. (2001). Where you going ah? *English Today, 17*(1), 46–53.

Quirk, R. (1990). Language varieties and standard language. *English Today, 21,* 3–10.
Richards, J. C. (1979). Rhetorical and communicative styles in the new varieties of English. *Language Learning,* 1–25.
Saw, S.-H. (2007). *The population of Peninsular Malaysia.* Singapore: Institute of Southeast Asian Studies Publications.
———. (2015). *The population of Malaysia* (2nd ed.). Singapore: Institute of Southeast Asian Studies Publishing.
Schneider, E. W. (2003). Evolutionary patterns of New Englishes and the special case of Malaysian English. *Asian Englishes, 6*(2), 44–63.
———. (2007). *Postcolonial English: Varieties around the world.* Cambridge: Cambridge University Press.
———. (2013). English as a contact language: The "New Englishes". In D. Schreier & M. Hundt (Eds.), *English as a contact language* (pp. 131–148). Cambridge: Cambridge University Press.
———. (2014). Asian Englishes—into the future: A bird's eye view. *Asian Englishes, 16*(3), 249–256.
Schreier, D. (2012). Second-language varieties: Second-language varieties of English. In A. Bergs & L. J. Brinton (Eds.), *English historical linguistics: An international handbook* (Vol. 2) (pp. 2106–2120). Berlin: De Gruyter Mouton.
Smith, L. (1982). Spread of English and issues of intelligibility. In B. B. Kachru (Ed.), *The other tongue: English across cultures* (pp. 75–90). Urbana, IL: University of Illinois Press.
Soo, K. (1990). Malaysian English at the crossroads: Some sign-posts. *Journal of Multilingual and Multicultural Development, 11,* 199–214.
Tan, R. S. K., & Low, E. L. (2010). How different are the monophthongs of Malay speakers of Malaysian and Singapore English? *English World-Wide, 31*(2), 162–189.
Tan, S. I. (2009). Lexical borrowing from Chinese languages in Malaysian English. *World Englishes, 28*(4), 451–484.
———. (2013). *Malaysian English: Language contact and change.* Frankfurt am Main: Peter Lang.
Tan, Y. S., & Santhiram, R. (2014). *Educational issues in multiethnic Malaysia.* Petaling Jaya, Selangor: Strategic Information and Research Development.
Tongue, R. K. (1974). *The Englishes of Singapore and Malaysia.* Singapore: Eastern Universities Press.
Walker, R. (2010). *Teaching the pronunciation of English as a lingua franca.* Oxford: Oxford University Press.

Linguistic Features

CHAPTER 2

Malaysian English: Evidence of Contact with Classifier Languages

Siew Imm Tan

Introduction

The emergence of a distinctive variety of English in Malaysia, widely known as ME, has been the subject of many studies. From the lexicon to the phonological system to the syntax, this variety has undergone the progressive nativisation commonly observed in varieties of English that were transplanted through colonisation into multilingual and multicultural settings and that have gone on to play significant roles and functions within the independent states (e.g. Lowenberg, 1984; Schneider, 2003; and Baskaran, 2005). The prolonged and intense contact between English and the other languages spoken in Malaysia, such as Malay, Chinese and Tamil, has produced systematic linguistic variation and change resulting in a local variety of English that is divergent from Standard English yet recognisable and relevant, especially to its speakers and others in the region.

A major aspect of the syntax of ME is the flexibility with which nominal countability is treated. In his acclaimed description of the English of Singapore and Malaysia, Tongue (1974) wrote that 'the most noteworthy distinction (between this variety and Standard English) in their use of nouns relates to the matter of "countability"' (p. 43). In McArthur's (1998, p. 759) entry on ME, the countable use of some usually uncountable nouns features prominently in his list of the syntactic features of this variety. Clearly a significant characteristic of ME, this variation is often attributed to processes of simplification similar to those observed in second or foreign language acquisition. For example, in her study of colloquial ME, Wong (1983) associated the tendency to 'apply the singular-plural distinction to all nouns, regardless of whether they are treated as countable or uncountable in standard English' (p. 129) with ME speakers' adoption of simplification strategies. Similarly, Lowenberg (1984), who detected the presence of this feature in acrolectal ME, interpreted it as evidence of nativisation 'due to the generalization of (grammar) rules' (p. 117).

Besides ME, similar tendencies have been found in many other new varieties of English. Kachru and Smith (2008) claimed that 'in African, Caribbean,

East, South, and Southeast Asian varieties of English, the complex system of marking count/mass distinction in English is simplified' (p. 90). More recently, Hall, Schmidtke and Vickers (2013) analysed the countable use of nouns that are generally non-count in Standard English across diverse Outer Circle and Expanding Circle Englishes. They found this variation to be '(a) *infrequent*, even for the most variable noun; but (b) *recurrent* compared with (Inner Circle) usage, where it is almost entirely absent; and (c) *widespread*, attestable across numerous L1 backgrounds and geographical regions' (p. 15). Furthermore, they found little evidence of substrate influence in this variability in usage, a finding which suggests that rule regularisation and simplification may have a bigger role to play.

Our understanding about the nature and potential causes of this syntactic variation derives, in part, from the way that we have analysed it. Earlier studies (e.g. Wong, 1983; Lowenberg, 1984) relied predominantly on randomly collected citations that were compared with either parallel structures found in substrate languages or patterns found within English itself. With such an approach, it is hardly surprising that interpretations involving processes of overgeneralisation and rule regularisation have been so dominant.

The present chapter proposes an alternative approach, one that considers the countable use of non-count nouns in ME (and possibly other Outer Circle varieties) to be a manifestation of variation in nominal classification. In order to understand the dynamics that promote this variation, this study used data extracted from the Malaysian English Newspaper Corpus (MEN Corpus) to investigate how common nouns are classified in ME. Two groups of nouns were targeted for analysis. The first group comprised a small subset of a group of nouns that are always non-count in Standard English, nouns that Allan (1980) referred to as 'true uncountables' (p. 560). The second group comprised count nouns that combine with the unit noun *piece* and its plural form *pieces*. By focusing on how these nouns were located within a noun phrase and how the noun phrase interacted with other parts of the sentence, it was possible to accurately detect examples of the countable use of non-count nouns and the uncountable use of count nouns in ME. These examples were then classified according to their pattern of divergence from Standard English. The utilisation of a corpus-based approach ensured that only authentic data were sampled and that for each noun studied, exhaustive data surrounding its use were extracted and analysed.

On the basis of the compilation of these patterns, I argue that variation in nominal classification in ME is driven not just by simplification strategies and rule generalisation but also by contact with the classifier languages spoken by many Malaysians. What is salient is not so much the occurrence of these patterns but what they signify collectively. Focusing on the influences of Malay and Chinese, this chapter demonstrates that these patterns of use represent nontraditional perceptions of countability and its role in nominal classification. Although infrequent, these nativised patterns are recurrent and provide competition for the far more common standard patterns because they do not significantly affect comprehension and are well tolerated within a society that is familiar with this alternative way of classifying common nouns. Such competition between nativised and standard patterns is characteristic of many contact situations that involve group second language acquisition and language shift (Winford, 2003, p. 236).

Methodology

The present study utilised a corpus-based approach to examine variation in nominal classification in ME. The data presented in this chapter were extracted from the MEN Corpus, a 5-million-word corpus of newspaper texts published between 1 August 2001 and 31 January 2002 in two of the most established English language newspapers in Malaysia—*The Star* and the *New Straits Times*. The corpus includes a balanced spread of topics and genres, comprising local and national news stories, regional and international pieces written by Malaysian correspondents, court and parliamentary reports, business, financial and sports news articles, and opinion pieces. Using Mike Scott's *Wordsmith Tools*, two categories of syntactic variation were extracted from the MEN Corpus for analysis—the countable use of nouns that are typically non-count in Standard English and the non-countable use of nouns that are generally regarded as count nouns in Standard English.

As mentioned earlier, one of the most frequently observed characteristics of ME is its tendency to pluralise non-count nouns. Although common, this is not the only syntactic pattern that reflects the countable use of non-count nouns. In order to uncover as many patterns associated with this propensity as possible, I extracted from the MEN Corpus all instances of 15 nouns that are typically non-count in Standard English but are known to be used countably in ME.[1] On the basis of the contexts of these nouns, all instances of their use as countable nouns were identified. Table 2.1 provides a summary of the results of this exercise. As can be seen, a total of 131 instances of the countable

---

1 This included instances of the adjectival use of these nouns (e.g., *information* folder) and where they form a part of a fixed expression (e.g. *information* technology, *Information* Minister).

use of the selected non-count nouns were identified. Although pluralisation of non-count nouns using the *–s* inflectional morpheme is the most common syntactic pattern which reflects variation in nominal classification, two other patterns were detected: the modification of non-count nouns using determiners that typically co-occur with singular count nouns and the modification of these nouns using determiners and verb forms generally used with plural count nouns.

TABLE 2.1   *Countable use of selected non-count nouns in the MEN Corpus*

Non-count noun	Countable use of non-count nouns		
	Plural *–s*	Singular determiners	Plural determiners
advice (n=356)	0	5	1
ammunition (n=54)	7	0	1
clothing (n=121)	7	0	1
equipment (n=506)	8	2	15
feedback (n=221)	5	2	0
furniture (n=151)	0	0	3
information (n=2371)	0	1	13
jewellery (n=260)	1	0	11
legislation (n=100)	6	10	0
luggage (n=57)	0	1	0
machinery (n=112)	4	0	0
scenery (n=39)	2	0	0
signage (n=25)	18	0	0
stationery (n=38)	2	0	0
terminology (n=12)	4	1	0
Total	**64**	**22**	**45**

In order to explore the non-countable use of count nouns in ME, I extracted all instances of the unit noun *piece* and its plural form *pieces* from the MEN Corpus.[2] In Standard English, the main function of *piece(s)*, either generally or with *of*, is to denote the quantity of a non-count referent, such as in '*a piece* of

---

2   Excluded were the adverbial expressions *a piece* (e.g. 'This US-made tyre costs RM1000 *a piece*') and *per piece* (e.g. 'The crabs are priced at RM49.90 *per piece*') as well as instances

bacon' and 'two *pieces* of advice' (Quirk, Greenbaum, Leech, & Svartvik, 1985, p. 249). It is also used with singular count nouns to express partition, as in 'a *piece* of a loaf' (Quirk et al., 1985, p. 250). However, *piece(s)* cannot combine with plural count nouns, including those that are invariably plural (e.g. *cattle*). In ME, the function of *piece(s)* extends beyond conveying the notion of partition and can in fact combine with singular and plural count nouns to express a whole. Table 2.2 lists all the count nouns that are used with *piece(s)* in the MEN Corpus.

These two categories of syntactic variation are further explored in the next section.

TABLE 2.2   *Count nouns that combine with piece(s) in the MEN Corpus*

Noun	Frequency	Noun	Frequency
disc	5	coupon	1
glove	5	dollar-note	1
pizza	5	forest	1
coin	3	garment	1
diaper	3	industrial lot	1
tyre	3	invention	1
bag	2	jersey	1
choker	2	lego set	1
mascara	2	log	1
monitor	2	mask	1
shirt	2	mattress	1
artefact	1	ornament	1
banana	1	painting	1
block	1	pendant	1
book cover	1	pin	1
bra	1	prawn	1
card	1	result slip	1
carpet	1	street bunting	1
clove	1	watch	1

where *piece(s)* combines with a localised word (e.g. *mooncake* and *bird's nest* 'edible swift's nest').

Data

Countable Use of Non-count Nouns

In Standard English, the nouns in Table 2.1 are considered non-count nouns. These are notionally lexical items that refer to things that cannot be counted; for example, Quirk et al. (1985) conceptualised them as 'denoting an undifferentiated mass or continuum', as opposed to count nouns, which denote 'individual countable entities' (p. 246). This is not entirely unproblematic. Most people would find the suggestion that *equipment* is 'an undifferentiated mass' in the same way that *water* is to be counter-intuitive. As Quirk and his colleagues (1985) acknowledged:

> The distinction between count nouns and non-count nouns is not fully explainable as necessarily inherent in 'real world' denotata.... Rather, the justification for the count/non-count distinction is based on the grammatical characteristics of the English noun. (p. 248)

Thus, while count nouns typically allow plural morphology, non-count nouns do not. Count and non-count nouns can also be distinguished by the determiners they take—some determiners can only be used with either count or non-count nouns, while others can be used with both. In the words of Huddlestone (1984), 'countability has to do with a noun's potential for combining with various types of determiner' (p. 246).

Therefore, in Standard English, constructions such as *ammunitions, jewelleries* and *signages* would be considered ungrammatical. In ME, these non-count nouns are regularly inflected with the morpheme *–s* to indicate plurality. The 15 non-count nouns studied here exhibited this pattern 64 times (see Table 2.1). The citations below illustrate the ways in which some of these inflected non-count nouns are used in ME:

1. Sessions Court judge Suraya Othman has fixed March 19 to 21 next year for the trial of two former commandos from the 22 Commando Regiment in Kuala Kubu Baru charged with committing armed robbery of a bank on Aug 2 and for the unlawful possession of *ammunitions*. (*The Star*, 12 October 2001)
2. Dr Jemilah said Mercy was trying to get a Royal Malaysian Air Force aircraft to fly in the volunteers, equipment and *clothings* to Quetta at the Pakistan-Afghanistan border. (*The New Straits Times*, 9 October 2001)

3. Sim said the Federation had obtained *feedbacks* from the aggrieved parties and have forwarded certain recommendations to the relevant government agencies in Sarawak asking for urgent action to be taken to resolve the problem. (*The Star*, 26 October 2001)
4. Dr Abubaker said the Government had also passed a number of *legislations* with the view of protecting investors in Yemen and pledged that Sana'a would provide all the support and security needed. (*The New Straits Times*, 2 August 2001)
5. 'Unlike in Sabah, the Sarawak BN is well prepared for this election. Their *machineries* are well organised and they are very experienced', he said here today. (*The New Straits Times*, 7 September 2001)
6. Along our journey, we met an avid photographer who makes seasonal pilgrimages to the park to capture the diverse *sceneries* for his website. (*The Star*, 28 October 2001)
7. Road users are advised to drive carefully and adhere to the *signages* along the project site. (*The New Straits Times*, 5 September 2001)
8. The Rotary Club of Damansara, together with the Persatuan Didik Muda Lembah Kelang donated uniforms, *stationeries* and books to 33 needy students of SJK (Tamil) Jalan Bangsar in Kuala Lumpur recently. (*The New Straits Times*, 7 September 2001)

A less widespread syntactic divergence in ME with regard to the 15 non-count nouns studied is their occurrence with determiners that are typically used to modify singular count nouns. In most cases, the uninflected non-count noun appears to have been reclassified to as a singular count noun through the use of determiners such as the indefinite articles *a* and *an*, the cardinal number *one* and the general ordinal *another*. Occurring a total of 22 times in the data examined in this study, this pattern of use is demonstrated in the citations below:

9. The guidelines on highland development may be turned into *a legislation* to prevent uncontrolled development which will affect the environment. (*The New Straits Times*, 16 August 2001)
10. 'Racing in the rain enables the bike to retain the original horsepower as the system cools down much faster and we also have *an* electronic *equipment* which serves as traction control to avoid spins'. (*The Star*, 18 October 2001)
11. The decision to allow passengers to carry only *one hand luggage* weighing less than five kilograms and compelling them to be at the Kuala Lumpur

International Airport early to board the flights from next week was welcomed by Malaysia Nanban. (*The Star*, 6 October 2001)
12. He also had *another advice*—some might even interpret as a warning—to re ellious MCA Youth chief Datuk Ong Tee Keat. 'I hope to meet Tee Keat again', he said. (*The Star*, 25 December 2001)

All the examples above demonstrate the reclassification of uninflected non-count nouns to singular count nouns. Paradoxically, in ME, uninflected non-count nouns are occasionally treated as inherently plural (and therefore countable). Some prototypical invariably plural nouns in Standard English include *cattle, people, police* and *vermin* (see Quirk et al., 1985, p. 303 for other examples). These nouns have no plural marking but are treated as plural nouns, taking plural determiners and agreement. Of the 15 nouns analysed in this study, only seven exhibit this pattern of variation—*advice, ammunition, clothing, equipment, furniture, information* and *jewellery*, of which only *equipment, information* and *jewellery* are regularly reclassified (see Table 2.1). The following are some examples of this syntactic pattern extracted from the MEN Corpus:

13. It is time to act on *those advice*. (*The Star*, 5 August 2001)
14. The *equipment*, which Noridah claims that Asum requested her to purchase in advance for the biennial Games, *include* two sets of diving manual order equipment, printing of score sheets for officials and other equipment. (*The New Straits Times*, 27 October 2001)
15. My eyes wander to the walls and the *furniture* that *decorate* the house that Luiz has made his home throughout his stay in Malaysia. (*The New Straits Times*, 12 August 2001)
16. Selected Stefan Hafner *jewellery are* available at The Carat Club in Suria KLCC and Bangsar. (*The Star*, 26 September 2001)
17. He advised women not to wear *too many jewellery* at public places and urged motorcyclists to secure their machines properly. (*The New Straits Times*, 26 November 2001)

Non-countable Use of Count Nouns

Piece(s) is one of the most productive unit nouns in the English language, combining with more than 100 different collocates (Biber, Johansson, Leech, Conrad, & Finegan, 1999, p. 250). In Standard English, it usually combines with non-count nouns to quantify an undifferentiated mass or a phenomenon and with count nouns to express a part of a whole. Therefore, *piece(s)* plays a strong partitive function in Standard English.

In ME, besides this function, *piece(s)* can also collocate with both singular and plural count nouns to denote either the entirety of the referent or the quantity of the referent. Data extracted from the MEN Corpus demonstrate the use of *piece(s)* with 38 count nouns ranging from *disc, glove* and *pizza* to *painting, pendant* and *pin* (see Table 2.2). This pattern occurs 61 times in the MEN Corpus. The following are some examples:

18. Twenty four premises were raided and 18,000 *pieces* of *CDs, VCDs and DVDs* worth RM100,000 were confiscated. (*The Star*, 10 January 2002)
19. Malaysia is the largest exporter of *natural rubber gloves* in the world, with 30 billion *pieces* produced in 1999. (*The New Straits Times*, 27 October 2001)
20. 'The *16.8gm silver coin* is made of sterling silver with .925 purity and only 2,500 *pieces* will be sold at RM150 a piece', he said after the launch at Bank Negara. (*The Star*, 30 January 2002)
21. He said the Japanese Judo Federation impressed with the development programme of the MJF have delivered about 400 *pieces* of *mattress* and other equipment. (*The New Straits Times*, 20 August 2001)
22. It virtually coated every *piece* of *prawn* in a spicy concoction of onions and garlic. (*The Star*, 20 October 2001)

This divergence in the function of *piece(s)* in ME appears to be related to variation in nominal classification. In Standard English, the –s plural morpheme in the nouns in examples 18 and 19 would have been sufficient to mark countability, as would the determiner *every* in example 22. In ME, the correlation between these grammatical contexts and nominal countability appears to be much weaker, and in some instances, this results in the nouns being treated as uncountable. In such a situation, the discreteness of these nouns is emphasised using unit nouns such as *piece(s)*.

Discussion

Where variation in nominal classification in ME is concerned, earlier studies have tended to focus on the pluralisation of non-count nouns, a characteristic often attributed to the generalisation of the singular-plural distinction in count nouns to non-count nouns. The present study demonstrates that this syntactic variation is more broadly manifested than we might have thought. While it is true that the pluralisation of non-count nouns is the most widespread of the patterns examined here, there are at least three other patterns that should be examined if we are to have a greater understanding of the dynamics that drive this variation in ME. These patterns include the reclassification of non-count nouns to singular count nouns, the reclassification of non-count nouns to plural count nouns and the use of the unit noun *piece(s)* with count nouns to denote either the entirety of the referent or the quantity of the referent.

I argue here that, collectively, these syntactic patterns suggest the influences of classifier languages spoken in Malaysia. In this section, I shall describe some principles of nominal classification in Malay and Chinese and demonstrate how these may have shaped the way that nouns are classified in the variety of English spoken in Malaysia. A good starting point is Wong's (1983) comment on the unpredictability of nominal countability: 'The count-non-count distinction in standard English is a grammatical rather than a logical one, which may be treated quite differently in another language' (p. 130). Kachru and Smith (2008) made a similar observation, noting the following:

> In English, mass nouns (*equipment, sugar*) are inherently singular, in Sinhalese and Swahili, they are treated as plural. In many languages, there is no distinction between a *shirt* and (*a pair of*) *trousers*. (p. 90)

The grammaticalisation of the distinction between count and non-count nouns is central to the system of nominal classification in the English language. For languages such as Malay and Chinese, nouns are classified according to complex classifier systems. In his seminal work on classifiers, Allan (1977, p. 285) defined them according to the following two criteria:

a. They occur as morphemes in surface structures under specifiable conditions; and
b. they have meaning, in the sense that a classifier denotes some salient perceived or imputed characteristic of the entity to which an associated noun refers (or may refer).

Thus, one would not be wrong in saying that the English language has classifiers. Words that function as classifiers in English include *head* in a *head of lettuce* and *pride* in *a pride of lions*. English is nevertheless not a classifier language in the way that Malay and Chinese are. In his analysis of 50 classifier languages, Allan (1977, p. 297) identified seven categories of classifiers, namely material, shape, consistency, size, location, arrangement and quanta, of which only the last two categories occur in English and other non-classifier languages. Furthermore, classifiers are not an obligatory component of a noun phrase in the English language. Count nouns, for instance, do not require classifiers (e.g. *three puppies*). The main function of classifiers in English is to individuate non-count nouns (e.g. three *cups* of coffee, a *drop* of water), but even these can occur without a classifier (e.g. *three coffees, some water*) (Lehrer, 1986, pp. 109–110). Most crucially, while classifier languages 'treat enumerable entities and enumerable quanta in much the same way', English grammaticalises 'the distinction between entity-denoting nouns and mass-denoting nouns' (Lyons, 1977, p. 463).

As such, most traditional grammars of English (e.g. Quirk et al., 1985, pp. 245–248; Biber et al., 1999, pp. 241–245) divide common nouns into two main groups, count nouns (e.g. *cat, tree* and *remark*) and non-count nouns (e.g. *water, money* and *equipment*), with a third group comprising nouns that can be either count or non-count depending on the intended referent. The noun *oak*, for instance, is a non-count noun when it is used to refer to a material (as in 'The daughter had to bring in logs of *oak* and pine'.) but a count noun when it is used to refer to the individual specimen (as in 'Well, we've got an *oak* out the front'.) (Biber et al., 1999, p. 242). Theoretically, the difference between count and non-count nouns has a semantic dimension—count nouns are supposed to denote discrete entities and non-count nouns, indistinct masses—but in reality, it is their morphological and syntactic properties that define them. So while count nouns allow plural suffixes, combine directly with numerals, and take determiners such as *every, each, a few* and *both*, non-count nouns do not allow plural suffixes, can only be modified by numerals that are accompanied by classifiers, and take determiners such as *little* and *much*.

Because of this, some scholars (e.g. Allan, 1980) speak of countability as a characteristic of the noun phrase rather than the noun. In other words, it is the morphosyntactic environment that the noun occurs in, rather than the noun itself, that determines its countability. Nevertheless, some nouns are generally to be found in countable noun phrases (e.g. *car, boat, beetle, table*, etc.), while others are more typically situated in uncountable noun phrases (e.g. *lighting, equipment, evidence, furniture*, etc.). Between these extremes are those that occur in both countable and uncountable noun phrases, and it is these nouns, according to Allan (1980, p. 548), that exhibit different levels of countability. Regardless of how we represent countability and nominal classification in English, what is clear is that this language 'requires that the countability of the (noun phrase) reference be known' (Allan, 1980, p. 542).

This is not the case with Malay and Chinese. In Malay, the root form of a common noun is neutral for number (Carson, 2000, p. 8). Although plurality can be indicated using reduplication (e.g. *buku-buku* 'books'; for details, see Nik Safiah, Farid, Hashim, & Abdul Hamid, 1993, pp. 133–136), this is not mandatory, and whether the noun is singular or plural is generally deducible from its context (Chung, 2000, p. 165). Another way of marking plurality in Malay is through the use of a cardinal number followed by a classifier. The following examples by Carson (2000, p. 7) demonstrate these two ways of marking plurality:

23. **Buku-buku** *ini* *berat*
 book-PL these heavy
 'These books are heavy'

24. *Dia* *ada* **tiga** **buah** **buku**
 she has three CL book
 'She has three books'

So, on the one hand, it can be said that the vast majority of Malay common nouns behave like English non-count nouns because they require classifiers to be transformed into countable entities (e.g. Carson, 2000, pp. 20–21). On the other hand, they are clearly different from English non-count nouns because they can be pluralised.

Like all classifier languages, Malay is equipped with a sophisticated classifier system comprising sortal and mensural classifiers (Lyons, 1977, p. 463). Sortal classifiers are semantically specific in that they capture the physical attributes of the nouns with which they are used. For instance, the classifier *orang* (literally, also 'person') typically precedes human nouns, while the classifier *buah* (literally, also 'fruit') is generally used for 'solid inanimate objects' (Hopper, 1986, p. 310). Other classifiers include *helai* (for objects that are in strands or layers, such as hair and clothing), *batang* (for cylindrical objects, but also meandering waterways), *bidang* (for referents that spread over a wide area, such as land or paddy fields), *rumpun* (for referents that grow in sheaves, such as paddy or lemongrass) and so on. A mensural classifier 'individuates' (Lyons, 1977, p. 463) the referent using units of measure. Hence, in the construction *dua kilogram epal* (literally, 'two kilogrammes of apple'), *kilogram* 'kilogramme' is used to express *epal* 'apple' as enumerable units.

Of the two types of classifiers, sortal classifiers are by far the more complex. Because they are semantically specific, they 'supply, or presuppose, a principle for individuating entities and grouping them into kinds' (Lyons, 1977, p. 464). This is most appropriately illustrated using the graphic representation of the classification of Malay common nouns produced by Nik Safiah et al. (1993), which is translated, adapted, and reproduced in Figure 2.1.

As can be seen, all common nouns in Malay can be classified into animate and inanimate categories. The former can be divided into human and non-human categories and the latter into institutional and non-institutional categories. The inanimate, non-institutional category can be further grouped into concrete and abstract nouns, of which only the abstract nouns are divided into count and non-count nouns. In short, nominal classification in Malay is based primarily on semantic properties (Nik Safiah et al., 1993, p. 100). Countability is a lower-order criterion that is relevant only to a very small group of nouns known collectively as inanimate, non-institutional abstract nouns. Within this last category, what distinguishes count nouns from non-count nouns is that the former can combine with a cardinal number without a classifier. It is therefore possible to say *satu senyuman* 'one smile' and *dua pendapat* 'two opinions'. Other classes of nouns require classifiers. These are generally class specific, although some classifiers may co-occur with several different noun classes (Aikhenvald, 2000, quoted in Goddard, 2011, p. 346). For instance, while the classifier *orang* is specific to human nouns, the classifier *buah* can be used for certain institutional nouns (e.g. dua *buah sekolah* 'two schools') as well as for some non-institutional, concrete nouns (e.g. tiga *buah buku* 'three

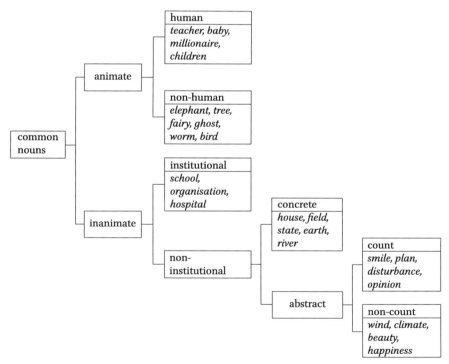

FIGURE 2.1   *Classification of common nouns in Malay (translated and adapted from Nik Safiah et al., 1993, p. 100).*

books'). A speaker of Malay is therefore required to 'categorize objects in their environment and pair them with the appropriate numeral classifier, using the language-specific classifier system' (Khazrivati & Winskel, 2009, p. 290).

Hokkien, Cantonese and Mandarin are also classifier languages. Like Malay, they do not make a grammatical distinction between count and non-count nouns, and plurality is indicated using cardinal numbers and classifiers. Unlike Malay, Chinese common nouns do not typically have plural morphology.[3] Some scholars have suggested that nouns in Chinese languages are all non-count nouns that have their 'plurality already built in' (e.g. Chierchia, 1998, p. 53). Others suggest that in Chinese, bare nouns (nouns without any determiners, classifiers or numerals) 'are neither singular nor plural, but somehow "neutral" or "unspecified" for number' (Rullmann & You, 2003, p. 1).

In his seminal work on Chinese grammar, Chao (1968, pp. 505–513) categorised Chinese common nouns according to the type of classifiers and measure words that they take. In his paper on classifier systems across diverse Chinese dialects and languages, Tai (1994) demonstrated how Chinese classifiers are linked to notions of animacy, shape, size and consistency (pp. 484–488) which surround nouns. Some of the classifiers examined by Tai include those used for animals (e.g. Hokkien 尾 *be*, Mandarin 只 *zhi*) and those associated with notions of length (e.g. Mandarin 根 *gen*, Cantonese 条 *tieu*, Hokkien 支 *ki*), flatness (e.g. Cantonese 块 *fai*, Mandarin 张 *zhang*) and roundness (e.g. Hokkien 粒 *liap*, Cantonese 粒 *lap*, Mandarin 粒 *li*).

The incongruence among English, Malay and Chinese in terms of how nouns are classified must have played a significant role in the two categories of syntactic variation examined in this study. While English distinguishes common nouns according to countability, Malay and Chinese classify nouns according to the classifiers that they take and, therefore, the semantic properties of the referents. ME users, most of whom are multilingual, straddle at least two systems of nominal classification—one which uses semantic cues and one which relies predominantly on morphosyntactic cues. Although it is possible that highly proficient speakers of ME are able to suppress the influences of their other languages when they are speaking in English, research has shown that in most cases, 'both languages are activated at some level *whenever* bilinguals speak—even when they speak in one language' (Myers-Scotton, 2006, p. 300).

The reliance on semantic cues can be observed in the three patterns associated with the countable use of non-count nouns in ME. Although the 15 nouns examined in this study are non-count in Standard English, they denote con-

---

3   For a possible exception, see Li's (1999) interpretation of the Mandarin 'plural morpheme' *-men*.

crete entities and are semantically very different from prototypical non-count nouns such as *water* and *mud*. ME speakers who are used to classifying nouns according to their semantic properties are likely to group *ammunition, clothing* and *equipment* together with count nouns such as *book, chair* and *house*. That the equivalents of these nouns are readily pluralised through reduplication in Malay (e.g. *senjata-senjata* 'ammunition-PL', *pakaian-pakaian* 'clothing-PL', *peralatan-peralatan* 'equipment-PL', *maklumat-maklumat* 'information-PL' and *barang-barang kemas* 'jewellery-PL') must also have a role to play, not only in the tendency to pluralise some of these nouns with the *–s* inflectional morpheme but also in the treatment of their uninflected forms as singular count nouns.

The possibility of such substrate influence does not negate the impact of processes of simplification. In fact, it is possible for the substrate structures to be reinforced by structures within the English language. The fact that all the non-count nouns analysed in this study can be expressed in countable terms, using either their count equivalents or unit nouns, must serve to reinforce their discreteness from the point of view of the Malay speaker. Thus, *machinery, scenery, signage* and *terminology* are non-count nouns, but their equivalents—*machine, scene, sign* and *term*—are count nouns. In some cases, the count equivalents are the names of various items subsumed under the non-count referent and are phonemically unrelated: *clothing* and *jewellery* are uncountable, but *skirt, dress, shirt, pendant, necklace* and *bracelet* are countable. *Information, luggage* and *advice* can be expressed in countable terms using the general unit noun *piece*, as in 'a piece of information'. *Clothing* and *underwear* can be realised as count nouns using the constructions *an article of* and *an item of*. Such structural ambiguities are common in the English language, and many Outer Circle varieties of English exhibit evidence of attempts at generalising patterns surrounding these features (see, for instance, Kirkpatrick, 2010, pp. 106–107). Thus, if *suitcase, bag, duffel, haversack* and *backpack* are count nouns, surely *luggage* must be as well. By the same token, if we can speak of *one suitcase*, surely we can say *one luggage*. By attributing countability to these non-count nouns, ME users are also legitimising the inflection of these nouns for plural and the use of articles, such as *a* and *an*, cardinal numbers such as *one* and general ordinals such as *another*, as their determiners.

The influence of classifier languages in ME can also be seen in the way that some uninflected non-count nouns are treated as invariably plural. In this pattern of use, the noun is not marked for plural but takes plural determiners and verbs. That the root form of a common noun in Malay and Chinese is neutral for number and can in fact be plural may have a role to play in this pattern of nativisation in ME. In Malay and Chinese, and to a certain extent in ME, whether the noun denotes a singular referent or a plural referent can be deduced from its context. This reliance on context can be seen in examples 13 to 17, which clearly provide for plural interpretations of the nouns. The fact that in Standard English, there is a group of nouns that are inherently plural (e.g. *people* and *cattle*) must reinforce the validity of the plural variants of nouns such as *equipment, furniture, information* and *jewellery* in ME.

The use of the unit noun *piece(s)* with singular and plural count nouns also seems to be triggered by the retention of Malay and Chinese classifier systems in ME. As mentioned earlier, in Malay and Chinese, the use of numerals to determine common nouns typically requires the concurrent use of classifiers. How the Malay and Chinese numeral + classifier + noun construction might have been transferred into ME is illustrated below:

25. Malay: 18,000   *keping*   CD
    Chinese: 18,000   片   CD
    Mandarin: 18,000   *pian*   CD
    Hokkien: 18,000   *pian*   CD
    Cantonese: 18,000   *p'in*   CD
                18,000   CL for thin objects   CD
    ME: 18,000   *pieces of*   CDS
                '18,000 CDS'

The present pool of data is too small to assess whether or not there is a correlation between the use of *piece(s)* and the physical attributes of the referent of the nouns: only 11 of the 38 nouns collocated with *piece(s)* more than once. With a much larger pool of data, it might be possible to establish whether *piece(s)* is used as a substitute for a specific Malay or a Chinese classifier. It is nevertheless clear that in ME, *piece(s)* sometimes plays the role of a quasi-classifier that emphasises the discreteness of count nouns.

Conclusion

This study demonstrates that variation in nominal classification extends beyond the commonly observed pattern involving the pluralisation of non-count nouns and is in fact manifested in at least three other syntactic patterns in ME: the reclassification of non-count nouns to singular nouns, the reclassification of non-count nouns to plural count nouns and the use of the unit noun *piece(s)* to emphasise the discreteness of count nouns.

Earlier studies have tended to interpret some of these patterns as outcomes of simplification strategies and rule regularisation. This chapter argues that although these processes are important, they do not operate alone in the formation of these nativised patterns. Instead, these patterns are driven by the interaction between these processes and the influence of classifier languages such as Malay and Chinese. Whereas English classifies common nouns according to countability, ME appears to have incorporated a system of classification that relies in part on semantic cues. The flexibility with which some of these nouns are treated reflects the tendency in Malay and Chinese for the root form of a common noun to be unspecified for number. That even prototypical count nouns occasionally need their discreteness emphasised through the use of the unit noun *piece(s)* demonstrates the significance of contact with classifier languages in ME.

Although not as prevalent as standard patterns, the nativised patterns underlying variation in nominal classification in ME are tangible and recurrent manifestations of language contact in ME. Their presence in newspaper English, a relatively formal domain of language use in Malaysia, is an indication of the influence of classifier languages in Malaysia. In spite of the widespread acquisition and use of the English language, classifier languages like Malay and Chinese have continued to play significant roles and functions within the society. The formal status and functions of Malay (see, for instance, Asmah, 1996, p. 526; Pillai, 2006, p. 64; Rajadurai, 2011, p. 27) and the social dominance of Chinese (see, for instance, Wong & Thambyrajah, 1991, p. 4; Cheng, 2003, p. 86; David, Cavallaro & Coluzzi, 2009, p. 162) mean that there is an intense and on-going interaction between these languages and English. Under such circumstances, syntactic variation, especially that which reflects the norms of the substrate languages, tends to be well tolerated. As such, although they may be ungrammatical in Standard English, they 'may well be acceptable to educated speakers of Malaysian or other non-native varieties of Standard English' (Lowenberg, 1992, p. 116).

Like the Outer Circle and Expanding Circle varieties examined by Hall, Schmidtke and Vickers (2013), ME appears to have a preference for standard patterns. This preference for standard forms led Hall et al. to suggest that 'there is little evidence... that countable usage is emerging as a new norm across or within (Outer Circle) or (Expanding Circle) varieties' (p. 18). I argue that the 'interaction and competition' among nativised and standard variants is characteristic of many contact situations that involve group second language acquisition and language shift. Winford (2003, p. 236) proposed that eventually some of these nativised features may be 'selected and conventionalized as part of the communal grammar, while others are discarded'. In the case of ME, the competition among the standard and the nativised patterns will continue as long as Malay and Chinese continue to be relevant to ME speakers.

References

Allan, K. (1977). Classifiers. *Language, 53*(2), 285–311.

———. (1980). Nouns and countability. *Language, 56*(3), 541–567.

Asmah, Haji O. (1996). Post-imperial English in Malaysia. In J. A. Fishman, A. W. Conrad, & A. Rubal-Lopez (Eds.), *Post-imperial English: Status change in former British and American colonies, 1940–1990* (pp. 513–533). New York: Mouton de Gruyter.

Baskaran, L. M. (2005). *A Malaysian English primer: Aspects of Malaysian English features*. Kuala Lumpur: University of Malaya Press.

Biber, D., Johansson, S., Leech, G., Conrad, S., & Finegan, E. (1999). *Longman grammar of spoken and written English*. Essex: Longman.

Carson, J. C. (2000). *The semantics of number in Malay noun phrases*. (Unpublished master's thesis). University of Calgary, Alberta, Canada.

Chao, Y. R. (1968). *A grammar of spoken Chinese*. Los Angeles: University of California Press.

Cheng, K. K. Y. (2003). Language shift and language maintenance in mixed marriages: A case study of a Malaysian-Chinese family. *International Journal of the Sociology of Language. 161*, 81–90.

Chierchia, G. (1998). Plurality of mass nouns and the notion of 'semantic parameter'. In S. Rothstein (Ed.), *Events and grammar* (pp. 53–103). Dordrecht: Kluwer.

Chung, S. (2000). On reference to kinds in Indonesian. *Natural Language Semantics, 8*, 157–171.

David, M. K., Cavallaro, F., & Coluzzi, P. (2009). Language policies—Impact on language maintenance and teaching: Focus on Malaysia, Singapore, Brunei and the Philippines. *The Linguistics Journal: Special Edition. Language, Culture and Identity in Asia*, 155–191.

Goddard, C. (2011). *Semantic analysis: A practical introduction* (2nd ed.). Oxford: Oxford University Press.

Hall, C. J., Schmidtke, D., & Vickers, J. (2013). Countability in world Englishes. *World Englishes, 32*(1), 1–22.

Hopper, P. J. (1986). Some discourse functions of classifiers in Malay. In C. Craig (Ed.), *Noun classes and categorization: Proceedings of a symposium on categorization and noun classification, Eugene, Oregon, October 1983* (pp. 309–325). Amsterdam/Philadelphia: John Benjamins.

Huddlestone, R. (1984). *Introduction to the grammar of English*. Cambridge: Cambridge University Press.

Kachru, Y., & Smith, L. E. (2008). *Cultures, contexts, and world Englishes*. New York: Routledge.

Khazriyati, S., & Winskel, H. (2009). An investigation into Malay numeral classifier acquisition through an elicited production task. *First Language, 29*(3), 289–311.

Kirkpatrick, A. (2010). *English as a lingua franca in ASEAN: A multilingual model*. Hong Kong: Hong Kong University Press.

Lehrer, A. (1986). English classifier constructions. *Lingua, 68*, 109–148.

Li, Y. -H. A. (1999). Plurality in a classifier language. *Journal of East Asian Linguistics, 8*, 75–99.

Lowenberg, P. H. (1984). *English in the Malay Archipelago: Nativization and its functions in a sociolinguistic area*. (Unpublished doctoral dissertation). University of Illinois, Urbana-Champaign.

———. (1992). Testing English as a world language: Issues in assessing non-native proficiency. In B. B. Kachru (Ed.), *The other tongue: English across cultures* (pp. 108–121). Urbana, IL: University of Illinois Press.

Lyons, J. (1977). *Semantics*. Cambridge: Cambridge University Press.

McArthur, T. (1998). *Concise Oxford companion to the English language*. Oxford: Oxford University Press.

Myers-Scotton, C. (2006). *Multiple voices: An introduction to bilingualism*. Malden, MA: Blackwell.

Nik Safiah, K., Farid, M. O., Hashim, M., & Abdul Hamid, M. (1993). *Tatabahasa Dewan* [The Dewan grammar]. Kuala Lumpur: Dewan Bahasa dan Pustaka.

Pillai, S. (2006). Malaysian English as a first language. In M. K. David (Ed.), *Language choices and discourse of Malaysian families: Case studies of families in Kuala Lumpur, Malaysia* (pp. 61–75). Petaling Jaya: Strategic Information and Research Development Centre.

Quirk, R., Greenbaum, S., Leech, G., & Svartvik, J. (1985). *A comprehensive grammar of the English language*. London/New York: Longman.

Rajadurai, J. (2011). Crossing borders: The linguistic practices of aspiring bilinguals in the Malay Community. *Australian Review of Applied Linguistics, 34*(1), 24–39.

Rullmann, H., & You, A. (2003, July). *General number and the semantics and pragmatics of indefinite bare nouns in Mandarin Chinese*. Paper presented at the International Workshop on Current Research in the Semantics-Pragmatics Interface, Michigan State University, East Lansing.

Schneider, E. W. (2003). Evolutionary patterns of new Englishes and the special case of Malaysian English. *Asian Englishes, 6*(2), 44–63.

Tai, J. H. Y. (1994). Chinese classifier systems and human categorization. In M. Y. Chen & O. J. L. Tzeng (Eds.), *In honour of William S. Y. Wang: Inter-disciplinary studies on language and language change* (pp. 479–494). Taipei: Pyramid Press.

Tongue, R. K. (1974). *The English of Singapore and Malaysia*. Singapore: Eastern Universities Press.

Winford, D. (2003). *An introduction to contact linguistics*. Malden, MA: Blackwell.

Wong, I. F. H. (1983). Simplification features in the structure of colloquial Malaysian English. In R. B. Noss (Ed.), *Varieties of English in Southeast Asia* (pp. 125–149). Singapore: Singapore University Press.

Wong, I. F. H., & Thambyrajah, H. (1991). The Malaysian sociolinguistic situation: An overview. In A. Kwan-Terry (Ed.), *Child language development in Singapore and Malaysia* (pp. 3–11). Singapore: Singapore University Press.

CHAPTER 3

The New [t] in Malaysian English

Toshiko Yamaguchi and Magnús Pétursson

Introduction

One salient characteristic feature of the pronunciation of ME is the replacement of the dental fricatives [θ] or [ð] with the stop [t]. This stop, or more precisely, dental stop, which is dubbed 'the new [t]' in this chapter, is a voiceless sound emerging from a voiced or voiceless dental fricative that differs acoustically from the ordinary alveolar stop [t]. The non-fricative realisation of [θ] or [ð] has been extensively reported in studies on different varieties of New English (Mesthrie, 2008, p. 318). In ME, it occurs sporadically; not all dental fricatives are transformed into the new [t], and their realisations vary among individuals and even within a single utterance by an individual. There seem to be several factors, thus far largely unexplained, which govern the new [t]'s robust appearance. The first part of this chapter summarises the highlights of two acoustic experiments we have conducted in recent years, parts of which have been reported in two papers (Yamaguchi & Pétursson, 2012; Yamaguchi, 2014). The tool employed to verify the stop consonants is the VOT, which refers to the time lag between the release of the stop closure and the onset of the voicing of the following vowel. As stated by Lisker and Abramson (1964) in their seminal work, VOT is the most important feature in the production of voiceless stop consonants, and its relevance has since been confirmed by a number of phoneticians (Cho & Ladefoged, 1999; Bijankhan & Nourbakhsh, 2009, among others). We measured the VOT values of the four voiceless stops ([p], [t], [k] and the new [t])[1] in two positions: word initial and medial. In the absence of a vowel, final positions were taken into account only when the substitution occurred. We employed Fougeron and Keating's (1997) 'articulatory strengthening' to explain why <th> is substituted with the new [t], why substitution with [d] is rare and why substitution almost exclusively occurs in the initial position. In the second part, we seek to explain how the new [t], whose presence is acoustically consistent, can be situated in the concept of nativisation, the central and most vibrant stage in the evolution of a language (Schneider, 2007, p. 40). In his 2003 paper focusing solely on ME, Schneider

---

[1] The new [t] is also presented graphically as [th>t] in this chapter.

explicitly stated that ME 'has progressed deeply into the third phase of "nativisation"' (p. 44). While this conception can certainly put ME in perspective vis-à-vis other varieties of New English, it remains to be seen exactly how the new [t], which exhibits a high degree of individual variation and irregularity, accords with nativisation. Inspired by Harder's evolutionary concept of 'collective facts' residing outside individual minds, we discuss primarily how it can explain the rise of [t].

Two Acoustic Experiments

The first experiment was conducted in 2010 and 2011 and the second in 2013. Each experiment was designed uniformly, consisting of four types of recording. Speakers first read a text (*The North Wind and the Sun* for Experiment 1 (Ex1) and *Alice in Wonderland* for Experiment 2 (Ex2)) followed by words and then sentences. The final section was 'free talk', in which speakers talked about topics informally (a topic related to their workplace or studies in Ex1; three topics, 'What I am currently thinking about', 'Weather' and 'Health', in Ex2). Speakers prepared for the free talk before the recording and were allowed to refer to brief notes on key words. Each recording session lasted about 7 to 10 minutes per speaker. Both recording sessions took place in a professional recording studio with technical support staff. Tables 3.1 and 3.2 illustrate the social, ethnic and linguistic background of the 24 speakers who participated in experiments 1 and 2. The speakers were either students pursuing a BA, MA or PhD at a local university or teachers working at a university in Kuala Lumpur (the capital of Malaysia) or in the surrounding area. Most of the speakers used English in the workplace, the exceptions being S11 in Ex2, who used Malay predominantly, and S10 and S12 in Ex2, who used Tamil and Malay more often than English. Speakers who were students at the time of recording also used English actively for their studies. All the speakers had in common the fact that English was not necessarily the dominant language at home and/or in their private communication (e.g. S12 in Ex1 used Malay or Tamil predominantly at home and privately). Their first language was often the language used at home. Where two languages are given in the tables below, it means that the speaker considered two languages as his or her second languages because he or she did not see any difference in terms of proficiency. To measure the data, we used the PRAAT programme, which is widely used in phonetic research (Boersma & Weenink, 2008).

TABLE 3.1   Social, ethnic and linguistic information of the 12 participants in Experiment 1

	Gender	Age	First language	Second language	Third language	Ethnicity
S1	Female	33	Chinese	English/Malay	–	Chinese
S2	Female	38	Chinese	English/Malay	–	Chinese
S3	Male	40	Chinese	English/Malay	–	Chinese
S4	Male	32	Chinese	English/Malay	–	Chinese
S5	Female	21	English	Malay	Chinese	Chinese
S6	Male	21	Chinese	English/Malay	–	Chinese
S7	Female	57	Chinese	English/Malay	–	Chinese
S8	Female	24	Chinese	English/Malay	–	Chinese
S9	Male	19	Chinese	English/Malay	–	Chinese
S10	Female	24	Malay	English	–	Malay
S11	Female	50	Malay	English	–	Malay
S12	Female	26	Tamil	Malay	English	Indian

TABLE 3.2   Social, ethnic and linguistic information of the 12 participants in Experiment 2

	Gender	Age	First language	Second language	Third language	Ethnicity
S1	Female	26	Chinese	English	Malay	Chinese
S2	Female	46	Chinese	English/Malay	–	Chinese
S3	Male	29	English	Malay	Chinese	Chinese
S4	Male	31	Chinese	Malay	English	Chinese
S5	Female	19	English	Malay	Chinese	Malay/Chinese
S6	Male	42	Malay	English	–	Malay
S7	Female	55	Malay	English	–	Malay
S8	Female	51	Malay	English	–	Malay
S9	Female	26	English	Malay	Tamil	Indian
S10	Male	47	Tamil	Malay	English	Indian
S11	Male	60	Tamil	Malay	English	Indian
S12	Male	57	Tamil	Malay	English	Indian

The Pronunciation of <th>

To reiterate, the most important and interesting phenomenon of stop consonants in ME is the inclusion of a dental stop [t] alongside the three ordinary stops [p], [t] and [k]. This new sound arises through changing the place and manner of the articulation of dental fricatives. This transformation was reported in Killingley's early study (1968). Killingley and two other early studies, namely Tongue (1974) and Platt and Weber (1980), revealed that dental fricatives were replaced by different sounds. More recently, Baskaran (2008) offered a comprehensive study of the phonology of ME, stating that dental fricatives are 'often realised by the corresponding alveolar stops [t] and [d] respectively' (p. 286). While this 'corresponding view' is taken as the main feature of ME's pronunciation of dental fricatives (Azirah & Tan, 2012), the actual pronunciations are apparently rich in variation, as recently demonstrated by Alias (2014). It is our fresh knowledge that the different roles of English, determined by respective governments after Singapore's independence from Malaysia in 1965, have rendered Malaysia and Singapore noticeably socio-politically distinct. It is worth mentioning, as Kirkpatrick maintained (2010, p. 122), that the two countries still have many linguistic features in common. One feature is undoubtedly <th> substitution, whose appearance in SE has been the focus of active research (Moorthy & Deterding, 2000; Wee, 2008, to name just two). An interesting fact is that while <th> is realised by different sounds in the two varieties, there are two salient phenomena that do not pertain to ME or, more accurately, to the data we obtained from the experiments: one is that [θ] tends to be replaced by [f] in SE, but this is very rare in our data; the other is that while [ð] tends to be replaced by [d] frequently in SE, this is not the case in ME. Scholars have to date offered perceptive reasons for <th> substitution. For example, they have pointed out that it is the uniqueness of the sounds that triggered the substitution; because these sounds are rare in the sound inventory of world languages, non-native speakers of English have difficulty pronouncing them, hence the rise of alternative sounds replacing them (Tongue 1974, p. 19; Deterding & Kirkpatrick, 2006, p. 395; Wester, Gilbers, & Lowie, 2007, p. 477; cf. Hanulíková & Weber, 2012, p. 614). Importantly, substitution is not restricted to New Englishes but occurs occasionally in Kachru's Inner Circle varieties. The most frequent substitution is that of [θ] with the fricative [f] (Hanulíková & Weber, 2012), and Lawson's recent study (2014) on Glasgow English sheds light on the emergence of [f] as a sociocultural feature of the Inner Circle variety.

General Characteristics of the New [t]

A total of 2,235 instances of the dental fricatives were recorded in the two experiments (880 in Ex1 and 1,355 in Ex2). There were 98 occurrences of the new [t] in Ex1 and 416 in Ex2. The new [t] has the following five characteristics.

THE NEW [T] IN MALAYSIAN ENGLISH

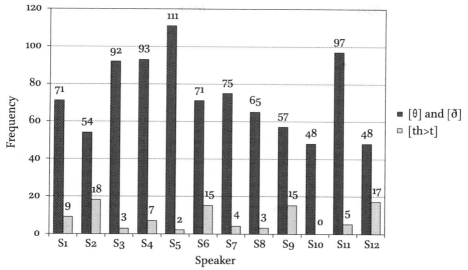

FIGURE 3.1 *Distribution of the standard norm ([θ] and [ð]) and the new [t] ([th>t]) in Experiment 1.*

First, the mean VOT value for all its occurrences is short, that is, 22.65 ms (22.7 ms in Ex1 and 22.6 ms in Ex2; see figures 3.3 and 3.4), and this value is much shorter than the mean 45.4 ms (48.9 ms in Ex1 and 41.9 ms in Ex2; see figures 3.3 and 3.4) for the original alveolar [t]. Second, all the speakers maintained the 'standard' pronunciation of <th>,[2] as shown by figures 3.1 and 3.2.

Third, the new [t] occurs most frequently in the word-initial position, as demonstrated in Tables 3.3 and 3.4. The two tables show the frequency of the new [t] in terms of number and percentage (shaded column) in Texts 1 to 3.[3] The two non-shaded columns for each text show the occurrences of the new [t] and dental fricatives in total. The percentages prove that the occurrence of the new [t] is concentrated in the initial position rather than the medial and final positions.[4]

---

2   The word 'standard' refers to the pronunciation of <th> as a voiced or voiceless dental fricative.

3   Because individual variations are prominent in free talk, we exclude Text 4 of Ex1 and Texts 4–6 of Ex2.

4   Two cases, marked by single and double asterisks, may counter this initial position hypothesis. However, this apparent threat can be eradicated. The single asterisk in Table 3.3 indicates that the new [t] in the final position was produced by a single speaker, which can be regarded as an individual variation. The double asterisk in Table 3.4 indicates that the new [t] produced in the medial position occurs almost exclusively in the pronunciation of *nothing*. One can suggest that this word consists of two words (*no* + *thing*) on the basis of the fact

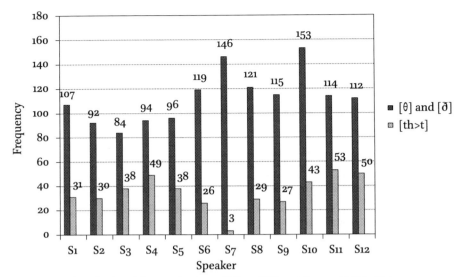

FIGURE 3.2 *Distribution of the standard norm ([θ] and [ð]) and the new [t] ([th>t]) in Experiment 2.*

TABLE 3.3 *Frequency of the new [t] and [θ] [ð] in different positions in Texts 1–3, Experiment 1*

	Text 1 The North Wind and the Sun			Text 2 (Words)			Text 3 (Sentences)		
	Frequency new [t]	[θ] [ð]	%	Frequency new [t]	[θ] [ð]	%	Frequency new [t]	[θ] [ð]	%
Initial	12	198	5.7	3	18	14.2	43	189	18.5
Medial	0	9	–	0	9	–	0	18	–
Final	4	36	*10	0	0	–	0	0	–

that a prolongation of the vowel [o] in the first syllable of *nothing* and a brief interruption before the articulation of <th> are observed in the spectrum. The pronounciation of <th> can thus belong to the initial position of a new word, *thing*. If this assumption is correct, the figures could be changed to 11 occurences of the new [t] and 55 occurences of dental fricatives, resulting in the percentage of 20%, thus tallying with our hypothesis.

TABLE 3.4 *Frequency of the new [t] in different positions in Texts 1–3, Experiment 2*

	Text 1 Alice in Wonderland			Text 2 (Words)			Text 3 (Sentences)		
	Frequency new [t]	[θ] [ð]	%	Frequency new [t]	[θ] [ð]	%	frequency new [t]	[θ] [ð]	%
Initial	50	231	17.8	24	55	30.4	136	418	24.5
Medial	18	55	**24.7	14	44	24.1	7	44	13.7
Final	5	44	10.2	11	44	20	15	88	14.6

Fourth, three speakers (S3 in Ex1, S5 in Ex1 and S7 in Ex2) produced the new [t] only a few times (Figures 3.1 and 3.2), and its occurrence was restricted exclusively to the free talk.[5] Fifth, due to the presence of the new [t], the VOT values of the original alveolar [t] are shortened. Consequently, the sequence of [p] and [t] is reversed, as shown in Figures 3.3 and 3.4. It is striking that, with the exception of [p], the mean values of the stops are much alike. It is even more striking that the VOT values of the new [t] are equally short. Figures 3.3 and 3.4 present the VOT values of the initial position of the four sounds.

The reverse between [p] and [t] can be contrasted with the universal claim that [p] has the shortest VOT values among all the stop consonants (Lisker & Abramson, 1964, p. 394). Although [t] and [th>t] are phonetically distinct, their sequential closeness caused by the aforementioned reverse might tell us that phonologically they can be the same sound (see Burquest, 2006, pp. 2–3 for a similar case involving [t]). In other words, speakers may not perceive the two sounds differently.

Individual Variations

Apart from the five general characteristics discussed above, the speakers substituted <th> with the new [t] in a highly idiosyncratic and unpredictable manner. In this section, we discuss two types of individual variations present throughout the data. The first is the variations found among the speakers. Recall Table 3.3, which shows the <th> substitution in terms of position. While

---

5 See Alias (2014, pp. 105, 109), who reported that the highest percentage of variants distant from the target phonemes [θ] and [ð] is produced in free conversations.

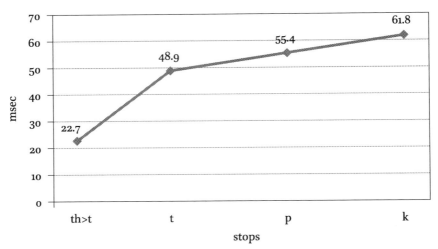

FIGURE 3.3 *Sequence of four stops with VOT values in Experiment 1.*

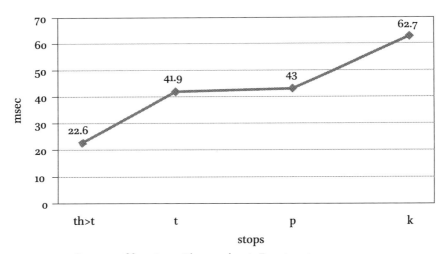

FIGURE 3.4 *Sequence of four stops with VOT values in Experiment 2.*

the high percentage of the occurrence of the new [t] in the word-final position is surprising, it is important to mention that the four occurrences of the new [t] were produced solely by a single speaker (S12 in Ex1); this means that all of the other speakers produced the standard pronunciation of <th> in the final position of the word *north*. If we look closely at Figure 3.1 again, S12 was not the speaker who most frequently produced the new [t], but neither S2, S6 nor S9, who produced nearly the same number of new [t]'s as S12, transformed

<th> into the new [t] in pronouncing *north*. This fact suggests that the different realisation of <th> is brought about by some specific quality of the individual speaker. Consider Figures 3.3 and 3.4 again. The addition of the new [t] to the three ordinary stops alters the universal sequence of the sounds. While it is noticeable that the mean values still show a significant acoustic gap between two types of [t], one speaker (S12) in Ex2 produced [th>t] and the ordinary alveolar [t] without much difference in VOT value. This did not happen with the other speakers in Ex2 or with any speaker in Ex1. For S12, the two sounds resemble each other very closely, which may result in a complete neutralisation of the two stops in the future. Table 3.5 presents the mean values of each sound at the initial and medial positions, which are averaged in the shaded column.

TABLE 3.5   *Mean VOT values for S12 in Experiment 2*

	[th>t]			alveolar [t]		
	initial	medial	mean	Initial	medial	mean
S12/Ex2	27.6	29.6	28.6	26	32.5	29.2

Another interesting speaker-specific variation was yielded by S11 in Ex2. In this case, the mean VOT values of [th>t] and the ordinary [t] were reversed; the latter was much shorter than the former. S11 was the only speaker to present this reversal over the course of the experiment. Table 3.6 presents the mean values of each sound in the initial and medial positions, which are averaged in the shaded columns.

TABLE 3.6   *Mean VOT values for S11 in Experiment 2*

	[th>t]			alveolar [t]		
	initial	medial	mean	Initial	medial	mean
S11/Ex2	16.6	25.6	21.1	17.1	13.3	15.2

The second type of variation is that found within a single speaker. Twenty-three speakers (the exception being S10 in Ex1, who did not produce any new [t]'s) produced the new [t]. It is intriguing that they not only produced this sound but also alternated between standard pronunciation and the new [t]. Alternation refers to a situation in which <th> is realised as [θ] or [ð] at one time and as [th>t] at another by the same speaker. Recall that we mentioned that three speakers (S3 and S5 in Ex1 and S7 in Ex2) produced the new [t] only in free talk. These speakers frequently alternated between the two pronunciations. S5 pronounced the <th> in *things* as [θ] first and then as [th>t]. S7 pronounced the <th> in *thunder* as [th>t] and the <th> in *think* as [θ]; both <th> pronunciations appeared in the same context, that is, [__V]. Similarly, in the context [__V], S3 produced [ð] and [th>t] for the definite article *the*. Because these three speakers produced [th>t] only in informal speech and not in Texts 1 to 3, which are structured formally, we propose that the new [t] is employed to express the speaker's internal/emotional state. However, this psychological account may be weakened in light of its irregular occurrence: for example, we may expect the <th> in *thankful* to be replaced by [th>t] in S7's speech, but this did not take place. It is also puzzling that S3 only replaced [ð] with [th>t] only for the <th> in *the summative assessment* and not for the <th> in *the formative assessment*. The underlined <th> in the speech extracts below signals the realisation of [th>t].

S3: 'there are two kinds of assessments **that** [tat] are used: one is **the** formative assessment and the other is **the** [tə] summative assessment'. (Ex1)

S5: 'You can hear people say some **things** that are quite out of the ordinary or when you listen back to what people have said it's just amusing to see why people say **things** [tɪŋs] **the** way they do...' (Ex1)

S5: 'sometimes **the** recorder is not placed [in] **the** proper place where everybody can speak clearly into **the** recorder...so **the** use of detective works sometimes, because you have to investigate, do some research online, like for instance, one [of] the recordings required me to check online about certain words in Burmese as **the** speaker used some Burmese terms and I was in charge of trying to figure out what was being said. So, in my **enthusiasm** [ɛntusiasm], I went online to do some research, to check what was **the** word **that** he said was, and it was interesting; at **the** end, I managed to find a word...' (Ex1)

S7: '**the** moment it rains, it will be so heavy, will be raining in sheets you know and **with thunder** [tʌndə], lightning you know, really scary... but I t̲h̲ink [tiŋk], I guess we have to be **thankful** for small mercies, because some people have to contend with hurricanes, typhoons, etc....' (Ex2)

In S3's speech, using [th>t] shows strong emotional commitment to the way he assessed his students. Likewise, in S5's first speech, she expressed her amusement by using [th>t]. In her second speech, she used [th>t] when talking about the efforts she had made to decode an unintelligible word in the speech she had recorded. S7 talked about fearful climate changes in Malaysia: by using [th>t], she disclosed her fear of *thunder* or *lightning*.

Sporadic Occurrence

The two above-mentioned types of individual variation can be subsumed under what Lehman (1992) called 'sporadic' or 'saltatory' changes. These changes take place irregularly because they do not conform to the patterns of a language. A fundamental principle, as stated by Campbell (2004, p. 27), is that language undergoes change, particularly sound change, in accordance with the structure of the language. No matter how the change occurs, at a phonemic or allophonic level, we can predict why that change is triggered or what conditioned it. Let us quote Campbell (2004, p. 17), who spelt out how regular sound change should occur:

> In fact, the most important basic assumption in historical linguistics is that sound change is regular,... Regular changes recur generally and take place uniformly wherever the phonetic circumstances in which the change happens are encountered. To say that a sound change is regular means that the change takes place whenever the sound or sounds which undergo the change are found in the circumstances or environments that condition the change. For example, original *p* regularly became *b* between vowels in Spanish (p > b / V__V); this means that in this context between vowels, every original *p* became *b*;...

However, Campbell recognised that there are cases in which changes do not affect all speakers and do not occur in all environments. He gave an example of sporadic change in the history of English (p. 27): the modern word *speech* was *spræc* in Old English. The change (loss of /r/) was sporadic in that other words in the same environment have not undergone the same sound change (e.g. *spring, sprig, spree*). While sporadic changes exist in language, the position Lehman and Campbell both take is that they are not found generally in the history of language. It is clear that the substitutions of <th> with [th>t] we have observed in the previous sections fall under the category of sporadic change in that their occurrence is not conditioned by the environments in which they are found. In light of this, it is reasonable to say that the changes we have witnessed in ME go far beyond regular sound changes.

According to Lehman (1992, p. 203), sporadic changes operate at a phonemic level and tend to correlate with the speaker's awareness of specific social dialects or styles. In other words, they are most likely to be caused by factors not inherent to language structure. The voicing of [t] in *water* in American English exemplifies such a phonemic change (from [t] to [d]), serving to express social dialect. Expression of emotion, the term we used in the previous section to illustrate irregular distributions of the new [t] in the speech of three speakers, can be viewed as individual style.

Articulatory Strengthening

It was concluded above that the change from <th> to the new [t] is not based on language structure but on sporadic alterations of phonemes. In this section, we look at changes from the perspective of articulatory strengthening (Fougeron & Keating, 1997).[6] We argue that this hypothesis can define conditions under which the new [t] comes into existence. The application of articulatory strengthening to explain variations differs essentially from the conventional viewpoint that variations are associated with sociocultural or sociolinguistic factors such as ethnicity or local languages (Kachru & Nelson, 2006, p. 35). In their seminal paper, Fougeron and Keating put forward the thesis that the pronunciation of the initial position requires more energy than other positions of a word or phrase. This is because the initial position shows more linguopalatal contact (contact between tongue and palate) than the medial or final positions do: for example, the [t] in *time* requires more energy than the [t] in *retire* or *kite*. This proposal is built on Fujimura (1990), who explicitly espoused that '[s]yllable initial position, as well as word or phrase initial position, seems to be generally characterised by more 'forceful' articulatory gestures along with reinforced source intensity' (also quoted in Fougeron & Keating, 1997, p. 3729). Although Fougeron and Keating's focus was on the positions of the sounds, the tenet of this hypothesis is applicable to the substitution of dental fricatives with the dental stop [t] in that the latter requires more linguopalatal contact, that is, more energy, than the former. Thus, the transformation of the fricatives

---

6   Our thanks to Michael Jessen for drawing our attention to this notion.

into stops can be seen as the result of strengthening the articulatory gesture of the dental fricatives. Put more simply, a stop like [d] requires more energy than [ð], and a stop like [t] requires more energy than [θ]. It follows, then, that these two stops are the best candidates for the sound in the word-initial position. As we saw in tables 3.3 and 3.4, the fact that the substitution occurs more frequently in the initial position provides strong evidence for the validity of articulatory strengthening as a factor accounting for the <th> substitution. When it comes to the contrast between voiced and voiceless stops, that is, [d] and [t], the latter is, as we saw above, the dominant substitute for both voiced and voiceless dental fricatives. This can also be explained using the same logic; owing to its voiceless quality, [t] requires more intense energy through tightening the contact between the tongue and alveolar ridge, whereas [d] does not as it is produced through vibration of the vocal folds, thus loosening the contact. Articulatory strengthening thus explains two questions fairly straightforwardly: first, why the new [t] is the best candidate for substituting voiced and voiceless dental fricatives; second, why the occurrence of the new [t] is concentrated in the first position. In sum, by selecting the new [t] as the substitute, the speaker maintains the same place of articulation, thereby creating a more perceptible contrast to the following vowel. In the syllable-initial position, a voiceless stop is more perceptible than a voiced stop or, alternatively, a dental fricative.

It has been mentioned above that the substitution of <th> with the voiceless labiodental fricative [f] rarely occurs in our dataset. But that is not to say that it never happens. We propose here that its rare occurrence is due to the process of assimilation but not to articulatory strengthening. To illustrate, S5 in Ex1 produced *truth* [tlʊf] in Text 2 and *mouth* [maʊf] in Text 3 but did not pronounce the [f] in *health* in Text 2 or *death* in Text 3. This substitution is probably due to the labial element present in the consonant (bilabial nasal for *mouth*) and in the vowel ([ʊ] and [aʊ]). Because the labial element continues to be effective throughout the articulation of <th>, it is transformed into [f] rather than the new [t]. This process can be understood as the economy of articulatory movement. Since the final position is least compatible with the effort of articulatory strengthening, the choice of [f] is absolutely logical.[7]

---

7 Blevins (2006, p. 12) stands by a very different claim, namely that the shift from the voiceless dental fricative [θ] to the labiodental fricative [f] is caused by misperception.

Thoughts on Nativisation

Schneider's (2003, 2007) Dynamic Model stipulates that there are five sequential stages, which are oriented towards sociopolitical events and contact situations in Kachru's (1985) Outer Circle countries, explaining the birth of postcolonial English and its unidirectional path to a fully differentiated language (e.g. American English, Australian English, etc., subsumed under Kachru's Inner Circle languages). Schneider locates ME in the third stage of his model, classified as nativisation. The hallmark of Schneider's model is to expound the evolution of a language, the genesis of which is the presence of a settler speech community (STL) and its contact with an indigenous speech community (IDG). Distinct from the Three Circles (Inner, Outer and Expanding) advocated by Kachru (1985), roughly corresponding to three levels of language acquisition (first, second and foreign), all languages are treated equally in the Dynamic Model regardless of the level of acquisition they manifest. The model demonstrates the process that underlies the evolution of postcolonial Englishes on the basis of different degrees of long-term contact situations between an STG and an IDG. During nativisation, contact between an IDG and an STL becomes remarkably weakened, and it is in this stage that one sees the seeds of a new language in the local community. Schneider (2007) described this stage as follows: 'Both parties involved realize that something fundamental has been changing for good' (p. 40). The STL no longer needs to be represented by the physical presence of STL English speakers, but it remains as an indicator of a social bond the local community has maintained with the English language. Factors for the creation of this metaphoric bond are various: the appreciation of English, its persistent presence with important functions or the desire to participate in international communication (Schneider 2007, p. 42). People in the local community thus acquire English as their second language without the presence of STL speakers (cf. Schreier, 2012). Consequently, learners in this environment constantly present a usage of the local language that deviates from the old norms of correctness. With regard to phonology, people speak the language with a marked accent, influenced by the phonology of indigenous languages. Unlike the next stage of endonormative stabilisation, in which the English language becomes culturally and linguistically independent of the language of the STL by being accepted as a local norm and codified in the form of dictionaries or grammar/usage books, the English language is still in a state of flux during nativisation but is deemed to be preparing for the next stage. Schneider incorporated the nativisation stage into the heart of his model as it bears witness to a variety of New English gradually becoming the language of local people. While Schneider took language-internal factors into account (2007, p. 98), his model is organised primarily in concert with language-external factors, that is, language contact and social criteria such as status and prestige (pp. 98–99). Linguistic factors are subordinate to sociolinguistic events. The aim of this section is to situate our experimental results in nativisation in order to define the status of English in present-day Malaysia.

At the macro level, Schneider's characterisation of nativisation is perfectly compatible with the results of our experiments. Nativisation predicts phonological innovations with which the emergence of the new [t] fits neatly. At this phase of development, there is also a discrepancy between speakers adopting IDG forms and speakers upholding norms of correctness. The coexistence of the standard pronunciation and the new [t] is a convincing example of this intermediate stage. Moreover, the influence of the new [t] on the sequential relationship between stop consonants, that is, the reversal between /p/ and the ordinary /t/, may indicate the beginning of structural nativisation in phonology.

However, looking at the model more closely at the micro level, there are a couple of issues that require more accurate analysis of the data before they fully agree with the concept of nativisation. The first issue concerns how adequately the model can justify the emergence of the new [t] if its occurrence is irregular. To the best of our knowledge, New Englishes have to date been characterised according to their marked features that are particularly distinct from the standard norm. Indeed, numerous scholars, including Mesthrie and Bhatt (2008), have correctly pointed out the substitution of <th> with alternative sounds. But it appears that no study has gone deeper than this. High rates of irregularity or non-uniformity, typical of ESL acquisition without the presence of an STL, as pointed out by Mesthrie (2008, p. 25), appear to represent non-native varieties of English, which can be a thorny issue for the nativisation account.

The second issue is that all the speakers in our experiments produced the standard pronunciation more often than the new [t]. Nativisation marks the weakening of the bond between the STL and the IDG, but in reality, standard pronunciations outnumber the pronunciations of the new [t], showing strong dependence on the STL. Acceptance of the external norm rather than the localised sound may locate ME in the exonormative stabilisation stage, a stage prior to nativisation. As there is virtually no STL in present-day Malaysia, exonormative stabilisation is not found. How then can we account for the presence of this 'British-cum-local' (Schneider, 2007, p. 38) identity in the theory of nativisation? The answer will be provided below.

The third issue is whether it is correct to presume that a language should evolve on the basis of external factors only. Our findings dictate that the new [t] occurs independent of the local language and hence irrespective of the first language of the speaker. The rise of the new [t] is clearly language internal, triggered by the phonetic laws of sounds combined with people's communicative needs in speech. Given that communication is an integral part of human cognition (e.g. Tomasello, 2008; Schneider, 2007, p. 98), the new [t] gives us the new insight that one aspect of a new variety is emerging on the basis of language-internal factors. How does Schneider's model deal with the new [t] and standard pronunciation? If it promotes the new [t], which it is expected to do, this will yield innumerable near-homophones, especially in the word-initial position (e.g. *three* versus *tree, thought* versus *taught, theme* versus *team, thank* versus *tank, thick* versus *tick, thin* versus *tin*). If the model chooses to promote standard pronunciation, this may contradict the dynamism of the model.

The implication of the third issue is important. We refer to Harder's (2010) functional-cognitive approach to the relationship between society and language. Harder's position is that the form of a language is not only based on the awareness of individual speakers but also on the niche, that is, outside individual minds. In other words, society is composed of two kinds of collective facts, one being accessible to individuals and the other not, despite the fact that together they contribute to the evolution of society. This particular causal pattern, which is operationally independent of the individual mind, is the crux of Harder's thesis. To illustrate this with an example in a socioeconomic context, inflation is a collective fact that individuals are not aware of despite their contribution at the individual level (purchase of goods). Beaver dams are another example since they are created as protection against predators; the formation of dams has the effect of blocking the flow of the river, but the original aim was to create ponds in the river and keep the water level high. This cause-effect relationship should not be neglected. The rise of the new [t] resembles the emergence of inflation or the construction of a beaver dam. High rates of standard pronunciation among all speakers denote their intention to pronounce <th> as a dental fricative, but they occasionally fail to do so: for instance, because of the efforts of articulatory strengthening or some assimilatory reality in the pronunciation. By the same token, beavers' efforts to block rivers may not always lead to the creation of dams precisely because it is not their intention. Similarly, it was not an intentional act that caused 23 of the speakers in our experiments to produce the new [t]; they were not aware of the presence of the phonetically distinct sound and its phonetic closeness to the ordinary alveolar [t]. In a nutshell, the pronunciation of dental fricatives operates over the individual speaker's head. To quote Harder (2010), 'in order to understand the position of the individual in a social context, it is not sufficient to address what is intuitively accessible (visible) from the individual perspective' (p. 157). This is a revealing social reality, enshrined in human communication, about which Schneider's model has little room for making assumptions (cf. Buschfeld, Hoffmann, Huber & Kautzsch, 2014).

Conclusion

This chapter started with a summary of two experiments, and the results of these experiments have been evaluated in terms of the nativisation in Schneider's Dynamic Model. The focus of this chapter was the three findings of the experiments: (i) the new [t] occurs highly sporadically; (ii) its acoustic values are the shortest of all stops (with the exception of one speaker); and (iii) the standard pronunciation of dental fricatives is still the norm.[8] We proposed that these phenomena be categorised as language-internal factors and that they can be elaborated upon using Harder's evolutionary thesis. The new [t] is the aggregate effect resulting from the efforts of individuals to pronounce dental fricatives following the standard norm that is coded in their minds. In the second language acquisition scenario without the physical presence of an STL, unconscious and conscious social acts may go parallel to the distinction between 'standard language' and language use. Harder's theory does not ignore the presence of the latter, but it places more emphasis on the former. Given that it is necessary to stipulate standard pronunciation for ME, such pronunciation should exhibit a system. As Harder (2010) explicitly claimed, if there is no standard language, that is, no collectively recognised norm in the niche, understanding among individuals will be a 'random accident' (p. 280). Itkonen (2003, p. 13) was on the same wavelength when he stated that

> [i]f language is nothing but endless individual variation, it is not possible. Therefore every single language is **not** just variation, **not** just a mass of individual disconnected facts, ... The existence of phonemes shows that

---

8   When TH is pronounced by Japanese speakers for whom English is a foreign language, it is realised customarily as [s]. This might suggest that unlike speakers of ME, Japanese speakers of English do not possess the standard pronunciation of dental fricatives in their sound repertoire. This difference might shed light on the classification of English as a New English and a foreign language.

behind the apparent infinite variations of sounds there are invariants. (emphasis in original)

Understood this way, choosing the [θ] or [ð] pronunciation of dental fricatives does not equal the reinforcement of the Inner Circle norm. Furthermore, pronouncing dental fricatives as [th>t] can be part of the system only when it carries predictable functions within the system. While many studies in the field have tended to prioritise individual speakers' variations to characterise a variety of English, we have pinpointed, on the basis of acoustic investigations of ME, that such individual variations may not occur in their own right but rather operate in conformity with the 'collective facts out there'.

References

Alias, A. G. (2014). Phonological variation in the speech production of Malaysian learners of English. In A. R. Hajar & A. M. Shakila (Eds.), *English in Malaysia: Postcolonial and beyond* (pp. 87–125). Bern: Peter Lang.

Azirah, H., & Tan, R. S. K. (2012). Malaysian English. In E-L Low & H. Azirah (Eds.), *English in Southeast Asia: Features, policy and language use* (pp. 55–74). Amsterdam: John Benjamins.

Baskaran, L. (2008). Malaysian English: Phonology. In R. Mesthrie (Ed.), *Varieties of English 4: Africa, South and Southeast Asia* (pp. 278–291). Berlin: Mouton de Gruyter.

Bijankhan, M., & Nourbakhsh, M. (2009). Voice onset time in Persian initial and intervocalic stop production. *Journal of the International Phonetic Association*, 39(3), 335–364.

Blevins, J. (2006). New perspectives on English sound patterns. *Journal of English Linguistics*, 34(10), 6–25.

Boersma, P., & Weenink, D. (2008). PRAAT: *Doing phonetics by computer*. Amsterdam, Netherlands: Phonetic Sciences, University of Amsterdam.

Burquest, D. A. (2006). *Phonological analysis: A functional approach* (3rd ed.). Dallas, TX: SIL International.

Buschfeld, S., Hoffmann, T., Huber, M., & Kautzsch, A. (Eds.). (2014). *The evolution of Englishes: The Dynamic Model and beyond*. Amsterdam/Philadelphia: John Benjamins.

Campbell, L. (2004). *Historical linguistics* (2nd ed.). Cambridge: Cambridge University Press.

Cho, T., & Ladefoged, P. (1999). Variation and universals in VOT: Evidence from 18 languages. *Journal of Phonetics*, 27, 207–229.

Deterding, D., & Kirkpatrick, A. (2006). Emerging South-East Asian Englishes and intelligibility. *World Englishes*, 25(3/4), 391–409.

Fougeron, C., & Keating, P. A. (1997). Articulatory strengthening at edges of prosodic domains. *Journal of the Acoustical Society of America, 101*, 3728–3740.

Fujimura, O. (1990). Methods and goals of speech production research. *Language and Speech, 33*(3), 195–258.

Hanulíková, A., & Weber, A. (2012). Sink positive: Linguistic experience with *th* substitutions influences non-native word recognition. *Attention, Perception & Psychophysics, 74*, 613–629.

Harder, P. (2010). *Meaning in mind and society: A functional contribution to the social turn in cognitive linguistics*. Berlin/New York: De Gruyter Mouton.

Itkonen, E. (2003). *What is language?: A study in the philosophy of linguistics*. Åbo: Åbo Akademis tryckeri.

Kachru, B. B. (1985). Standards, codification and sociolinguistic realism: The English language in the outer circle. In R. Quirk & H. G. Widdowson (Eds.), *English in the world: Teaching and learning the language and literatures* (pp. 11–30). Cambridge: Cambridge University Press.

Kachru, Y., & Nelson, C. (2006). *World Englishes in Asian contexts*. Hong Kong: Hong Kong University Press.

Killingley, S. Y. (1968). The phonology of Malayan English. *Orbis, 17*(1), 57–87.

Kirkpatrick, A. (2010). *English as a lingua franca in ASEAN: A multilingual model*. Singapore: NUS Press.

Lawson, R. (2014). 'Don't even [θ/f/h]ink about it': An ethnographic investigation of social meaning, social identity and (θ) variation in Glasgow. *English World-Wide, 35*(1), 68–93.

Lehman, W. P. (1992). *Historical linguistics: An introduction* (3rd ed.). London: Routledge.

Lisker, L., & Abramson, A. S. (1964). A cross-language study of voicing in initial stops: Acoustical measurements. *Word, 20*, 384–420.

Mesthrie, R. (2008). Introduction: Varieties of English: Africa, South and Southeast Asia. In R. Mesthrie (Ed.), *Varieties of English: Africa, South Asia and Southeast Asia* (pp. 23–31). Berlin/New York: Mouton de Gruyter.

Mesthrie, R., & Bhatt, M. (2008). *World Englishes: The study of new linguistic varieties*. Cambridge: Cambridge University Press.

Moorthy, S. M., & Deterding, D. (2000). Three or tree: Dental fricatives in the speech of educated Singaporeans. In A. Brown, D. Deterding, & E. L. Low (Eds.), *The English language in Singapore: Research on pronunciation* (pp. 76–83). Singapore: Singapore Association for Applied Linguistics.

Platt, J., & Weber, H. (1980). *English in Singapore and Malaysia*. Kuala Lumpur: Oxford University Press.

Schneider, E. W. (2003). Evolutionary patterns of New Englishes and the special case of Malaysian English. *Asian Englishes, 56*(2), 44–63.

———. (2007). *Postcolonial English: Varieties around the world*. Cambridge: Cambridge University Press.

Schreier, D. (2012). Second-language varieties: Second-language varieties of English. In A. Bergs & L. J. Brinton (Eds.), *English historical linguistics: An international handbook* (pp. 2106–2121). Berlin/Philadelphia: De Gruyter Mouton.

Tomasello, M. (2008). *Origins of human communication.* Cambridge, MA: The MIT Press.

Tongue, R. (1974). *The Englishes of Singapore and Malaysia.* Singapore: Eastern University Press.

Wee, L. (2008). Singapore English: Phonology. In R. Mesthrie (Ed.), *Varieties of English 4: Africa South and Southeast Asia* (pp. 259–277). Berlin/New York: Mouton de Gruyter.

Wester, F., Gilbers, D., & Lowie, W. (2007). Substitution of dental fricatives in English by Dutch L2 speakers. *Language Sciences, 29,* 477–491.

Yamaguchi, T. (2014). The pronunciation of TH in word initial position in Malaysian English. *English Today, 30*(3), 13–21.

Yamaguchi, T., & Pétursson, M. (2012). Voiceless stop consonants in Malaysian English: Measuring the VOT values. *Asian Englishes, 15*(2), 60–79.

CHAPTER 4

How do We Stress? Lexical Stress in Malaysian and British English

Rachel Siew Kuang Tan

Introduction

Researchers working on ME in the past have claimed that ME differs significantly from native-speaker varieties of English such as BE in terms of pronunciation (Baskaran, 2008; Gaudart, 2000; Zuraidah, 2000). Although based on impressionistic methods, the findings of these researchers nevertheless laid the foundations for research on the pronunciation of ME. Later work on the pronunciation of ME extended to instrumental analysis to confirm if these earlier claims could be supported via acoustic analysis. Over the last few years, research in this area has been growing steadily, and the published acoustic research on ME includes work done on vowels (Tan & Low, 2010; Pillai, Zuraidah, Knowles, & Tang, 2010; Yap, Wong, & Abdul Aziz, 2010), consonants (Yamaguchi & Pétursson, 2012), prosodic marking (Gut, Pillai, & Zuraidah, 2013), intonation patterns (Noor Fadhilah & Setter, 2011) and rhythm (Tan & Low, 2014). This study extends the work on ME to lexical stress.

Review of Literature

Lexical Stress
Stress refers to strong prominence on a particular syllable (Trask, 2007) and is a suprasegmental feature that applies to whole syllables (Ladefoged & Johnson, 2011). While phoneticians are not exactly in agreement regarding the definition of stress, it is commonly believed that stress is caused by a combination of physical attributes such as pitch movement (fundamental frequency), length (time), increased loudness (amplitude) and vowel quality and that this combination varies across different languages. In English, stressed syllables tend to be louder, have a higher pitch, and be longer than unstressed syllables (Trask, 2007).

While sentence stress can vary since it is 'the placement of the nuclear intonational tone' resulting in the word becoming the most prominent in the intonational pattern of the sentence in order to emphasise it, lexical stress follows a fixed pattern of prominence (Laver, 1994, p. 514). In the context of this study, lexical stress is the actual placement of stress on the syllable of a word. In other words, it is the 'actual physical occurrence' of prominence assigned to a part of a word.

Different languages have different phonetic realisations of stress, but the common factor across languages that have stress is that stressed syllables are different from unstressed ones and this difference is seen as a difference in prominence (Lass, 1987). Fry (1955, 1958, 1965) investigated the acoustic and perceptual qualities of lexical stress in English noun/verb word pairs such as *OBJect/obJECT* and *PERmit/perMIT* and was able to show that in terms of perception, the pitch cue was most influential, followed by duration, intensity and lastly segmental quality. Fox (2000) reported that Lieberman (1960) and Morton and Jassem (1965) found pitch, amplitude and duration to be the most important cues to stress. More recently, Tan (2005) claimed that British speakers tend to perceive prominence following the rules for lexical stress in BE (e.g. the first syllable of disyllabic nouns is stressed if the final syllable contains a short vowel and one or no final consonant; Roach, 2009), while Singapore speakers tended to perceive final syllables as prominent, especially if they are lengthened, even when the syllable-final prominence does not follow the standard stress rules in BE. Tan (2006) found that Singaporean speakers perceive higher pitched, louder and longer syllables as more prominent compared to lower pitched, softer and shorter syllables. In determining the relative strength of the different parameters in judging stress, she found that intensity or loudness tends to be the most dominant perceptual cue for prominence, followed by pitch. Duration was found to be the weakest perceptual cue for stress.

The literature survey shows that although past researchers have clearly shown that in the older varieties of English, the most prominent cues to stress are pitch and duration, the claims by Tan (2005, 2006) that amplitude is also an important cue warrant closer attention. Thus, amplitude as a cue to stress in ME will be investigated as a correlate of stress along with duration and pitch, and each of these cues will be compared with the realisation of stress by speakers of BE.

Lexical Stress in Malaysian English

Researchers of ME have claimed that there is much variation in the patterns of word stress in ME when compared with the more established varieties of English, and this sometimes causes a lack of intelligibility (Wong, 1981; Gaudart, 2000; Schneider, 2003). This variation in the stress pattern is especially marked in informal speech (Baskaran, 2008). Previous work on ME has shown that in ME, the placement of stress within a word with more than two syllables (polysyllabic words such as *intellectual*) is different from that in BE (Platt & Weber, 1980; Baskaran, 2005, 2008). Others have claimed that stress placement in ME is random (Wong, 1981). Thus, a word like *blackbird* that is stressed on the first syllable if it is a compound noun but on the second syllable in the noun phrase *black bird* in BE might not have the same pattern of lexical stress in ME. Rajadurai (2006) put forward the notion that the difference in lexical stress in ME could be influenced by ME speakers' tendency to realise reduced vowels as full vowels. It has also been suggested that Malay speakers tend to shift stress to the final syllables accompanied by vowel lengthening, especially when they speak using the colloquial variety of English (Rajadurai, 2004). Many of the previous claims on word stress place in ME, however, appear to be based on auditory analysis as well as the production of words in citation forms. A citation form of a word takes place in isolation, and as it is not embedded in a sentence, the stress placement might be different from the lexical stress of words in sentences (Low, 2000).

While there have not been any claims made about stress placement in compound nouns and noun phrases in ME, Rajadurai (2006) did posit that due to the narrower pitch range used by ME speakers, prominence in formal speech, though detectable, is not always clearly marked and ME speakers may use other features of pronunciation, such as length, to signal lexical stress.

English as a Lingua Franca

As English is regarded as an international language, there is a need for speakers to understand each other's English to enable ease of communication. In Malaysia's case, English is important as it is needed for international communication as well as for communication within Malaysia; this is because, despite the status of Malay as the national language, English is still very much the lingua franca in many organisations in the private sector in Malaysia. Thus, a high proficiency in English increases students' chances of being employed later on when they enter the world of work and also enhances their promotion prospects. While consideration of proficiency in English encompasses the different productive and receptive skills, speaking skills are not only important for the workplace: they are also often critical for gaining employment. Admittedly, pronunciation is just one aspect that contributes to intelligibility; nevertheless, it is an important factor as how one articulates is critical in any oral interaction. Limited pronunciation skills not only undermine learners' self-confidence but also restrict their ability to interact in different contexts and give a negative reflection of their credibility and ability. If learners are limited in their pronunciation skills, this not only hinders their communicative skills but also leads to communication breakdown due to a lack of intelligibility.

Work done in the area of English as a lingua franca (ELF) have encouraged practitioners in the area of English language teaching to reconsider their models and goals for the teaching of pronunciation, especially since many non-native speakers of English tend to communicate more with other non-native speakers of English compared with native speakers, particularly because the former outnumber the latter. Work done in the field of World Englishes has shown that varieties of English in Outer Circle countries such as Singapore and Nigeria are contributing to the growth in the use of English, and such norms of speaking are increasingly accepted by learners from Expanding Circles of English such as Japan and Korea as models of pronunciation (Murphy, 2014). All these developments show that endonormative patterns of pronunciation of English are now viewed more favourably. However, the fact remains that while endonormative norms of pronunciation are increasingly accepted, certain norms of pronunciation patterns still need to be maintained to enable intelligibility and comprehensibility, especially when communicating at the international level. While researchers like Jenkins (2000, pp. 158–159) have proposed some forms of 'simplified phonological systems' to be the focus of pronunciation teaching to non-native speakers so that the intelligibility of their speech will not be greatly affected, earlier researchers have been divided about whether the variations in the realisation of segmental or suprasegmental features such as word stress, intonation and rhythm contribute more to intelligibility.

Intelligibility

Intelligibility has often been generally used to mean the 'intelligible production and felicitous interpretation of English' (Nelson, 1995, p. 274). More recently, this term has been used to mean the formal recognition of the meaning of an utterance based on the decoding of the word or words, while comprehensibility refers to the listener's understanding of the meaning of words or utterances in specific contexts (Pickering, 2012). The extent to which the utterances of a speaker are intelligible to listeners depends on a number of factors, such as the listeners' attitudes, attentiveness, and level of fatigue as well as their familiarity with the topic and the variety of the language produced (Pickering, 2006).

Connected to the issue of the intelligibility of non-native speakers of English is whether it is more important for the language produced by these speakers to be intelligible to native speakers of English or non-native speakers of English (Murphy, 2014). At the same time, if the language produced is intelligible to others in the same speech community, does this automatically mean that the language will be intelligible to non-native speakers with a different first language from other countries? Answers to these issues should determine the goals of English classes, specifically, those of pronunciation teaching. These issues are not easily answered, and perhaps the goals of pronunciation courses must be achievable as well as determined by the needs of the users.

Work on intelligibility in the past has shown that suprasegmental features are more essential for clear communication than segmental features (Field, 2005; Murphy, 2014). The suprasegmental features highlighted in Murphy's study that were deemed to contribute to intelligibility were intonation, rhythm, and stress or prominence (Murphy, 2014). Intelligibility can be very much hindered if the suprasegmental features of a speaker's speech are very different from expected norms. This is especially true for native speakers of English, who tend to rely more on suprasegmental features to help them decode and structure speech (Rajadurai 2004). As word stress is a major component of suprasegmental speech, non-standard word stress can seriously affect the intelligibility and comprehensibility of a speaker's speech (Checklin, 2012). It has been found, for instance, that intelligibility is impaired when non-standard word stress is used (Lepage & Busà, 2014). Researchers such as Jenkins (2002) and Deterding (2005), on the other hand, have shown that non-native speakers of English tend to focus more on segmental features when trying to comprehend oral communication. Thus, it appears that while native speakers tend to rely more on suprasegmental cues for intelligibility, non-native speakers tend to rely more on segmental cues. To be intelligible to both native and non-native speakers of English, Malaysians would need to ensure that their speech conforms with the standard suprasegmental and segmental features of English.

Word stress in English is largely predictable as it follows a set of complex rules (Roach, 2009). When comparing the lexical stress placement of SE and BE, Low found that SE speakers realise compound nouns differently from BE speakers (Low, 2000). While no difference was found in stress placement in terms of duration, a difference between the two varieties of English was found for Fo. For BE, there was a step down between the offset of syllable 1 and the onset of syllable 2 for compounds, while for phrases, there was a step up between the offset of syllable 1 and the onset of syllable 2. In SE however, the pattern was the same for both compounds and phrases: there was a step up between the offset of syllable 1 and the onset of syllable 2.

From the ESL perspective, when word-stress information is different, native speakers may perceive the quality of the ESL speaker's speech as intelligible or fully functional as well as easy to comprehend, partially intelligible or difficult to understand, requiring much from the listener for comprehension, or totally unintelligible, resulting in communication breakdown (Murphy, 2004). In cases where the speaker's speech is difficult to comprehend, the listener then has to put in more effort and rely more on the context to comprehend the meaning of the utterances. Lepage and Busà's (2014) work on the intelligibility of French and Italian accented English, for instance, showed that a leftward misplacement of lexical stress is more detrimental to intelligibility than a rightward misplacement as the reaction time to identify tokens correctly was longer, implying that listeners require more effort to comprehend tokens with leftward misplaced stress.

While it has been noted that most suprasegmental features are difficult to acquire, the same is not always true for word stress since it is relatively stable and specific rules can be learned (Hung, 2002). On the same note, the word stress of two or three syllable words is important for intelligibility as these words can be misinterpreted, as in the case of (to) *insult* versus (an) *insult* or even *impotence* versus *importance*, unless the meaning is clear from the context. Another reason for the learning of lexical stress information is that it is an essential part of an ESL learner's experience of learning a new word because as new vocabulary is taught, learners need to be exposed to the form, meaning and use of the word (Murphy, 2004). Lexical stress is an integral part of the knowledge of the spoken form of a word. The aim of lexical stress teaching should not be confined to teaching rules of word stress. McCartan (2001), as cited by Murphy (2004), recommended that the goals of ESL instruction should include helping learners to develop an awareness of how rhythmic patterns occur at the word level as well as teaching them a manageable range of common lexical stress patterns. Through such instruction, learners are trained to be able to recognise the stress patterns of new words they come across, empowering them to be more autonomous, as well as intelligible, users of English.

It should also be noted that although this paper focuses on pronunciation, mutual intelligibility does not rest solely on pronunciation as other aspects, such as lexis and syntax, as well as cultural issues are equally important. At the same time, with respect to pronunciation, other than accent, factors such as clarity and voice projection that result in good articulation are just as important factors for intelligibility as it is possible for a person with an internationally intelligible accent such as British English or American English to be unintelligible if their speech is poorly articulated (Hung, 2002).

Methodology

Acoustic Analysis

Twenty subjects (10 ME speakers and 10 BE speakers) were recorded in quiet rooms reading 20 sentences (see Appendix). They were asked to read the list of sentences as clearly as they could, and no information was provided about the context of the sentences. The recordings were done directly onto a computer with the aid of a clip-on microphone.

Due to the linguistic diversity in Malaysia, ethnic Malay subjects from the Klang Valley, which is located in the central region of Peninsular Malaysia, were selected to limit the variables that could influence the data since the Malays form the largest ethnic group. Furthermore, to control for the education variable, the students selected were all studying at universities in Malaysia. The British speakers in the study were all undergraduate speakers of Southern BE who were selected to represent a comparable group of BE speakers.

The speakers read sentences from Low (2000) which consisted of 10 compound nouns in carrier sentences. Ten noun phrases were included by replacing the first syllables of the compound nouns with an adjective (e.g. *schoolyard* with *cool yard*). Compound words consist of two nouns which are stressed on the first syllable in BE: for example, the word *BLACKboard* has a greater stress on the first syllable if it refers to the board that is used for teaching purposes. Noun phrases, on the other hand, are stressed on the second syllable (*slack BOARD*). The compound nouns and noun phrases were also placed in sentence-final position as, according to Fudge (1984), lexically stressed syllables are not always assigned more prominence unless they coincide with the nucleus of the sentence. Bearing this in mind, the compounds were placed in sentence-final positions, where they were expected to carry nuclear stress when the sentence was produced out of any context. All the test items were placed in similar sentences, such as *She discovered a new bird*, and were always in the phrase-final position. A list of the sentences used can be found in the Appendix.

Questionnaire
The second part of the study was a questionnaire; some Malaysian students were asked to give their views of how they stressed syllables in a word and how disyllabic compound nouns and noun phrases were stressed. The subjects were asked to tick what they thought were the most appropriate answers.

Data Analysis
Four hundred tokens (200 ME and 200 BE) were analysed. Measurements were done for duration, amplitude and pitch using Praat version 4.4.22 (Boesma & Weenink, 2006). The spectral splice and the spectrums were used as a guide to syllabification, and the segmentation was confirmed through auditory perception. In cases of ambiguity in the syllable boundary between the segments, the pitch line indicator in the Praat programme was also used as an indicator

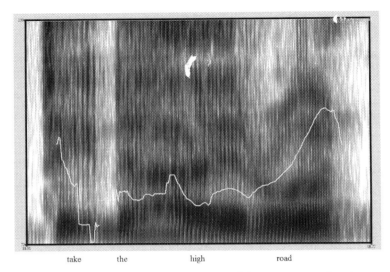

FIGURE 4.1 *Example of the use of pitch line to aid the segmentation of a token.*

in addition to observing the changes in the spectral splice as well as the spectrums. The segmentation was finally confirmed through perception.

Results

The results of the measurements in terms of duration, amplitude and fundamental frequency are reported first, followed by the findings from the questionnaire.

Duration
The measurements taken showed that the second syllables were longer for both compound nouns and noun phrases for both ME and BE. The average durations of the first syllables of the compound nouns and noun phrases realised by both the ME and BE speakers were shorter than those of the second syllables.

Table 4.1 lists the average duration of the first and second syllables. Percentages were calculated to enable a comparison of the syllables in proportion to the entire disyllabic noun phrases or compound nouns for both ME and BE. The percentages obtained implied that the proportions of the durations of the syllables of both compound nouns and noun phrases are similar for

TABLE 4.1 *Average duration (ms) of first and second syllables for compound words and noun phrases*

	Compound Words			
	1st syllable		2nd syllable	
	Average duration	Percentage	Average duration	Percentage
ME	237	43.9%	303	56.1%
BE	213	40.3%	330	59.7%
	Noun Phrases			
	1st syllable		2nd syllable	
	Average duration	Percentage	Average duration	Percentage
ME	259	45.0%	316	55.0%
BE	231	40.0%	346	60.0%

both ME and BE. Thus, it appeared that both the ME and BE speakers did not differentiate noun phrases and compound nouns in terms of the duration of the first and second syllables of the two categories of words investigated.

Amplitude

The measurements taken showed that the average amplitude of the first elements was louder than the average amplitude of the second elements for compound nouns and noun phrases for both ME and BE, as can be seen in Figure 4.2. The increase in the amplitude between the first syllable and second syllable of all the compound nouns was compared with the increase in amplitude between the first and second elements of noun phrases produced by the ME speakers using a paired *t*-test. The results of the *t*-test did not show any significant difference (t=1.18, p=0.23, df=99, ns, paired *t*-test). A similar comparison done for the amplitude of the first and second syllables of compound nouns and noun phrases produced by the BE speakers also showed a similar

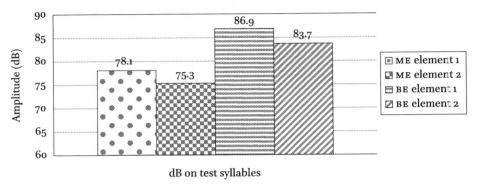

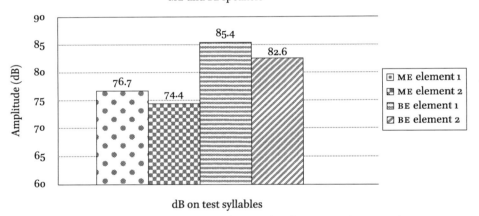

FIGURE 4.2 *Average amplitude of the ME and BE speakers for compound nouns and noun phrases.*

pattern. No difference was found between the decrease of amplitude between the first and second elements of compound nouns compared to the decrease between the first and second elements of noun phrases produced by the BE speakers (t= 0.93, p=0.35, df=99, ns, paired *t*-test). This implies that there was no difference in the way the ME and BE speakers stressed the first and second syllables in both noun phrases and compound nouns in terms of amplitude.

Fundamental Frequency

The values obtained for the fundamental frequency measurements for males and females are reported separately due to the difference in male and female voices. The results obtained for the male speakers are listed in Table 4.2. As can be seen from Figures 4.3 and 4.4, the stress pattern realised by the male ME speakers for both compound nouns and noun phrases are similar in that there was a slight step up between the offset of syllable 1 and the onset of syllable 2, implying that there was no difference in the stress pattern of compound nouns and noun phrases in the pronunciation of the male ME speakers. As for the male BE speakers, there was a slight step down between the offset of syllable 1 and the onset of syllable 2 for compound nouns, whereas for the noun phrases, there was a step up between the offset of syllable 1 and the onset of syllable 2, indicating that there was a difference in how the BE male speakers stressed noun phrases and compound nouns.

As for the female speakers, Figure 4.6 shows that both the ME and BE female speakers seemed to exhibit similar patterns in the lexical stress placement for noun phrases. There was a step up between the offset of syllable 1 and the onset of syllable 2. However, the change in the fundamental frequency for the female ME speakers was smaller compared to the change in the fundamental frequency of the female BE speakers. There appeared to be a difference in how the two groups of female speakers realised compound nouns, as shown in Figure 4.5. While a step down from the offset of syllable 1 to the onset of syllable 2 was seen in both the ME and the BE speakers, the fundamental frequency of the ME speakers was lower at the offset of syllable 2, whereas an increased fundamental frequency was seen at the offset of syllable 2 for the BE speakers. This appears to indicate that the female ME speakers did not have the same pattern of stress as the female BE speakers for compound nouns.

TABLE 4.2 *Average fundamental frequency of male speakers for compound nouns and noun phrases*

	Fundamental frequency (Hz) for compound nouns (Males)				Fundamental frequency (Hz) for noun phrases (Males)			
	Syllable 1		Syllable 2		Syllable 1		Syllable 2	
	Fo onset	Fo offset	Fo onset	Fo offset	Fo onset	Fo offset	Fo onset	Fo offset
ME	120	124	126	109	124	115	123	99
BE	90	86	82	79	86	80	89	83

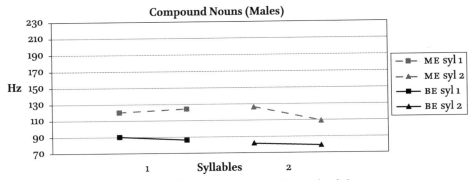

FIGURE 4.3 *Average fundamental frequency of compound nouns (males).*

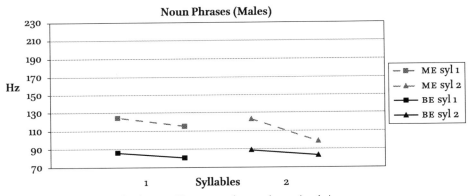

FIGURE 4.4 *Average fundamental frequency of noun phrases (males).*

In order to ascertain if there was an overall difference in the stress placement for both noun phrases and compound nouns realised by all the ME and BE speakers, paired *t*-tests were conducted comparing how each speaker realised compound nouns against the same speaker's realisation of noun phrases. The difference in the fundamental frequency from the offset of syllable 1 to the onset of syllable 2 for compound nouns was compared against the difference in the fundamental frequency of the noun phrases realised by all the speakers. The results of the paired *t*-test showed that there was no difference in the way the ME speakers realised noun phrases and compound nouns (t=1.49, df=99, p=0.14, paired *t*-test, two-tailed, ns), while a difference was seen in the realisation of noun phrases and compound nouns by the BE speakers (t= 4.06, df=99, p=0.000098, paired t-test, two-tailed). Benferroni adjustment confirmed that this was significant at the alpha level of 0.001. This indicates that there was a difference in the stress pattern of compound nouns between the ME and the BE speakers.

TABLE 4.3 *Average fundamental frequency of female speakers for compound nouns and noun phrases*

	Fundamental frequency (Hz) for compound nouns (Females)				Fundamental frequency (Hz) for noun phrases (Females)			
	Syllable 1		Syllable 2		Syllable 1		Syllable 2	
	Fo onset	Fo offset	Fo onset	Fo offset	Fo onset	Fo offset	Fo onset	Fo offset
ME	216	204	198	164	225	199	203	164
BE	197	191	165	176	178	168	196	186

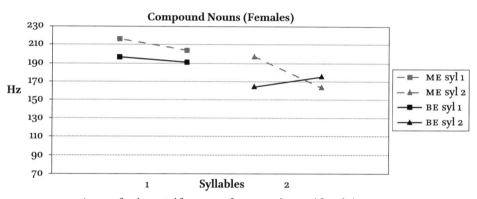

FIGURE 4.5 *Average fundamental frequency of compound nouns (females).*

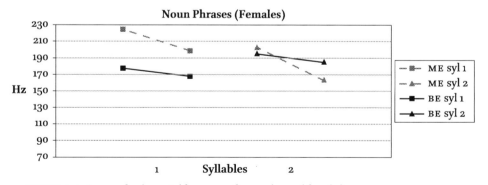

FIGURE 4.6 *Average fundamental frequency of noun phrases (females).*

Questionnaire

A total of 52 Malaysian students returned the questionnaire. The responses of the students regarding how they considered stress to be signalled are summarised in Table 4.4. The students were asked to tick all the features they used to signal stress in an utterance.

From the answers given by the respondents in the survey, it can be seen that the students had very varied notions of how to signal a stressed syllable. Out of the 11 different permutations of answers returned, 25% of the 52 students said that a stressed syllable is longer, higher pitched and louder. The second most popular option was louder and longer (17.31%), and the third most popular option was higher pitch (15.38%).

In their response to the question 'How do you stress a two-syllable compound noun?', 36.5% of the subjects said that stress should fall on the first syllable, while 40% said they did not know. In their responses to the question on the stress placement in noun phrases, 36.5% said that stress should fall on the first syllable, while 44.2% said that they did not know the answer. The answers obtained appear to indicate that many of the respondents were not sure of the pattern of lexical stress for compound nouns and noun phrases. The similarity in the opinions given for stress falling on the first syllable in compound nouns and noun phrases confirmed that the Malaysians do not make any distinction in their stress pattern for compound nouns and noun phrases.

TABLE 4.4   *Respondents' answers to the question 'How do you signal stress in an utterance?'*

Signal of lexical stress	No. of responses	Percentage
Higher pitch	8	15.38
Softer	1	1.92
Louder	5	9.62
Longer duration	3	5.77
Louder, higher pitch	6	11.54
Louder, longer duration	9	17.31
Louder, lower pitch, longer duration	3	5.77
Louder, higher pitch, longer duration	13	25
Louder, higher pitch, shorter duration	1	1.92
Higher, longer pitch	1	1.92
Louder, lower pitch, shorter duration	2	3.85

TABLE 4.5 *Respondents' answers to How They Stress Two-syllable Compound Nouns and Noun Phrases*

	How do you stress a two-syllable compound noun?	How do you stress a two-syllable noun phrase?
Stress 1st syllable	19 (36.5%)	19 (36.5%)
Stress 2nd syllable	12 (23.1%)	10 (19.2%)
Don't know	21 (40.4%)	23 (44.2%)

TABLE 4.6 *Summary of key findings of acoustic analysis*

	ME	BE
Duration	No difference between compound nouns and noun phrases	
Amplitude	No difference between compound nouns and noun phrases	
Fo	No difference between compound nouns and noun phrases	Difference between compound nouns and noun phrases

Discussion and Conclusion

A summary of the key findings of the first part of the study is provided in Table 4.6.

The results of the study confirm the finding of earlier perceptual studies that Malaysians do have a different stress pattern for compound nouns compared to BE speakers. As shown in Table 4.5, the responses of the informants in the survey seem to imply that lexical stress placement is more likely to be random as the informants claimed to have varied patterns of lexical stress. These variations in stress patterns in the pronunciation of Malaysians can lead to communication breakdown.

Discussions on the patterns of pronunciation to be adopted, especially for new varieties of English such as ME, need to strike a balance between the need for national identity, which is connected to accent, and intelligibility in international contexts. While the need for certain distinctive pronunciation features that mark one's identity has its merits, to achieve the nation's aspirations, Malaysia as a developing nation needs to be pragmatic and adopt pronunciation patterns that enable Malaysians to be intelligible in English. Inevitably, there is a need for some common standards, such as some phonological core as the Lingua Franca Core (which are essential pronunciation features that are crucial to the intelligibility of non-native speakers), to facilitate international intelligibility (Jenkins, 2000). While the Lingua Franca Core emphasises segmental features and does not recommend teaching the full range of lexical stress, it nevertheless does recommend providing learners with general guidelines on word stress (Jenkins, 2000, p. 151). Work by researchers such as Field (2005) suggests that it is suprasegmental features that are considered to be more critical for intelligibility by native speakers, implying that lexical stress, which is one of the elements of suprasegmental features, is important for communication with native speakers of English. Although comprehensibility is 'co-constructed' in that it is the interaction between the speaker, hearer and the linguistic and social contexts, it has been shown by previous research that the speaker's accent is the most significant factor for comprehension in international contexts (Pickering, 2006). When a speaker's pronunciation is difficult to understand, listeners will need to utilise more contextual cues in their effort to comprehend. As a nation that desires to develop human resources that are able to function effectively in the international arena, Malaysia can ill afford to ignore the need to develop speakers of English who are intelligible and comprehensible to both native and non-native speakers of English.

Examination of the curriculum for teaching English in Malaysian primary and secondary schools shows that the teaching of pronunciation is indeed among the list of skills to be imparted to primary and secondary school students. Specific features of segmental and suprasegmental speech are listed in the English language curriculum for each year of study from Year One in primary school to the end of secondary school education: for example, stress in compound words and two- and three-syllable words is listed as the sound patterns to be taught in the Form Two syllabus (Kementerian Pendidikan Malaysia [Ministry of Education, Malaysia], 2003, p. 30). Past research, however, has revealed that despite the fact that specific aspects of pronunciation have been listed in the English curriculum of Malaysian primary and secondary classes, teachers, in their rush to complete the syllabus, tend to sideline the teaching of pronunciation as pronunciation is not an important element of the major government examinations (Nair, Krishnasamy, & de Mello, 2006; Jayapalan & Pillai, 2011). Nair et al. (2006) also highlighted the fact that some teachers also avoid teaching pronunciation as they are not confident in this area of teaching. Another reason commonly cited is the fact that teachers tend to focus more on other aspects of English, such as writing and reading comprehension, that are frequently tested in the major government examinations. Given that pronunciation contributes much to intelligibility, there should perhaps be greater focus on the teaching of pronunciation in teacher training courses as well as more time allocated to pronunciation lessons in normal English classroom lessons.

The Malaysian Education Blueprint (2013–2025) documents the Ministry of Education's goal of developing students who are proficient in English. Among the targets listed is the aim of developing individuals 'that are equipped to work in a globalised economy where the English Language is the international language of communication' (Ministry of Education, 2013, p. 4–10) and operationalised as being independently proficient, as defined by the Common European Framework of Reference. A number of measures have been put forward to enable the achievement of this goal, among which are steps to improve the quality of English teachers and increase the time allocated for the teaching of English and the proposal to make English a mandatory pass at the end of secondary school examination by 2016. Although the aim of improving the overall proficiency of students in schools has been clearly stated, little has been mentioned about pronunciation. It appears that the assumption is that if students are proficient, they are automatically intelligible; thus, pronunciation may still be overlooked in the future unless greater focus is placed on the teaching of pronunciation. Clear pronunciation is an important aspect of intelligibility. Jenkins convincingly showed through her work that pronunciation is the biggest factor causing loss of intelligibility and comprehensibility, especially among those who do not belong to the categories of native and bilingual English speakers. This group of speakers tends to rely much more on the acoustic signals or what they actually hear in communications, and this bottom-up approach tends to be prevalent even among those who are competent in the use of English (Jenkins, 2000). As such, although lexical stress is not the only aspect affecting intelligibility, it should be emphasised in the English classroom as it can help improve intelligibility. Given the aim of the Ministry of Education to equip Malaysians to be able to function effectively at the international level, some measures need to be taken. The need for Malaysia to produce a workforce that is able to communicate clearly and intelligibly in English is even more acute given the greater fluidity in the flow of goods and services, including labour, that will occur after ASEAN integration is implemented in 2015. Malaysian workers will need to be able to function competently in English as in a more liberalised market, they will need to compete with workers from other ASEAN nations for jobs. In such a scenario, spoken intelligibility, which essentially involves clear pronunciation, is critical, and specific steps should be put in place to bring about change.

While it has been noted that the teaching of the suprasegmental features of English can be difficult, teaching word stress is not necessarily so. Students with lower proficiency in English can be made aware of lexical stress, while students with higher proficiency in English can be taught the rules of word stress to help them become more intelligible. More support for the teaching of word stress has come from researchers such as Murphy (2004), who noted that as learners of English are made aware of the common patterns of lexical stress, regular rules and patterns of the English stress system are internalised. This acts as a form of scaffolding enabling learners to better perceive the patterns of new words they learn and integrate them into the vocabulary they normally use.

Looking ahead, further investigation should focus on whether the realisation of word stress in ME affects intelligibility and comprehensibility in non-native contexts where English is the lingua franca. Another area that can be focused on is the effectiveness of the methods used to teach and learn word stress. The results of such studies may have an impact on the classroom teaching of pronunciation as well as the intelligibility of ME.

References

Baskaran, L. (2005). *A Malaysian English primer: Aspects of Malaysian English features.* Kuala Lumpur: University of Malaya Press.

———. (2008). Malaysian English: Phonology. In R. Mesthrie (Ed.), *Varieties of English 4: Africa, South and Southeast Asia* (pp. 278–291). Berlin/New York: Mouton de Gruyter.

Boersma, P., & Weenink, D. (2006). *Praat: Doing phonetics by computer* (version 4.4.22). Retrieved from http://www.fon.hum.uva.nl/praat/

Checklin, M. (2012). What in the world do we know about word stress? A review of what it is and how to teach it. Retrieved from http://www.tesol.org.au/files/files/267_martin_checklin.pdf

Derwing, T. M., & Munro, M. J. (1997). Accent, comprehensibility and intelligibility: Evidence from four L1s. *Studies in Second Language Acquisition, 19*, 1–16.

———. (2005). Second language accent and pronunciation teaching: A research-based approach. *TESOL Quarterly, 39*, 379–397.

Deterding, D. (2005). Listening to Estuary English in Singapore. *TESOL Quarterly, 39*, 425–440.

Field, J. (2005). Intelligibility and the speaker: The role of lexical stress. *TESOL Quarterly, 39*(3), 398–423.

Fox, A. (2000). *Prosodic features and prosodic structure*. Oxford: Oxford University Press.
Fry, D. B. (1955). Duration and intensity as physical correlates of linguistic stress. *Journal of the Acoustical Society of America, 27*, 765–768.
———. (1958). Experiments in the perception of stress. *Language and Speech, 1*, 126–152.
———. (1965). The dependence of stress judgments on vowel formant structure. In E. Wirner & W. Bethge (Eds.), *Proceedings of the 6th International Congress of Phonetic Sciences* (pp. 306–311). Basel: Karger.
Fudge, E. C. (1984). *English word stress*. London: Allen and Unwin.
Gaudart, H. (2000). Malaysian English, can or not? In H. M. Said & K. S. Ng (Eds.), *English is an Asian language: The Malaysian context* (pp. 47–56). Kuala Lumpur: Persatuan Bahasa Moden Malaysia and Macquarie Library.
Gut, U., Pillai, S., & Zuraidah, M. D. (2013). The prosodic marking of information status in Malaysian English. *World Englishes, 32*(2), 185–197.
Hung, T. T. N. (2002). English as a global language and the issue of international intelligibility. *Asian Englishes, 5*(1), 4–17.
Jayapalan, K., & Pillai, S. (2011). The state of teaching and learning English pronunciation in Malaysia: A preliminary study. *Malaysian Journal of ELT Research, 7*(2), 63–81.
Jenkins, J. (2002). A sociolinguistically based, empirically researched pronunciation syllabus for English as an international language. *Applied Linguistics, 23*, 83–103.
Kementerian Pendidikan Malaysia [Ministry of Education, Malaysia]. (2003). Huraian sukatan pelajaran kurikulum bersepadu sekolah menengah Bahasa Inggeris Tingkatan 2. [Curriculum Development Centre, Ministry of Education, Malaysia. Curriculum Specifications English Form 2, Integrated Curriculum for Secondary Schools]. Kuala Lumpur.
Ladefoged, P., & Johnson, K. (2011). *A course in phonetics* (6th ed.). Boston, MA: Wadsworth Cengage Learning.
Lass, R. (1987). *The shape of English: Structure and history*. London: Dent.
Laver, J. (1994). *Principles of phonetics*. Cambridge: Cambridge University Press.
Lepage, A., & Busà, M. G. (2014). Intelligibility of English L2: The effects of incorrect word stress placement and incorrect vowel reduction in the speech of French and Italian learners of English. In *Proceedings of the international symposium on the acquisition of second language speech, Concordia Working Papers in Applied Linguistics, 5*, 387–400.
Low, E. L. (2000). Is lexical stress placement different in Singapore English and British English? In A. Brown, D. Deterding, & E. L. Low (Eds.), *The English language in Singapore: Research on pronunciation* (pp. 22–34). Singapore: Singapore Association for Applied Linguistics.
Ministry of Education. (2013). *Malaysia education blueprint 2013–2025 (pre-school to post-secondary)*. Kuala Lumpur: Ministry of Education Malaysia.

Murphy, J. M. (2004). Attending to word-stress while learning a new vocabulary. *English for Specific Purposes, 23*(1), 67–83.

———. (2014). Intelligible, comprehensible, non-native models in ESL/EFL pronunciation teaching. *System, 42*, 258–269.

Nair, R., Krishnasamy, R., & de Mello, G. (2006). Rethinking the teaching of pronunciation in the ESL Classroom. *The English Teacher, 35*, 27–40.

Nelson, C. (1995). Intelligibility and world Englishes in the classroom. *World Englishes, 14*, 273–279.

Noor Fadhila, M. N., & Setter, J. (2011). *The intonation patterns of Malay speakers of English: A discourse intonation approach*. International Congress of Phonetic Sciences, Hong Kong.

Pickering, L. (2006). Current research on intelligibility in English as a lingua franca. *Annual Review of Applied Linguistics, 26*, 219–233.

———. (2012). Second language speech production. In S. M. Gas & A. Mackay (Eds.), *The Routledge handbook of second language acquisition* (pp. 335–348). New York: Routledge.

Pillai, S., Zuraidah, M. D., Knowles, G., & Tang, J. (2010). Malaysian English: An instrumental analysis of vowel contrasts. *World Englishes, 29*(2), 159–172.

Platt, J., & Weber, H. (1980). *English in Singapore and Malaysia: Status, features, functions*. Kuala Lumpur: Oxford University Press.

Rajadurai, J. (2004). The faces and facets of English in Malaysia. *English Today, 20*(4), 54–58.

———. (2006). Pronunciation issues in non-native contexts: A Malaysian case study. *Malaysian Journal of ELT Research, 2*, 42–59.

Roach, P. (2009). *English phonetics and phonology* (4th ed.). Cambridge: Cambridge University Press.

Schneider, E. (2003). Evolutionary patterns of New Englishes and the special case of Malaysian English. *Asian Englishes, 6*(2), 44–63.

Tan, R. S. K., & Low, E. L. (2010). How different are the monophthongs of Malay speakers of Malaysian and Singapore English? *English Worldwide, 31*(2), 162–189.

———. (2014). Rhythmic patterning in Malaysian and Singapore English. *Language and Speech, 57*(2), 196–214.

Tan, Y. Y. (2005). Observations on British and Singaporean perception of prominence. In D. Deterding, A. Brown, & E. L. Low (Eds.), *English in Singapore: Phonetic research on a corpus* (pp. 95–103). Singapore: McGraw Hill.

———. (2006). Is the stressed syllable stressed? The perception of prominence in Singapore English. In H. Azirah & N. Hassan (Eds.), *Varieties of English in Southeast Asia and beyond* (pp. 133–152). Kuala Lumpur: University of Malaya Press.

Trask, R. L. (2007). *Language and linguistics: The key concepts* (2nd ed.) (P. Stockwell, Ed.). New York: Routledge.

Wong, I. F. H. (1981). English in Malaysia. In L. Smith (Ed.), *English for cross-cultural communication* (pp. 94–107). London: Macmillan.

Yamaguchi, T., & Pétursson, M. (2012). Voiceless stop consonants in Malaysian English. *Asian Englishes, 15*(2), 60–79.

Yap, N. T., Wong, B. E., & Abdul Aziz, A. Y. (2010). Representation of English front vowels by Malay-English bilinguals. *Pertanika Journal of Social Sciences & Humanities, 18*(2), 379–389.

Zielinski, B. W. (2007). The listener: No longer the silent partner in reduced intelligibility. *System, 36,* 69–84.

Zuraidah, M. D. (2000). Malay + English → A Malay variety of English vowels and accent. In H. M. Said & K. S. Ng (Eds.), *English is an Asian language: The Malaysian context* (pp. 35–46). Kuala Lumpur: Persatuan Bahasa Moden Malaysia and Macquarie Library.

Appendix
Sentences for Lexical Stress

1	a	He loves this armchair.
	b	It resembled an old chair.
2	a	It will be held in the schoolyard
	b	Behind the house was a cool yard.
3	a	He is writing on the blackboard.
	b	The floor had a slack board.
4	a	The party has no dress code.
	b	He was complimented for devising the best code.
5	a	He wanted to take the high road.
	b	He had good light and a dry road.
6	a	You need to plant it in the greenhouse.
	b	They admired the clean house.
7	a	That house is having a whitewash.
	b	Her hair needs a nice wash.
8	a	This shop sells dogfood.
	b	She needs a drink and some hot food.
9	a	He was wearing a wetsuit.
	b	She came in a red suit.
10	a	That is definitely a bluebird.
	b	She discovered a new bird.

Language Attitudes

CHAPTER 5

Attitudes towards Malay, English and Chinese among Malaysian Students: A Matched Guise Test

Paolo Coluzzi

Introduction

Malaysia is a multilingual and multi-ethnic state boasting around 140 different historical languages (Ethnologue). In spite of this enormous linguistic diversity, the only official language in Malaysia is Standard Malay (Bahasa Malaysia), whereas English, the former colonial language, could be considered a de facto second language. The position of English is very strong in Malaysia, with a noticeable presence in many high domains, including the mass media (see Coluzzi, forthcoming). English also tends to be the preferred language of inter-ethnic communication, particularly among educated people (Asmah, 1992, 2003).

The scheme in Table 5.1 may be seen as representing the linguistic repertoire of Malaysia.

TABLE 5.1 *The Malaysian Linguistic Repertoire*

English: inter-ethnic communication, modernity, economic opportunities, foreigners/tourism
Standard Malay: inter-ethnic communication, nationalism, economic opportunities, Islam
Mandarin Chinese: communication within the Chinese community, identity for the Chinese, economic opportunities
Arabic: Islam
Tamil: communication within the Tamil community, identity for the Tamil
Other minority languages, including other Indian languages and the languages of the Dayaks and Orang Asli (aboriginal Malaysians): communication within the ethnic group, local identity
Other Malay and Chinese dialects: local communication and identity

It is not an easy task to assess the level of prestige that a language enjoys, also considering the fact that different languages may enjoy different degrees of prestige among different individuals and ethnic groups. On the basis of my own research and observations, however, I have attempted to rank these languages according to the prestige they seem to enjoy among the majority of their speakers (from more to less). The most prestigious varieties also tend to be the ones that enjoy more official support. As can be seen, English has arguably been placed in first position. Standard Malay also enjoys quite high prestige and shares with English many high domains, apart from being used widely in low domains among the Malays and other bumiputeras. It is also used as a language of inter-ethnic communication, but normally only when one of the speakers is Malay and not fluent in English (Asmah, 2003, pp. 121–122). Education is mostly in Malay, although many Chinese and Indians attend national-type Chinese and Tamil primary schools where Malay is only taught as a subject. Mandarin Chinese also enjoys high prestige in spite of lacking official recognition as a language of Malaysia. Arabic is spoken by few people, but it retains a high level of prestige among the Muslim community thanks to its religious significance. The remaining languages (including the Chinese dialects) occupy the low position in a diglossic relationship with English, Standard Malay and Chinese and are used mostly in non-official/family settings. In Malaysia, the phenomenon of code-mixing and code-switching between speakers' first languages and English and/or Malay is widespread (Asmah, 1992).

The level of prestige indicated in Table 5.1 is obviously the author's own assessment based on his and other academics' observations, on the answers provided by a sample of Malaysian students in a survey on language use and attitudes conducted by the author in 2011 at the University of Malaya (Kuala Lumpur) and on research on the linguistic landscape in Kuala Lumpur, both of which will be referred to later in this chapter. As a matter of fact, the prestige of English and other languages in Malaysia is a hotly debated issue. Saying that English appears to have higher prestige among educated Malaysians than Malay, the national language, seems to be politically incorrect given the high status that the Malaysian state is trying to uphold for Malay. As for the aforementioned survey, it cannot be denied that answers given in questionnaires are not always reliable as personal, political and ideological motives may sometimes lead to underestimation or overestimation. A more reliable way to detect the level of prestige a language enjoys may be through research on the linguistic landscape (e.g. on signs found in an urban area, particularly the bottom-up or private ones) as this provides insights into the linguistic repertoire of a given area—not so much into the languages actually spoken perhaps (some of which, especially 'low' varieties like minority languages, may not appear in the linguistic landscape at all), but definitely into the status and the level of prestige these languages enjoy. In Landry and Bourhis's (1997, p. 26) words: 'The predominance of one language on public signs relative to other languages can reflect the relative power and status of competing language groups'.

Another way to evaluate language attitudes and the prestige the languages of a given repertoire enjoy may be through a matched guise test as this is more likely to show, for example, respondents' attitude towards a language without them realising it. To my knowledge, this is the third time matched guise testing has been carried out in Malaysia. A paper was presented at the 'International Conference on Minority and Majority: Language, Culture and Identity' in Kuching (Sarawak) in November 2010 (Ting & Puah), and another article based on the results provided by matched guise testing was published in 2012 (Lam & Kamila). However, both of these works only involved Chinese varieties. This may be the first time the three most used languages in Malaysia—Malay, English and Chinese—have been involved in a study using matched guise testing.

Matched guise testing, developed by Wallace Lambert and his associates in the early 1960s (Agheyisi & Fishman, 1970, p. 145; Fasold, 1984, p. 150), is an indirect way to gauge respondents' attitudes towards the languages involved, as they are asked to evaluate the speaker and not the languages, as is the case in direct methods such as questionnaires and surveys (Agheyisi & Fishman, 1970; Fasold, 1984).

After this introduction, the chapter goes on to outline the methodology employed and to analyse the data obtained, comparing the results provided by the Chinese and Malay students. Then, the results are discussed and compared with the data provided in another matched guise test carried out in Singapore in 2009 (Cavallaro & Ng) and with the author's previous research. The chapter closes with some general conclusions.

Methodology

A trilingual Chinese student in the Italian Division of the Department of Asian and European Languages of the University of Malaya was selected for the test[1] as she appeared to be one of the few students who had mastered Malay, English and Mandarin. Whereas very few non-Chinese can speak Mandarin, all Chinese in Malaysia can speak Malay as, together with English, it is the language with the highest visibility in the linguistic landscape and the media and is a compulsory subject in all schools. The problem is that many Chinese

---

1   A good part of the author's teaching hours at the University of Malaya are spent teaching in the Italian Division, whose students he knows particularly well.

may not be very fluent in Malay as they do not often use it actively, and the majority retain a Chinese accent when they speak it. On the other hand, the student selected (born in 1993) is fluent in Malay and can speak it with no detectable Chinese accent. This is because even though she attended Chinese national-type schools before entering university, she comes from a small town in the Kelantan region with a mostly Malay population, with whom the small Chinese community has to interact regularly. Obviously, finding perfectly balanced bilinguals, let alone trilinguals, is very difficult, but this student was the closest to a balanced trilingual I was able to find. Three other students from the Italian Division were chosen as 'distractors'.[2]

Three passages on the same subject were selected from three different versions of Wikipedia. The first paragraph of the entry on Kuala Lumpur was printed out from Wikipedia in Malay (http://ms.wikipedia.org), Wikipedia in English (http://en.wikipedia.org) and Wikipedia in Mandarin Chinese (http://zh.wikipedia.org) (see Appendix).

As the Mandarin included some traditional characters, pinyin transcriptions were provided for the characters students are not used to (in Malaysian Chinese schools, only simplified characters are used).[3] The idea was to have a passage of similar length, register and content without having to resort to translations, which may have made the text sound less natural.

The students were given time to familiarise themselves with the written passages before being recorded. If the flow of the reading was interrupted for any reason, the recording was repeated, but the inevitable small 'indecisions' and 'hitches' in the reading were left as long as the reading was flowing and sounded natural.

The passage in the three languages was recorded six times in total, twice in Malay, twice in English and twice in Chinese, by the four students. One of the four students, the stimulus speaker, was recorded three times in the three different languages, while one of my Malay students read only the Malay version, one of my Chinese students read the Chinese version and another of my students of mixed Kadazan and Chinese parentage read the English version. Therefore, the English version clearly sounded like local English (and this may have had implications for the results, as commented on below).

In order to prevent the participants in the testing, the judges, from realising that the same speaker was reading three of the passages, the recordings were

---

2 I would like to thank my students, Ching Fei Yee, Fazilah binti Sunmy, Yong Lin Li and Shaflina binti Mohd Gazali Fong, for their help with the recordings.

3 I would like to thank my colleague Rie Kitade for her invaluable help both in providing pinyin transcriptions and assessing the quality of the Chinese recording and in helping with the actual recording of the passages.

ordered in the following way: (1) Malay read by the stimulus speaker, (2) Malay read by the Malay 'distractor', (3) English read by the Kadazan-Chinese 'distractor', (4) English read by the stimulus speaker, (5) Chinese read by the Chinese distractor and (6) Chinese read by the stimulus speaker.

A questionnaire was then prepared with ten 7-point semantic differential scales to be filled in for each recording. The verbal anchors were as follows:

Intelligent—stupid[4]
Confident—insecure
Hardworking—lazy
Sincere—insincere
Reliable—unreliable
High social class—low social class
Friendly—unfriendly
Polite—rude
Efficient—inefficient
Modern—old-fashioned

The participants, who were told to try and evaluate six different Malaysian students by listening to their voices, ticked their scores on the scales (10 for each of the six versions) while and/or after listening to the readers, thereby assigning points: 1 for the lower end (e.g. 'stupid') and 7 for the higher end (e.g. 'intelligent').

In total, 50 students from the University of Malaya studying Japanese, Spanish or German,[5] whose ages ranged from 20 to 24[6] years, participated in the testing. Ten of these students were Malay[7] and 40 were Chinese;[8] the vast majority were girls.

---

4   No consideration was taken of political correctness in the selection of terms such as *stupid*, *lazy* or *rude*. What was deemed to be most important was that the participants, very few of whom had English as their first language, would be able to understand the words clearly.
5   I would like to thank my colleagues Kitade Rie, Woo Wai Sheng, Ricardo Reyes and Michael Freutel for allowing me to carry out the testing in their classes. Some of their students were also tested directly in my own office.
6   There was only one student who was 28.
7   Only one of these was a Bajau from Sabah (a Dayak ethnic group living in Northern Borneo), but I included him among the Malay group for the following reasons: He spoke perfect Malay and was a Muslim and therefore would supposedly be more integrated into the Malay community.
8   It would have been ideal to have had many more Malay students carry out the testing, but the great majority of the students in the Department of Asian and European Languages of the University of Malaya happen to belong to the Chinese ethnic group.

Results

Table 5.2 shows the overall results of the testing for the stimulus speaker's readings.

TABLE 5.2 *Overall results of the matched guise testing*

Verbal anchors	Malay	English	Chinese
Intelligent	4.98	4.8	4.02
Confident	4.74	4.52	4.28
Hardworking	4.74	4.8	4.66
Sincere	4.28	4.48	4.34
Reliable	4.84	4.7	4.04
High social class	4.62	4.46	4.1
Friendly	3.64	4.44	4.54
Polite	4.62	4.6	4.48
Efficient	4.66	4.46	3.8
Modern	4.48	4.94	4.2
Total average	4.56	4.62	4.24

Interestingly, overall, there was not a great difference among the results obtained for the three languages even though, on the whole, English seemed to fare slightly better than the other two languages, with Chinese coming last. This seems to clash with personal observation and with the results obtained in Coluzzi's survey (Coluzzi, 2012): In the latter, in response to the question 'Which language would you say is the most important (usefulness, 'beauty', etc.)?', 44 out of the 88 respondents replied English, 29 replied Chinese and only four replied Standard Malay; even though those opting for Chinese were all ethnic Chinese and those choosing Malay were all ethnic Malay, the majority of both the Chinese and Malay respondents chose English (37 Chinese and six Malays, Coluzzi, 2012, p. 124).[9] In the matched guise testing, however, only one verbal anchor (*friendly*)

---

9 It is interesting to notice that in this survey, as many as 10 students of different ethnic backgrounds declared that their first language was English (Coluzzi, 2012, p. 124). The fact that there is a small but growing number of Malaysian parents who decide to speak English to their children can also be seen as a sign of the prestige this language enjoys in Malaysia (see also David, 2001, 2006 and Low et al., 2010).

gave Chinese a higher score than both English and Malay, while for five verbal anchors (*intelligent, confident, reliable, polite and efficient*), Malay scored higher than English. These results are very interesting, particularly considering that the great majority of the respondents were ethnic Chinese. In contrast, the results provided by my own research on the linguistic landscape in places of worship in the Kuala Lumpur area seem to prove a higher presence of English than Malay (with Chinese as the third most used language), which seems to reflect the relative prestige these three languages enjoy. The research, carried out in seven different places of worship representing the main religions followed in the Kuala Lumpur area (one mosque, one Theravada Buddhist temple, two churches, one Chinese temple, one Hindu temple and one Sikh temple or Gurdwara), showed that as many as 151 signs (out of 306) were in English, whereas the scripts in Malay amounted to barely 20% of the total (60 out of 306). Two of these places of worship (the Gurdwara and the Hindu temple) did not have any signs in Malay whatsoever in their compounds, whereas Chinese writings were present in 37 signs found in four different places of worship (the two churches, the Buddhist temple and the Chinese temple, where they amounted to 75% of the total number of signs) (Coluzzi & Kitade, 2015).

Coming back to the present research, if we look at the overall results of the testing divided by ethnic group (Table 5.3: M. for Malay and C. for Chinese), a more varied and interesting state of affairs is revealed.

TABLE 5.3   *Results of the matched guise testing by ethnic group*

Verbal anchors	Malay	English	Chinese
Intelligent	M. 4.6 / C. 5.07	M. 5.1 / C. 4.72	M. 4.5 / C. 3.9
Confident	M. 4.6 / C. 4.77	M. 4.8 / C. 4.45	M. 4.9 / C. 4.12
Hardworking	M. 3.9 / C. 4.95	M. 5.2 / C. 4.7	M. 5.1 / C. 4.55
Sincere	M. 3.3 / C. 4.52	M. 4.4 / C. 4.5	M. 4.1 / C. 4.4
Reliable	M. 4.0 / C. 5.05	M. 4.9 / C. 4.65	M. 4.6 / C. 3.9
High social class	M. 4.1 / C. 4.75	M. 4.5 / C. 4.45	M. 4.5 / C. 4.0
Friendly	M. 3.2 / C. 3.75	M. 4.8 / C. 4.35	M. 4.3 / C. 4.6
Polite	M. 4.8 / C. 4.57	M. 4.7 / C. 4.57	M. 5.1 / C. 4.32
Efficient	M. 4.0 / C. 4.82	M. 4.7 / C. 4.4	M. 4.8 / C. 3.55
Modern	M. 4.1 / C. 4.57	M. 5.3 / C. 4.85	M. 4.8 / C. 4.05
Total average	**M. 4.06 / C. 4.82**	**M. 4.84 / C. 4.56**	**M. 4.67 / C. 4.13**

In fact, the Malay respondents assigned the lowest score to their own language (in its standard form), whereas a similarly higher score was assigned to English and Chinese, though a little more to the former than the latter. The Chinese respondents, on the other hand, assigned the highest score to Malay, the second highest to English and the lowest score to Chinese; the score assigned to Chinese was significantly lower than the scores of the first two languages. In short, both ethnic groups seem to value their own language significantly less than the other two varieties. It appears as if English is the only language both ethnic groups seem to find most prestigious, as reflected in the above-mentioned survey.

As can be observed, some of the verbal anchors chosen can be related more closely to the spheres of affectivity and solidarity (family and friends), while others can be related more to status and prestige (work and officialdom). If we group together the overall scores provided for the anchor words 'sincere', 'friendly' and 'polite' on the one hand and 'confident', 'hardworking' and 'efficient' on the other, an unexpected outcome can be observed (Table 5.4): English is generally perceived as more 'intimate' than the other two languages, whereas Malay would appear to be the language perceived as the most useful and prestigious.

TABLE 5.4   *Results for the anchor words divided into those related to affectivity and solidarity and those related to work and officialdom*

Verbal anchors	Malay	English	Chinese
Sincere, friendly, polite	4.18	4.5	4.45
Confident, hardworking, efficient	4.71	4.59	4.24

If these results are divided according to the ethnic group of the respondents (Table 5.5), Malay again becomes the language scoring the lowest for the Malay respondents but the highest for the Chinese respondents as far as the anchor words related to work and officialdom are concerned, with Chinese scoring the highest for the Malay respondents and the lowest for the Chinese respondents. In the more intimate sphere, however, the ranking provided by the Malay and the Chinese respondents seems to coincide: English is ranked first, followed by Chinese and then Malay. It is interesting to note that it is only in this more intimate sphere that the respondents' perception of the prestige these languages enjoy seems to reflect the overall prestige that these languages enjoy in Malaysian society (as noted above).

TABLE 5.5 *Results for the anchor words divided into those related to affectivity and solidarity and those related to work and officialdom as provided by the Malay and Chinese respondents*

Verbal anchors	Malay	English	Chinese
Sincere, friendly, polite	M. 3.76 / C. 4.28	M. 4.63 / C. 4.47	M. 4.5 / C. 4.44
Confident, hardworking, efficient	M. 4.16 / C. 4.84	M. 4.9 / C. 4.51	M. 4.93 / C. 4.07

Discussion

How can these results be explained? One would have expected English to rank the highest in Table 5.2 and the ethnic 'roofing languages' of each ethnic group,[10] together with English, to score the highest in Table 5.3. However, there may be an explanation for the results obtained. First of all, the fact that the respondents were all students and the testing was carried out within the compounds of a state university may have led the respondents to reply in a way that was felt to be closest to the role that these languages and their speakers enjoy within the university and Malaysian society and according to official state policies—Malay is the only official language whose knowledge is indispensable in many domains, whereas Chinese is officially seen as having relatively low value as an 'ethnic' and 'foreign' language (see Fasold, 1984, p. 160; Cavallaro & Ng, 2009, pp. 155–156). Perhaps more important than this is the fact that the official status of Malay and its importance are continuously reiterated by the authorities and the media, with campaigning to make any other language official not only being forbidden but even conducive to detention (see Coluzzi, forthcoming; see also Cavallaro & Ng, 2009, p. 155, on official campaigning for English). Linked to this is the possibility that matched guise testing, at least in South East Asia where state control tends to be stronger than in the West, may be measuring overt prestige more than covert prestige. In Cavallaro and Ng's (2009, p. 155) words:

---

10 'Roofing language' is the most common English translation for Kloss's term *Dachsprache*, an 'umbrella language' that is used as a standard by speakers of related nonstandard varieties. In Malaysia, the roofing language for the Chinese speaking different Chinese varieties (Cantonese, Hokkien, Hakka, etc.) is Mandarin, while for the Malays speaking Malay dialects such as Kelantan Malay or Kedah Malay, the roofing language is standard Malay.

In responding to the MG [matched guise] surveys, participants could be evaluating the role of the language in the public domain—that is, how others may feel about it, how it is generally perceived. However, in using the variety and expressing positive orientation to the variety, they are evaluating their own personal beliefs.

In fact, in Cavallaro and Ng's own research based on matched guise testing, they unexpectedly found that Standard SE scored higher than the local variety of English, Singapore Colloquial English, even along the most intimate dimensions ('solidarity' variables). In both their and my research, the local varieties tend to score lower even when related to anchor words that denote more intimate relations.

This would explain the answers given by the Chinese respondents in my own research which ranked the languages in a sort of 'official' and 'hegemonic' manner, with Malay at the top followed by English and finally Chinese (but, interestingly enough, not in the more intimate sphere, where the respondents may have felt freer to report their own personal beliefs), but it would not explain the answers provided by the Malay respondents. Another reason for the Chinese respondents valuing Mandarin so low might have something to do with the fact that the stimulus reader's rendering of Mandarin could be clearly recognised as local, and it seems as if many Chinese believe that their own version of Mandarin is not as good as the official Mandarin spoken in China, to which they are exposed through the media. Similar considerations may apply for English, which would have probably have scored even higher if the passage from the English Wikipedia had been read by a native speaker from the United Kingdom, the United States or Australia.

Unlike the Chinese respondents, the Malay respondents might not have felt under so much pressure to report official standings and might have felt freer to express their own feelings about the actual prestige and usefulness of the three languages through the evaluation of their speakers. After all, Malay is first of all their own language before being the official language of the country, and not being able to understand Chinese and distinguish a local accent from that of a native speaker from China might not have affected the aura of prestige that Chinese enjoys as the language of China and of a wealthy and dynamic sector of Malaysian society (in addition to being, together with English, the most spoken language in the world). In short, the targets of the Malay state's efforts to uphold Malay as the national language are mainly the non-bumiputeras who do not speak it as a first language. In any case, the relatively low number of Malay respondents who took part in the testing makes these considerations provisional and tentative.

Conclusions

According to the results obtained, it seems as if matched guise testing in Malaysia, Singapore and perhaps other countries in Southeast Asia may be measuring overt prestige rather than covert prestige. In Malaysia, this may be due to the constant official campaigning for an official language, Malay, which is only a second language for a large proportion of Malaysians, and to the lack of public debate on anything that may question the privileges of the Malay majority, including the language. On the other hand, the ranking provided by the Chinese respondents as far as the more intimate sphere is concerned seems not to differ much from that provided by the Malay respondents, which may be interpreted as an expression of covert prestige. For some reason, the anchor words 'sincere', 'friendly' and 'polite' (i.e. those related to affectivity and solidarity) seem to have elicited 'deeper' answers, less influenced by official and hegemonic concerns. It would be interesting to repeat the matched guise testing with a larger number of respondents, including more Malays and also working people of different ages and backgrounds rather than only students, to see whether different outcomes are obtained. In the meantime, the results obtained in this research seem to point once again to the absolute high prestige of English among all Malaysians as the language of globalisation and economic opportunities and also as the preferred lingua franca among educated Malaysians. They also point to the relative prestige of Malay as the national and official language of the country, even though it continues to be largely the everyday language of Malays only.[11]

References

Agheyisi, R., & Fishman, J. A. (1970). Language attitude studies: A brief survey of methodological approaches. *Anthropological Linguistics, 12*(5), 137–157.

Asmah, Haji O. (1992). *The linguistic scenery in Malaysia*. Kuala Lumpur, Malaysia: Dewan Bahasa dan Pustaka.

———. (2003). *Language and language situation in Southeast Asia: With a focus on Malaysia*. Kuala Lumpur, Malaysia: Akademi Pengajian Melayu Universiti Malaya.

Cavallaro, F., & Ng, B. C. (2009). Between status and solidarity in Singapore. *World Englishes, 28*(2), 143–159.

---

[11] However, nowadays, the younger generations of Dayaks who live in the big coastal towns of Sabah and Sarawak (East Malaysia) also tend to use mostly Malay in 'low' domains.

Coluzzi, P. (2012). Modernity and globalization: Is the presence of English and of cultural products in English a sign of linguistic and cultural imperialism? Results of a study conducted in Brunei Darussalam and Malaysia. *Journal of Multilingual and Multicultural Development, 33*(2), 117–131.

———. (forthcoming). Language planning for Malay in Malaysia: A failure or a success case? *International Journal of the Sociology of Language,* 244.

Coluzzi, P., & Kitade, R. (2015). The languages of places of worship in the Kuala Lumpur area: A study on the 'religious' linguistic landscape in Malaysia. *Linguistic Landscape. An International Journal, 1*(3), 243–267.

David, K. M. (2001). *The Sindhis of Malaysia: A sociolinguistic account.* London: Asean.

———. (2006). Language choice in Sindhi families. In M. K. David (Ed.), *Language choices and discourses of Malaysian families* (pp. 3–21). Petaling Jaya: Strategic Information and Research Development Centre.

Ethnologue (Malaysia). Retrieved from http://www.ethnologue.com/country/MY.

Fasold, R. (1984). *The sociolinguistics of society.* Oxford: Blackwell.

Jí lóng pō (n.d.). In *Wikipedia.* Retrieved April 28, 2014, from http://zh.wikipedia.org.

Kuala Lumpur (n.d.). In *Wikipedia.* Retrieved April 28, 2014, from http://en.wikipedia.org/wiki/Kuala_Lumpur.

———. (n.d.). In *Wikipedia.* Retrieved April 28, 2014, from http://ms.wikipedia.org/wiki/Kuala_Lumpur.

Lam, K. C., & Kamila, G. (2012). An online community-based language attitude study on Chinese varieties. *Journal of Malaysian Chinese Studies, 15,* 65–84.

Landry, R., & Bourhis, R. Y. (1997). Linguistic landscape and ethnolinguistic vitality: An empirical study. *Journal of Language and Social Psychology, 16*(1), 23–49.

Low, H. M., Howard, N., & Wales, R. (2010). A sociolinguistic profile of 100 mothers from middle to upper-middle socio-economic backgrounds in Penang-Chinese community: What languages do they speak at home with their children? *Journal of Multilingual and Multicultural Development, 31*(6), 569–584.

Ting, S. H., & Puah Y. Y. (undated). Language attitudes of Hokkien speakers towards Hokkien and Mandarin. Retrieved from https://www.academia.edu/1788145/language_attitudes_of_hokkien_speakers_towards_hokkien_and_mandarin.

Appendix

The texts used for the matched guise test, taken from Wikipedia (Kuala Lumpur/Jílóngpō), were as follows:

Malay
Kuala Lumpur (singkatan: KL) atau nama penuhnya Wilayah Persekutuan Kuala Lumpur, ialah ibu negara dan bandar terbesar di Malaysia. Kawasan Wilayah Persekutuan ini yang meliputi tanah seluas 244 km2 (94 batu^2), diduduki 1.63 juta orang mengikut banci tahun

2010. Kuala Lumpur tergolong dalam sebuah kawasan metropolitan besar yang turut meliputi sebahagian besar negeri Selangor, iaitu Lembah Klang, sebuah kelompokan bandar yang diduduki 7.2 juta orang, dan juga kawasan metropolitan yang paling pesat membangun di negara dari segi bilangan penduduk dan ekonomi.

English
Kuala Lumpur, often abbreviated as K.L., is the federal capital and most populous city in Malaysia. The city covers an area of 243 km2 (94 sq mi) and has an estimated population of 1.6 million as of 2010. Greater Kuala Lumpur, also known as the Klang Valley, is an urban agglomeration of 6.9 million as of 2010. It is among the fastest growing metropolitan regions in the country, in terms of population and economy.

Chinese
吉隆坡（馬來語、英語：Kuala Lumpur, 舊稱州府地）是马来西亚的首都兼最大城市，常被簡稱為「KL」。據 2012 年統計，該城市面積達 243 平方公里（94平方英里），人口約有 160 萬人。大吉隆坡也稱為巴生河流域，是一個有 720 萬人的大都會區，也是馬來西亞人口和經濟成長最快速的都會區。
吉隆坡位在馬來半島西岸，為雪蘭莪州環繞。吉隆坡划轄於吉隆坡聯邦直轄區，為马来西亚三个聯邦直轄區之一，由联邦政府直接管辖。

Pinyin transcription
Jílóngpō (mǎ lái yǔ, yīngyǔ: Kuala Lumpur, jiù chēng zhōu fǔ dì) shì mǎláixīyà de shǒudū jiān zuìdà chéngshì, cháng bèi jiǎnchēng wéi 'KL'. Jù 2012 nián tǒngjì, gāi chéngshì miànjī dá 243 píngfāng gōnglǐ (94 píngfāng yīnglǐ), rénkǒu yuē yǒu 160 wàn rén. Dà jílóngpō yě chēng wéi bā shēng hé liúyù, shì yígè yǒu 720 wàn rén de dà dūhuì qū, yěshì mǎláixīyǎ rénkǒu hé jīngjì chéngzhǎng zuì kuàisù de dūhuì qū.
Jílóngpō wèi zài mǎlái bàndǎo xī'àn, wéi xuělán'é zhōu huánrào. Jílóngpō huà xiá yú jílóngpō liánbāng zhíxiá qū, wéi mǎláixīyà sān gè liánbāng zhíxiá qū zhī yī, yóu liánbāng zhèngfǔ zhíjiē guǎnxiá.

CHAPTER 6

English for the Indigenous People of Sarawak: Focus on the Bidayuhs

Patricia Nora Riget and Xiaomei Wang

Introduction

Sarawak covers a vast land area of 124,450 km² and is the largest state in Malaysia. Despite its size, its population of 2.4 million people constitutes less than one tenth of the country's population of 30 million people (as of 2015). In terms of its ethnic composition, besides the Malays and Chinese, there are at least 10 main indigenous groups living within the state's border, namely the Iban, Bidayuh, Melanau, Bisaya, Kelabit, Lun Bawang, Penan, Kayan, Kenyah and Kajang, the last three being collectively known as the Orang Ulu (lit. 'upriver people'), a term that also includes other smaller groups (Hood, 2006). The Bidayuh (formerly known as the Land Dayaks) population is 198,473 (State Planning Unit, 2010), which constitutes roughly 8% of the total population of Sarawak. The Bidayuhs form the fourth largest ethnic group after the Ibans, the Chinese and the Malays. In terms of their distribution and density, the Bidayuhs are mostly found living in the Lundu, Bau and Kuching districts (Kuching Division) and in the Serian district (Samarahan Division), situated at the western end of Sarawak (Rensch et al., 2006). However, due to the lack of employment opportunities in their native districts, many Bidayuhs, especially youths, have migrated to other parts of the state, such as Miri in the east, for job opportunities and many have moved to parts of Peninsula Malaysia, especially Kuala Lumpur, to seek greener pastures.

Traditionally, the Bidayuhs lived in longhouses along the hills and were involved primarily in hill paddy planting. Traditionally, the Bidayuh community held matters concerning land close to their hearts as the land is looked upon as a direct source of sustenance. In the same way, paddy planting became a natural activity (regarded as part of Bidayuh life) and thus needed to be treated with great care and respect. Today, the majority of the Bidayuhs, particularly those living in rural villages, continue their agricultural activities, but they are less involved in paddy planting. They have gradually switched to planting cash crops such as rubber, cocoa, oil palm and pepper, in addition to investing their time and energy in orchards that produce fruits such as durian, rambutan and bananas and many vegetables (Minos, 2000, pp. 45–47). The main reason for the change in agrarian activity is that cash crops provide them with better income.

Over the years, with better access to formal education, more Bidayuhs have found employment in government offices and private businesses, most of which are located in Kuching (Hood, 2006, p. 89). Indeed, in the 1960s, the majority of Bidayuh parents began to believe that education was the key to obtaining a job in the government service. In fact, nowadays, the two areas in which many Bidayuhs are involved are teaching and health services. Nevertheless, according to Minos (2000, p. 44), the Bidayuh community is still economically backward compared to the other major races of Malaysia as only about 10% of Bidayuhs, primarily those who are well educated and have expertise, work for the government or private sectors, and only a handful of them are practising liberal professions such as medicine, the law or accountancy.

In terms of religious belief, the Bidayuhs used to practice animism. According to Minos (2000, pp. 117–118), the Bidayuhs can be considered 'naturalists' or believers in nature. Minos further explained that, being land-based people, the Bidayuhs who practised animism in the past paid respect to the land, including the hills and mountains, the woods, the forests, the rivers and many other things connected with nature and the environment. However, nowadays, the majority of Bidayuhs are Christians, most belonging to the Catholic or Anglican churches and a few to the Seventh Day Adventist Church. The Bidayuhs' conversion to Christianity began with the arrival of the first Christian missionaries to the island of Borneo in the 19th century during the Rajah Brooke regime. Hence, it is quite common nowadays to see one or more churches in each Bidayuh village.

Regarding the use of languages, most of the Bidayuh speak languages belonging to a common family of languages traditionally called 'Land Dayak' (Hudson, 1970); more specifically, it is called 'Bidayuh' (Rensch et al., 2006). All these languages belong to part of the Austronesian family. There are five major varieties of Bidayuh, sometimes referred to as dialects: Bidayuh Serian (traditionally called Bukar-Sadong), Bidayuh Bau (traditionally called Bau-Jagoi), Bidayuh Biatah (encompassing dialects spoken in the Penrissen and Padawan regions), Rara Bakati and Salako. Not all of these are mutually intelligible. The Salako, though politically and culturally of Bidayuh ethnicity, speak a language more closely related to Malay.

Bidayuh People and Formal Education

Earlier records show that Sarawak does not have a long history of formal education (Noeb & Ridu, 2006, p. 11). Besides the Malay traditional religious schools, formal education was introduced in Sarawak after the arrival of James Brooke. The missionaries began establishing schools in Kuching very soon after they first arrived, but for a long time they did little to bring education to the villages where most Bidayuhs lived. In fact, during the Brooke regime (1841–1941), the policy towards education in Sarawak used by the three White Rajahs was largely laissez-faire. Affairs regarding non-Muslim indigenous education were left entirely to the Christian missionaries, and due to a lack of resources, almost all Anglican and Catholic mission schools were in urban areas. Thus, very few non-Muslim indigenous children could afford to attend school. As such, non-Muslim indigenous pupils who lived in the rural areas, such as the Bidayuh pupils, did not benefit much from these earlier educational establishments.

Formal education, according to Minos (2000), was first introduced to the Bidayuhs in the late 1880s, but only in two Bidayuh areas, namely the Singgai area in the Bau District and the Quop area in Kuching District. It was the Christian missionary movement that brought the first primary schools to these two areas. Thus, the first and better educated Bidayuhs came from these two areas. For this reason, the earliest Bidayuh civil servants, teachers, graduates and professionals were from the Singgai and Quop areas, especially the former. Consequently, the Singgai and Quop groups became leaders for the Bidayuh population in the field of education.

Traditionally, the Bidayuh people, being an agrarian community, did not bother much about formal education, while the British colonial masters did little to push the reluctant Bidayuhs to gain an education. According to Minos (2000), among the reasons given by Bidayuh parents for not wanting to send their children to school, especially in the 1940s, were firstly that they needed their children to help them with farm work and secondly that they did not want their children to be far away from home and influenced by outside ideas, customs and traditions. Earlier records show that the Anglican mission established a school at Ta'ee, a Bidayuh village in Serian, in 1916, whereas the Seventh Day Adventist mission built a school that provided academic and agricultural training for the Serian Bidayuhs at the foot of the Stabun Mountain (near Serian) in 1933. In the same year, the Roman Catholic Church built a small school in Serian where a number of Bidayuhs came to learn how to read and write.

It is recorded that in Sarawak there were 29 mission schools in 1930 and 41 such schools in 1938 (P. L. Ong, P. H. Ong, Sivapalan, Marsitah, & Badariah, 2014). After the Japanese occupation (1942–1945), the number of mission schools in Sarawak increased to 58, with a total enrolment of 5,087 students, in 1947 (Ong et al., 2014). In total, towards the end of Brooke rule in Sarawak in 1941, there were 11 Anglican mission schools, 27 Roman Catholic Schools, three

Seventh Day Adventist schools, 33 Government-supported Malay schools, 144 Chinese schools and one Iban school (Noeb & Ridu, 2006, p. 12). It was only after the Second World War in 1945, and especially in the late 1940s and early 1950s, that the Bidayuhs started to realise the importance of formal education. From then on, both the government under the British and the Christian missionaries made some efforts to educate Bidayuh villagers.

As a result, more and more of the Bidayuh villages had primary schools, especially those close to Kuching and larger districts such as Bau and Serian. In the early 1950s, a number of secondary schools were built by the British colonial government under the Colombo Plan. One such school is the Dragon School (now called Kolej Tun Abdul Razak), located at the 24th mile of the Kuching-Serian Road. The setting up of government primary schools in even the remotest Bidayuh villages, such as the very interior parts of Lundu, Bau, Kuching and Serian districts, where there were no early mission schools, came about from 1963 onwards under the then newly formed Federation of Malaysia Government. Today, every Bidayuh village has its own primary school and every Bidayuh district where the Bidayuhs are the majority has at least two or three secondary schools: for example, SMK[1] Lake and SMK Bau for the Bau district, SMK Serian and SMK Tebekang for the Serian district, SMK Siburan and SMK Padawan for the Padawan district and SMK Lundu and SMK Sematan for the Lundu district. Nevertheless, it should be noted that the Bidayuhs had their first contact with the English language via the mission schools, as the medium of instruction in these schools at that time was English.

After Malaya achieved independence from the British in 1957, there were great changes in the educational policy of the country. These changes came about much earlier in West Malaysia (formerly Malaya) than in East Malaysia due to the special status of Sarawak and Sabah, which did not join the federation until 1963. The 1957 Education Ordinance was aimed at establishing a national system of education for all the people of the federation and making Malay the national language of the country. Subsequently, the Education Act of 1961 continued to place emphasis on monolingual education. As a result, many Chinese schools were converted to government schools from 1962 onwards, and these schools adopted English as a medium of instruction. In 1967, the Malaysian parliament passed the National Language Act, which stated that Malay was the national language and the sole official language in West Malaysia. This meant that after 1967, English lost its official status in West Malaysia, and this later had a great impact on its education system. As a result, all English-medium schools at elementary and secondary levels were

---

1   SMK refers to *Sekolah Menengah Kebangsaan* in Malay, meaning 'National Secondary School'.

converted into Malay-medium schools by the end of 1982 in West Malaysia. It was claimed that this conversion was driven by the imperatives of nation building (Asmah, 1982).

The situation in East Malaysia was slightly different from that in West Malaysia as 'by constitutional agreement, the administration of education in Sabah and Sarawak... remained under state jurisdiction' (Rudner, 1977, p. 30). Sarawak joined Malaysia in 1963 when British colonial rule ended. As the people of Sarawak continued to receive an English-medium education, there was a need to retain this common language (Ting & Sussex, 2002). Therefore, the official status of English in Sarawak was retained until 1985 (Asmah, 1996). Despite the loss of its official status, English is still used in law courts and state parliamentary sessions and is the 'de facto official language in the commercial sector' (Ting, 2001, p. 55). In Sarawak, the Malay language was taught as a school subject only from 1969. Later on, in 1977, the medium of instruction in primary schools started to gradually change from English to Malay and English became a subject in national schools. The conversion up to secondary Form 6 level was completed in 1989 (Ting, 2001), 7 years later than in West Malaysia. Since then, education in Sarawak has shown a great degree of conformity with West Malaysia, and it is claimed that this gradual harmonisation has been an integral part of nation building.

The Present Situation of the English Language among the Bidayuhs

One of the consequences of closing English schools was the perceived drop in the level of English proficiency among Malaysians (Gill, 2005). Later, due to the effects of globalisation in the 1990s, the value of English in the global market was highlighted once again. As a result, starting in 2003, a reversal of policy towards English in the education domain began, with emphasis being placed on the role of English as the medium of instruction for mathematics and science subjects in primary and secondary schools (Gill, 2005). Although the policy was withdrawn in 2012 due to various reasons, such as the poor academic performance of students, the low level of teachers' English proficiency and the disparity between schools in rural and urban areas (Tan & Santhiram, 2014), the government continued to strengthen English in its subsequent policy, with slogans such as 'to uphold Bahasa Malaysia, to strengthen the English language' (Nor Liza, Obaidul, & Moni, 2011). Under this new policy, the teaching hours for English in schools were increased: for instance, the teaching time for English became 300 minutes (10 periods) per week in national primary schools and 150 minutes (5 periods) in national-type primary schools (Nor Liza et al., 2011).

This policy was implemented to balance the planning of Malay and English, consolidating the status of Malay as the national language and strengthening the role of English as the global language.

The Bidayuh community has experienced the above changes in educational policy together with other communities in the country. Due to these dramatic changes, proficiency in English and Malay among the Bidayuh youth has changed. According to Ting (2001), young Sarawakians are more proficient in Malay than in English. In other words, compared with the minority of Bidayuh students who received an English-medium education up to the late 1970s, their attitude towards English may not be the same.

This Study

The current study attempted to investigate the attitude of Bidayuh youths towards English through a questionnaire (see Appendix). The focus of the survey was the motivation for learning English and attitudes towards English. A 5-point Likert scale was used for the questions on motivation, and triple-choice questions ('Agree', 'Disagree' and 'Don't Know') were used for the questions on attitude. A total of 70 respondents, 59 females and 11 males, returned their questionnaires. Most of the respondents were upper secondary or college students. All the respondents were from Kuching, thus representing Bidayuh youth in urban areas. Due to the sample size, no claim is made that the results reflect the views of the entire Bidayuh youth population in Sarawak. Nevertheless, in this preliminary study, the tendencies within the Bidayuh youths' attitude towards English can be seen. To complement the questionnaire survey, interviews with representatives from the Bidayuh community were conducted in English. Seven interviewees aged over 30 expressed their opinions about the English language. The results from these surveys and interviews are reported and discussed in detail in the next section.

The Results

English as Home Language and Best Language
Of the 70 respondents, only three claimed that they spoke English at home. This shows that English is not preferred in the family domain. Most respondents stated that they spoke Bidayuh with their family members (N=55, 78.6%). This finding is similar to the results of the survey by Coluzzi, Riget and Wang (2013), in which 83.5% of the respondents (N=266) spoke only Bidayuh at home and

none of them used English as their sole home language. When the respondents were asked about their best language, six of them chose English. Most of the respondents regarded Bidayuh as their best language (N=45, 64.3%). It was noticed that Malay had become the respondents' second best language (N=16, 22.9%); this may be the effect of the current language policy in education. As mentioned in the previous section, the medium of instruction in schools in Sarawak changed from English to Malay in the 1980s, so Bidayuh children have been receiving their education in Malay since their enrolment in primary schools. This has contributed to their command of Malay being better than their command of English. Coluzzi et al. (2013) also reported that 30.8% of their respondents from four Bidayuh villages in Sarawak spoke Bidayuh and Malay equally fluently.

Most respondents claimed that their English level was 'good', 'very good' or 'excellent' (N=45, 64.3%). This self-reported result may reflect their positive attitude towards English on the one hand and their wish to upgrade their English level on the other. This can be seen in the respondents' comments on English learning (R refers to an individual respondent):

1. The ruling government should be very supportive of the use of English as an educational tool. (R 1)
2. English should be given just as much priority as Bahasa Malaysia. (R 7)
3. I hope that the English language will be a compulsory subject in Malaysia. (R 63)
4. English should be highlighted in all education in Malaysia. (R 64)
5. I hope that the English language will be made a compulsory subject to make it easier to pass in public examinations. (R 66)
6. I hope that English learning will be a crucial subject in Malaysia. (R 70)

These comments show that they believed that English should receive more support from the government in the education domain and that it should be treated equally with Malay, the national language. These views may also indicate that Bidayuh children need more English input in schools, which can be seen in the choice of medium of instruction for science and maths in their schools. Out of the 28 respondents who responded to the question pertaining to the medium of instruction for science and maths in their schools (Q 8 and Q 9, Part A in the Appendix), 18 mentioned that their schools employed English as the medium of instruction for these two areas of the curriculum, whereas 10 respondents mentioned Malay. Among these respondents, 25 mentioned that their schools offered five periods of English classes, while six mentioned that their schools offered six periods per week.[2] As will be shown in the next section, many of the respondents agreed with the statement that English should be the medium of instruction in secondary schools in Malaysia.

Motivation to Learn English

Nine reasons for learning English (Table 6.1) were listed in the questionnaire for the respondents to rate (Part B in the Appendix). A 5-point Likert scale with the following descriptions was used for rating: 'very important', 'important', 'of some importance', 'of little importance' and 'not important'. Table 6.2 shows the responses of the respondents.

TABLE 6.1 *Motivation to learn English*

1. Because I will be able to search for information and materials in English on the Internet.
2. Because it will make me a more knowledgeable person.
3. Because it is a school/university requirement.
4. Because I hope to further my education.
5. Because it will enable me to get a job easily.
6. Because I would like to make friends with foreigners.
7. Because other people will respect me more if I have knowledge of a foreign language.
8. So that I can understand English-language films, videos, TV or radio.
9. Because my parents tell me to study it hard.

---

2 The term *period* refers to a teaching session for each subject taught in national schools in Malaysia. Each period lasts around 35 minutes.

TABLE 6.2 *Respondents' responses to the questions on motivation to learn English (N=70)*

Statement	Very important	Important	Of some importance	Of little importance	Not important
1	39	23	8	–	–
2	43	24	2	1	–
3	35	27	7	1	–
4	42	25	1	2	–
5	42	20	5	2	1
6	23	28	14	2	3
7	19	23	16	7	5
8	39	21	7	2	1
9	34	19	10	4	3

In general, the respondents gave positive responses to statements 1, 2, 3, 4, 5 and 8. In contrast, statement 6, 7 and 9 received some negative responses. The results reveal that the respondents tended to associate English with knowledge and education. They regarded English as a tool to retrieve information and knowledge. In addition, they saw English as a tool that can help them in obtaining employment. However, it is not always treated as a bonus for self-esteem or reputation. This motivation for English learning corresponds to what the government has promoted in the 'Strengthening English Policy' in the Malaysian Education Blueprint (Ministry of Education, 2013). When the respondents were asked to make further comments on English learning in the final open-ended question, some of them highlighted the importance of English as an international language: for instance, '(English can) create a connection with a wider range of the world's population' (R 22); 'learning English can help when travelling to other countries, so that I can speak with other people from different regions' (R 37); 'it is crucial to know how to speak the English language as it is an international language' (R 67). In fact, the view of English as an international language is also shared by other minority groups in Malaysia such as Chinese and Indians (Wang, Riget, Supramani, & Koh, 2015).

It should be noted that as the sample for the current study came only from urban areas, it may not reflect the situation in rural areas. In fact, there are many issues with indigenous education. As pointed out by the Malaysian Education Blueprint (Ministry of Education, 2013, pp. 4–21), the drop-out rate of indigenous students in secondary schools is alarming at around 70%.

This meant that only 30% of these students are able to complete secondary school education. The situation in remote areas is even worse than this. One of the reasons given by the Ministry of Education is that Bahasa Malaysia, the medium of instruction, is not the mother tongue of these indigenous students (*Orang Asli* in Malay) (Ministry of Education, 2013, pp. 4–21). Another possible reason is the quality of teachers. Indeed, one of the respondents in the current study pointed out that 'teachers are not so knowledgeable about English terminology'.

Generally speaking, the instrumental value of English is highlighted among the Bidayuh youth, especially in urban areas. This generation has undergone a national education which uses Malay as the medium of instruction, which is different from the previous mission schools. Therefore, it is not entirely unexpected that proficiency in English has dropped gradually. This situation is reflected in the comments made by one of the interviewees (aged 54): 'the older generation that studied in the sixties and seventies are able to converse well in English, but the English proficiency of those who studied in the eighties and nineties is low'. She further commented that even if they use English, it would be mostly 'English synonyms or in short form only'. Meanwhile, another interviewee (aged 60) estimated that 'about 80% of Bidayuh youths are facing difficulties in conversing in English' and pointed out that 'English was only widely used among the Bidayuhs in the 60s and earlier'. Another interviewee (aged 56) further added that 'for the rest of their lives, many (Bidayuh youths) will never be able to converse and write in decent English'. Even children in the cities are 'still shy about speaking openly (in English)' (interviewee aged 54). Obviously, the perception of the older generation in the sample was that the English level of the younger generation has dropped dramatically.

This drop is due to the change in the education system over the years and in the status of English in Malaysia. As stated by one of the interviewees (aged 56), '[o]ur educational system is a tragedy occurring to our children'. This statement was further emphasised by another interviewee (aged 47): 'The youth today are not that fluent (in English) due to our Malaysian education system that uses Bahasa Malaysia (BM) as the medium of instruction'. Does the younger generation have the same perception? This will be discussed in the next section.

Attitudes towards English

In the questionnaire, the respondents were asked about their attitudes towards the use of English in government and business offices, schools and entertainment (Part C in the Appendix). Table 6.3 lists the eight statements presented to the respondents, who were required to give one of three responses to each statement: 'agree', 'disagree' or 'don't know'. Table 6.4 summarises the results.

TABLE 6.3 *Attitudes towards English*

1. The development of our country is made possible mainly by educated people who have a good command of English.
2. The use of English in government and business offices helps in getting things done easily.
3. English should not be a compulsory subject in secondary schools in Malaysia.
4. English should be the medium of instruction in secondary schools in Malaysia.
5. English should be used to teach science subjects at the secondary level in Malaysia.
6. The number of hours dedicated to the teaching of English in Malaysian schools is sufficient.
7. English films are more enjoyable than films in any other language.
8. When I hear someone speak English well, I wish I could speak like him/her.

TABLE 6.4 *Respondents' responses to the statements on attitudes towards English (N=70)*

Statement	Agree	Disagree	Don't know
1	52	8	10
2	60	6	4
3	10	50	10
4	47	13	10
5	59	5	6
6	29	26	15
7	43	15	12
8	64	3	3

From the perception of the respondents, English is very important in official domains, as reflected in their responses to statements 1 and 2. The majority of the respondents (74.3%, N=52) agreed that knowing English is crucial when dealing with Malaysian government agencies and in business circles. The better educated people are all perceived to have been educated in English and to able to speak good English. As for the education domain, 84.3% of the respondents (N=59) agreed that English should be the medium of instruction for science (statement 5) and 67.1% of the respondents (N=47) supported the view that English should be used as the medium of instruction in secondary schools in Malaysia (statement 4). As for the teaching hours allocated for English, less than half of the respondents (N=29, 41.4%) contended that the number of teaching hours is sufficient. For entertainment, most of the respondents preferred films in English. In Malaysia, the original soundtrack of imported movies is retained and subtitles in Malay and Chinese are provided. Statement 8 examined the respondents' intention to upgrade their English level: 91.4% of them showed a keenness to improve their proficiency in the English language.

Concerning ways to improve the level of English among Bidayuh youths, the interviewees gave the following suggestions:

1. The language faculty at institutions (of higher learning) should organise a seminar or workshop in Sarawak at least once a year to analyse the proficiency of the Bidayuh.
2. There should be more English lessons in schools.
3. Our kids should be given a kick-start by being given English exercises as early as kindergarten level. Maintain a balance of intensity between English and national language usage in all learning modules and levels in our schools and later in our working professions.
4. Encourage our children, especially our youth, to speak English at home, school or university. Parents should also speak English to their children. Buat (Do) English Campaign. Workshops organised at kampong (village) level by those experts.
5. Give extra classes or tuition for English. Provide venue for them (Bidayuh youths) to communicate in English.
6. Create awareness. Watch more English movies. Listen to English songs. Provide English workshops with English speakers.
7. Encourage them (Bidayuh youths) to speak English instead of mixing Malay and Bidayuh. Promote English through the radio. Get assistance from foreigners.

The above suggestions given by the older generation of Bidayuhs convey a message that English learning should be enhanced among the Bidayuh community. English is indeed, according to one of the interviewees (aged 37), a very important tool to have in order 'to seek better jobs and access economic opportunities'. This respondent further added that other ethnic groups in Sarawak would respect the Bidayuh people more if 30 to 40 % of them could speak, understand and write English very well.

As it is still important and widely used in Sarawak (Ting, 2001), English is one of the most popular lingua francas for cross-ethnic communication. As commented by one of the interviewees (aged 56), English has been 'of paramount importance as a means of communication and a learning tool since the colonial days'. Similarly, another interviewee (aged 50) commented that 'being able to speak in English is an advantage as you are not limited to only communicating among Bidayuh people; rather, you can also converse with others in the local and international community'. She further added that 'being able to speak English automatically gives the impression that you are knowledgeable and smart'. During our fieldwork in different Bidayuh villages, it was not difficult to find people who were fluent in English. However, these English speakers were all educated in English and in their fifties or sixties. The younger generation tends to speak more Malay than their parents. This raises the contention that a language shift towards Malay is happening; studies on this area are left for future research.

Summary and Conclusion

This chapter has explored the evolution and effect of English language education among the Bidayuhs, more specifically, the Bidayuh youths' motivation to learn English and their attitudes towards English. The results from the questionnaire survey and the interview data reveal that, overall, both the older and younger generations of Bidayuhs have a positive attitude towards the English language and that mastering English is still considered important, if not very important. Nevertheless, one can also conclude from the results of the interviews that the English level among young Bidayuhs is perceived to have dropped dramatically. Of course, it would be valuable to investigate the extent to which standards of English really have fallen. The interview data also show that the perceived drop in English proficiency levels among Bidayuh youths is due primarily to changes in the medium of instruction in the Malaysian school system.

Although the findings from previous studies conducted on the Bidayuhs and language shift (Dealwis, 2008; Norazuna, 2010; Coluzzi et al., 2013) have shown that the occurrence of a language shift among the Bidayuhs is from

Bidayuh to Bahasa Melayu, Sarawak Malay dialect and English in school, at work and at home, this phenomenon mostly occurs among the Bidayuhs in the urban areas. As for the majority of the Bidayuh youths living in Bidayuh villages in the Bidayuh belt, their home language is Bidayuh and their daily contact with the English language is limited to subjects taught in English in schools or to English programmes, movies and songs on television, radio and other social media. English is also used by the Bidayuh youths during church services when they sing hymns.

Historically (since the late 1880s), the Bidayuhs had a good head start with English learning via the mission schools, and yet this advantage has been cut short by the change in the medium of instruction from English to Malay. Nevertheless, one should not conclude that the dramatic drop in English level that was claimed to have occurred among the Bidayuh youths is due only to the change in the medium of instruction in the country's school system. The lack of access to the Internet and cable television in the majority of the Bidayuh villages should also be taken into consideration. Indeed, in villages where access to cable television is non-existent, the only channels that they have access to are national television channels (e.g. TV1, TV2, TV3, 8TV and NTV7[3]). The majority of the programmes on these channels are either in Malay (the exception being movies, series and reality shows, which are often broadcast in English) or in Chinese. Hence, apart from their English lessons in schools, Bidayuh children's contact with English is rather limited. Yet, in order for the Bidayuh youths to be able to compete with the major ethnic groups in the country for jobs both in the government and private sectors, and to give them more cultural and educational opportunities (for example, the range of subjects and genres available in books in Malay is very limited), mastering English should be made a priority for them. For this to happen, all stakeholders should work together towards attaining that objective.

References

Asmah, Haji O. (1982). *Language and society in Malaysia*. Kuala Lumpur: Dewan Bahasa dan Pustaka.

———. (1996). Post-imperial English in Malaysia. In J. A. Fishman, A. W. Conrad, & A. Rubal-Lopez (Eds.), *Post-imperial English: Status change in former British and American colonies, 1940–1990* (pp. 513–533). Berlin: Mouton de Gruyter.

---

3   NTV7 derives from the name of the broadcasting company known as 'Natseven TV Private Limited'.

Collins, J. (2004). Malayic languages of Sarawak. In H. O. Asmah (Ed.), *Encyclopedia of Malaysia: Languages and literature* (Vol. 9) (pp. 32–33). Singapore: Editions Didier Millet.

Coluzzi, P., Riget, P. N., & Wang, X. (2013). Language vitality among the Bidayuh of Sarawak (East Malaysia). *Oceanic Linguistics, 52*(2), 375–395.

Dealwis, C. (2008). *Language choice among the Dayak Bidayuh undergraduates* (Unpublished doctoral dissertation). University of Malaya, Kuala Lumpur.

Gill, S. K. (2005). Language policy in Malaysia: Reversing direction. *Language policy, 4*, 241–260.

Hood, S. (Ed.). (2006). *Encyclopedia of Malaysia: People and traditions* (Vol. 12). Singapore: Editions Didier Millet.

Hudson, A. B. (1970). A note on Selako: Malayic Dayak and Land Dayak languages in western Borneo. *Sarawak Museum Journal, 18*, 301–318.

Ministry of Education, Malaysia. (2013). *The Malaysian education blueprint (2013–2025)*. Putrajaya: Ministry of Education Malaysia.

Minos, P. (2000). *The future of the Dayak Bidayuhs in Malaysia.* Kuching: Lynch Media and Services.

Norazuna, N. (2010). *Language choice of Bidayuh graduates in Kuching-Samarahan Division* (Unpublished doctoral dissertation). University of Malaya, Kuala Lumpur.

Nor Liza, A., Obaidul, H. M., & Moni, K. (2011). English in primary education in Malaysia: Policies, outcomes and stakeholders' lived experiences. *Current Issues in Language Planning, 12*(2), 147–166.

Ong, P. L., Ong, P. H., Sivapalan, S., Marsitah, M. R., & Badariah, S. (2014). The making of Malaysian solidarity: A historical look at education and social cohesion in Sarawak. *Malaysian Journal of Society and Space, 10*(1), 36–48.

Rensch, C. R., Rensch, C. M., Noeb, J., & Ridu, R. S. (2006). *The Bidayuh language: Yesterday, today and tomorrow.* Kuching: Dayak Bidayuh National Association.

Rudner, M. (1977). Education, development and change in Malaysia. *South East Asian Studies, 15*(1), 23–62.

State Planning Unit. (2010). *Sarawak: Facts and figures.* Kuching: Chief Minister's Department.

Tan, Y. S., & Santhiram, R. (2014). *Educational issues in multiethnic Malaysia.* Kuala Lumpur: Strategic Information and Research Development Center.

Ting, S. H. (2001). When is English not the right choice in Sarawak. *English Today, 17*(1), 54–56.

Ting, S. H., & Sussex, R. (2002). Language choice among the Foochows in Sarawak, Malaysia. *Multilingua, 21*, 1–15.

Wang, X., Riget, P. N., Supramani, S., & Koh, Y. C. (2015). Constructing identities through linguistic landscape: A comparison between Chinatown and Little India in Kuala Lumpur. In N. Norazuna & Haji O. Asmah (Eds.), *Linguistic minorities: Their existence in larger communities* (pp. 120–142). Kuching, Sarawak: Universiti Malaysia Sarawak Press.

Appendix
The Students' Questionnaire

The purpose of this questionnaire is to collect data on Bidayuh students' motivation and attitudes towards learning English. The data collected will be used for an article that we are currently working on entitled 'English for the Indigenous People of Sarawak: Focus on the Bidayuhs'.

Instructions: For the following items, please indicate your answer with a tick (√) in the spaces provided. Where a line is provided, please write your answer, if applicable.

A) Background Information

Please tick (√) in the appropriate space.

1. What is your age?

3–15 years	
16–18 years	
19–23 years	
Over 23 years	

2. What is your gender?

Male	
Female	

3. What is your mother's ethnic group?

Bidayuh	
Malay	
Chinese	
Other Bumiputra groups	

4. What is your level of study?

Lower secondary	
Upper secondary	
College/University	
Other (please specify)	

5. What language do you speak at home?

Bidayuh	
Malay	
English	
Other languages (specify)	

6. What is your best language?

Bidayuh	
Malay	
English	
Other languages (specify)	

7. How do you rate your current level in English?

Bad	
Ordinary	
Good	
Very good	
Excellent	

Note: Questions 8 & 9 below are to be answered by lower & upper secondary school respondents.

8. There are ___ periods of English classes in my school.

9. The medium of instruction for science and maths in my school is _____.

B) **Motivation to Learn English**

What are your reasons for learning English? Please rate the following reasons according to their importance. Please tick (√) the appropriate box:

Reasons for learning English	**Very important**	**Important**	**Of some importance**	**Of little importance**	**Not important**
1) Because I will be able to search for information and materials in English on the Internet.					
2) Because it will make me a more knowledgeable person.					

Reasons for learning English	Very important	Important	Of some importance	Of little importance	Not important
3) Because it is a school/university requirement.					
4) Because I hope to further my education.					
5) Because it will enable me to get a job easily.					
6) Because I would like to make friends with foreigners.					
7) Because other people will respect me more if I have knowledge of a foreign language.					
8) So that I can understand English-language films, videos, TV or radio.					
9) Because my parents tell me to study it hard.					
10) Others (please specify)					

C) Attitudes toward Learning English

What are your attitudes towards the following issues? Please tick (√) the appropriate box:

Issues	Agree	Disagree	Don't know
1) The development of our country is made possible mainly by educated people who have a good command of English.			
2) The use of English in government and business offices helps in getting things done easily.			
3) English should not be a compulsory subject in secondary schools in Malaysia.			
4) English should be the medium of instruction in secondary schools in Malaysia.			
5) English should be used to teach science subjects at secondary level in Malaysia.			
6) The number of hours dedicated to the teaching of English in Malaysian schools is sufficient.			
7) English films are more enjoyable than films in any other language.			
8) When I hear someone speak English well, I wish I could speak like him/her.			

Do you have any comments that you would like to add with regard to English learning?

_____
_____
_____
_____
_____

End
Thank you very much for your time and cooperation.

Malaysian English Online

CHAPTER 7

English and Other Languages in the Online Discourse of East Malaysians

James McLellan

Introduction

Research studies into language choice and use in multilingual Malaysia too often focus on West Malaysia (*Semananjung*, the Malay Peninsula) alone and tend to marginalise or ignore the East Malaysian states of Sabah and Sarawak, located in the north of Borneo Island, where the ethnolinguistic mix is different and more diverse. In an attempt to counter this imbalance, this chapter focuses exclusively on issues of online language choice and use in Sabah and Sarawak (see Figure 1.1 in Chapter 1). The chapter offers an analysis of textual data examples from public websites, including government and commercial sites, ethnolinguistic community sites, discussion forums and readers' responses to reports posted on the webpages of East Malaysian newspapers, blogs and social media sites. Texts taken from social media sources (e.g. Facebook™ status updates and asynchronous discussions) are limited to those available publicly to any reader with Internet connectivity so as to comply with ethical norms.

This study of language use and choice also subsumes language alternation (code-mixing), defined here as the appearance of more than one language in the same electronically mediated discourse text. The co-occurrence of English, Bahasa Malaysia (BM) and other languages of Sabah and Sarawak within the same text is of interest in this study as it enables comparison with spoken discourse in which the use of more than one language is unmarked and unsurprising.

Brief Literature Review and Analytical Framework

There are very few previous studies addressing the particular issues of EMD and online language choice and use in East Malaysia. Stephen (2006) has discussed language choice in Kadazandusun-related websites, where the language choice may not necessarily be Kadazandusun. There is only one study, that of Gupta (2006), on the use of English in Borneo-based websites. However, there is a growing body of scholarship on EMD worldwide, and the linguistic and sociocultural complexities of Sabah and Sarawak have been the focus of much scholarly attention.

The term *electronically mediated discourse* (EMD) is used in this chapter to refer to texts on the World Wide Web (WWW) since EMD encompasses all types of communication accomplished through the medium of information and communication technologies (ICTs). This decision is informed by Crystal's (2011, pp. 1–3) discussion on issues of terminology in *Internet Linguistics*. Crystal (2001, 2011) has claimed that an initial fear of the WWW favouring the further spread of powerful global languages such as English and Spanish has been largely overcome. The spread of Internet connectivity has been concomitant with an awareness that the WWW can support any language (Androutsopoulos, 2013; Danet & Herring, 2003, 2007), even those which do not yet have a fixed writing system, since it can serve as a repository for audio and video files.

Sebba's (2009) concepts of regulated and unregulated spaces are applicable to the analysis of the language choice decisions made by EMD text producers. In regulated spaces, a measure of control is expected and exercised by gatekeepers, including language planning agencies that are tasked with prescribing standard norms.

A kueh lapis (layer cake) analogy is used by Noor Azam and McLellan (2014) to discuss multilingualism in Borneo contexts. This enables consideration of the interactions between the various indigenous and immigrant languages within each of the four polities of Borneo. This chapter aims to uncover some of these layers of language use in Sabah and Sarawak EMD.

Background

The language ecologies of Sabah and Sarawak are distinct from that of West Malaysia, with both states having a greater range of indigenous languages and complex patterns of individual and societal multilingualism (King, 1994; Ting, 2012). Sabah and Sarawak also differ from each other, both in their earlier histories of settlement and colonisation and in more recent patterns of migration and language shift. It is claimed that Sabah and Sarawak have 54 and 52 languages, respectively (Lewis, Simons, & Fennig, 2014). Overlaying these languages are Malay in both its Sabah and Sarawak varieties, standardised BM and English, all of which may serve as lingua francas in the different EMD contexts.

Languages of Sabah

The demography, and hence also the language ecology, of Sabah has changed dramatically over the past 25 years (Kamal Sadiq, 2005), with an influx of migrants from the neighbouring southern Philippines and Indonesia (see Figure 1.1). Reliable demographic information is hard to find given the political sensitivities of this issue, which is currently being investigated by a Royal Commission of Inquiry. The figures for 2010, cited by Wikipedia and sourced from the Population and Housing Census, Malaysia Department of Statistics, are shown in Table 7.1.

TABLE 7.1 *Ethnic groups of Sabah*

Ethnic group	% of total Sabah population
Kadazandusun	17.8
Murut	3.2
Bajau	14.0
Brunei Malay	5.7
Other bumiputera (indigenous)	20.6
Chinese	9.1
Other non-bumiputera	1.5
Non-Malaysian citizen	27.8

These figures represent declared ethnicity. They differ from those cited in Chapter 1 of this volume (Table 1.2) which only show Bumiputera. The non-Malaysian citizen category is by some way the largest. The figure for the Kadazandusun, formerly the largest indigenous group, shows a reduction from the 1960 figure of 32%. Apart from the small Brunei Malay community, no figure is given for 'Malay', yet Sabah Malay functions as the principal lingua franca for the whole population. These figures differ from those given in Chapter 1 of this volume, which are derived from a different source, and they do not provide an accurate account of which languages are spoken by the various communities. The Ethnologue listing, which includes all the languages of Malaysia (Lewis et al., 2014), classifies 39 out of Sabah's total of 54 languages as 'threatened' and five as 'shifting'. The latter classification signals a language at great risk of imminent loss.

Languages of Sarawak

Sarawak, by contrast, shows more stable demographic patterns. Population by ethnic group, cited by Wikipedia from the Sarawak Department of Statistics, is shown in Table 7.2.

TABLE 7.2   *Ethnic groups of Sarawak*

Ethnic group	% of total Sarawak population
Iban	29
Chinese	24
Malay	23
Bidayuh	8
Melanau	6
Orang Ulu	5
Others	5

As with the Sabah figures, these figures represent declared ethnicity. Twenty six of the 52 Sarawak languages are described as threatened and three as shifting by Lewis et al. (2014), all of them indigenous languages of the Austronesian family. Sarawak Malay, as distinct from 'Peninsular Standard' Malay, serves as Sarawak's major lingua franca alongside Iban and English. Mandarin serves this function among Sarawak's Chinese community, who form 25.5% of Sarawak's population and whose heritage languages include Hokkien, Hakka and Foochow (Ting, 2012, p. 384). It is necessary to distinguish between Sarawak Malay as the L1 of the Malay community, who comprise about 23% of the state's total population, and Sarawak Malay as a unifying lingua franca (McLellan, 2014; Ting, 2012).

Juxtaposed with the economically and politically powerful languages in Sabah and Sarawak's complex multilingual ecosystem, the minority indigenous languages of the Austronesian family can be considered as endangered. Even Iban is perceived as 'marginalised' by Ariffin Omar and Teoh (1994), despite the Iban being the largest ethnic group, representing 29% of the state's population, and despite the Iban language having relatively little dialectal diversity. Bidayuh, the fourth largest Sarawak language in terms of number of speakers (about 8% of the total population of the state), is also perceived as endangered, partly because it is not a unified language and is extremely diverse in terms of its five major varieties (McLellan & Campbell, 2015; Rensch, 2006; Topping, 1990). Other Sarawak indigenous groups include the Melanau (6% of the Sarawak state population) and the groups collectively labelled *Orang Ulu* ('upriver people'), who comprise 5% of the population.

Improved connectivity in terms of road systems facilitates rural-urban migration and thus increases the potential for language shift in both states. But improved rural Internet connectivity through the Malaysian government's *kampung tanpa wayar* ('village wifi') scheme could possibly contribute towards language maintenance (McLellan, 2014, pp. 19–20). Thus, there are contrary tendencies exerting influence on patterns of online language use in East Malaysia.

Methods

Purposive and convenience sampling were the main methods used for selecting websites which originate from East Malaysia. For the different categories of website, small-scale textual corpora were collected and analysed. For the different categories of website, small-scale textual corpora were collected and analysed, mostly manually. Corpus analysis allowed for initial quantitative analysis, such as how many texts there were in each language and how many texts showed any measure of language alternation. Some of these texts were then analysed and discussed in greater detail in terms of their language choices. Because the texts were mostly anonymous, or pseudonymous in the public discussion forms, it is only possible to offer analysis of the product, not of the processes by which the texts were produced, edited and uploaded.

Findings

Language choice and use in seven categories of website are described in this section. All the websites discussed in this section are listed with their urls in the Appendix.

National and State Government and Government-linked Websites

In the East Malaysian states, government ministries and departments can be classified into those which are under federal (West Malaysian) jurisdiction and those which are under the jurisdiction of the respective states. Education, for example, is under federal control, whereas land is a state matter; hence, the respective *Jabatan Tanah dan Survei* (land and survey departments) are answerable to the Sabah and Sarawak state governments. In terms of language choice, one expects government and government-linked websites (e.g. those of statutory bodies) to adhere to Malaysian national language policy and BM to be the default choice.

An online search for the websites of two government secondary schools, one each in Sabah and Sarawak, came up with *Sekolah Menengah Kebangsaan Sandakan* (Sandakan National Secondary School) in Sandakan town in the East Coast Residency of Sabah and *Sekolah Menengah Kebangsaan Katibas* (Katibas National Secondary School) in Song sub-district in central Sarawak. Both these schools' websites are in BM only, in compliance with Malaysia's national language policy.

The Sarawak Land and Survey Department has parallel websites in BM and English carrying the same information, with a toggle enabling switching between the languages. The Sabah Land and Survey Department website homepage has three language options: English, BM and Chinese. Clicking on the Chinese option brings up a version that has been machine-translated using Google Translate™.

The websites of the port authorities of Sabah and Kuching (state capital of Sarawak) serve as examples of government-linked organisations. The Sabah Ports Authority controls all seaports in Sabah state; its website is bilingual BM and English but with some of the information in English and some in BM. The pulldown menus on the homepage are all in English, as is the featured promotional video clip which has a commentary in a standard variety of English spoken in an educated (acrolectal) Malaysian accent. Only the announcements and some of the media reports are in BM. The *Lembaga Pelabuhan Kuching* (Kuching Port Authority) has a bilingual BM/English interface with a toggle for switching between languages, similar to the Land and Survey Department websites; hence, all information is available in both BM and English.

Commercial Websites: Online Media Classified Advertisement Texts

This section includes promotional texts from private-sector businesses and individuals, particularly classified advertisements (CAs) appearing in online editions of Sabah and Sarawak newspapers. Different priorities apply here, contrasting with those of government-linked websites. The predominant role of the Sabah and Sarawak Chinese communities in the private sector is reflected in the greater frequency of Chinese-language commercial websites and in the use of Chinese in online media advertisements. Both Sabah and Sarawak have Chinese-language newspapers with online editions: the *See Hua Daily News* (http://www.seehua.com) is published in both Kuching, Sarawak and Kota Kinabalu, Sabah.

Online editions of *The Borneo Post*, *Utusan Borneo* and the *New Sabah Times* newspapers include the same classified advertising as their print editions. Classified advertising texts involve negotiation between sellers and potential buyers. As such they are an accurate reflection of popular language preferences.

For this part of the study, three mini-corpora were collected, one from each newspaper, as shown in Table 7.3.

TABLE 7.3 *Classified advertisements corpora*

Newspaper	Date	Number of CAs
The Borneo Post	27 July 2010	174
Utusan Borneo	27 July 2010	76
New Sabah Times	2 December 2011	144

An analysis of language choices within the CAs revealed the following:

TABLE 7.4 *Language choice in online CAs in three newspapers*

Newspaper	English only	BM only	BM-English code-mixing	Others
The Borneo Post	139 (79.8%)	8 (4.6%)	15 (8.6%)	Eng/Chinese = 12
Utusan Borneo	43 (56.6%)	17 (22.4%)	10 (13.1%)	Eng/Chinese = 3; BM/Eng/Chinese = 2; Iban = 1
New Sabah Times	24 (16.7%)	37 (25.7)	83 (57.6%)	–

One striking finding here is that the BM- and Iban-language *Utusan Borneo* has a majority of CAs in monolingual English. Also surprising is the fact there are no instances of Kadazandusun in the *New Sabah Times*' CAs and only a single example of Iban in the *Utusan Borneo*, even though these newspapers have daily sections in these Borneo languages. Code-mixed BM and English is the most common choice in the *New Sabah Times* CAs. In the two Sarawak newspapers, *The Borneo Post* and *Utusan Borneo*, Chinese is sometimes found in the names of businesses (e.g. hotels and restaurants) and in the names of dishes served in restaurants. One example of this is text 1:

1. 黑　　鸡　　　人参　　　汤
    black　chicken　ginseng　soup
    double boiled black chicken (Ginseng soup with dried seafood)
    (*Utusan Borneo* CA, 27 July 2010)

Other examples of BM/English language alternation in CA texts include the following, in which the words in BM have interlinear glosses:

2. a. *We supply wrought iron material, hollow section, flat bar.*
        Harga　　Termurah
        price　　lowest

    b. Terdapat jawatan kosong di cawangan Miri: *Office boy cum delivery*
        got　　　position vacant in branch　　(city)
        driver　(lelaki)　*Cashier*　(perempuan)
        　　　　　male　　　　　　　　female

    c. *Waiter* (mesti　ada　pengalaman). *Cook–Malay/Western/Chinese*
        　　　　　must　have　experience
        (mesti　ada　bukti　pengalaman　kerja)
        must　have　proof　experience　work

    d. Terbuka　kepada　kakitangan　kerajaan　(*Federal and State*) &
        open　　to　　　staff　　　　government
        berpencen
        pensioner

(Source for 2a–d: *The Borneo Post*, 27 July 2010)

It is evident that the newspapers, themselves bi- or tri-lingual, do not regulate classified advertisement texts in terms of their language choices. Clearly the language choices, mixed or not, are not random since the text producers have time to plan before submitting them for publication in the newspapers. Text producers aim for maximum intelligibility whilst observing the constraints of the CA genre: Since the newspapers charge by the word or by the line, their product or service must be described succinctly and must target the likeliest buyers, or applicants if it is a job advertisement. These factors may be part of the explanation for the language choices, including alternation, found in the CAs. Kirkpatrick and McLellan (2011) used parts of the same CA corpus to analyse the discourse of Borneo CAs within a World Englishes framework.

Ethnolinguistic Community Websites

Ethnolinguistic community association websites in East Malaysia are potential sites for the online use of the languages of the respective communities. The Sarawak Dayak Iban Association (SADIA) has a public Facebook page and a blog (see Appendix for the urls). Information posted on both of these sites is in English only. The same applies for the Dayak Bidayuh National Association website and the Kadazandusun Language Foundation (KLF) website.

Reasons for the predilection for English include the community associations' motivation for maintaining these websites: as a window for outsiders, including researchers, to find information about the communities, including their languages. The potential for in-group communication, especially for linking with diaspora group members living away from their home area, is now being realised more within social media sites, especially Facebook (discussed under that subheading below).

Discussion Forums

Online discussion forums have been available for around 20 years. The online interface allows for threaded asynchronous postings (Crystal, 2001; 2011) on a topic nominated by the initial message poster, to which other registered participants may choose to reply. If the forum is public, then the texts of postings are visible to anyone. An earlier study of language choice and language alternation (McLellan, 2000) analysed two small corpora of 20 main-language English and 20 main-language BM texts from the Sarawak Talk discussion forum (formerly hosted at www.malaysia.net/sarawak). The findings showed a higher percentage of English insertions in main-language BM texts (14.6%) compared to Malay insertions in main-language English texts (4.4%). In terms of language choice within the threads of related postings, only 3.4% of the threads showed a switch in the main language away from that of the initial posting: if the initial posting was in BM, the responses tended to be in BM also.

TABLE 7.5 *Language choice in responses to initial posting*

Language of initial posting	Number of postings	Language change in responses	%
BM	195	7 (6>Eng, 1> Iban)	3.6
English	315	10 (10>BM)	3.2

A small number of code-mixed texts were found in the two corpora. These were both intersentential, where the language changes between sentences or utterances, and intrasentential, where switching occurs within the same sentence or utterance. Examples of the latter category include the following extracts:

3. a. *Fed up* dengar dia olang cakap
      hear   3P   talk
   'Fed up of hearing them talk'

   b. Aku   boleh kontrol *market VCD, 34K net* sebulan, *you*
      1S   can   control   a.month
      'I can control the market for VCDs, 34K a month you (know)'

   c. …buktikan   kebenaran   bahan/cerita   yang ditulis
         AV.prove truth   material/story REL   PASS.write
      otherwise shut up!!!
      'Prove the truth of the story material written, otherwise shut up'
(Data source: McLellan, 2000, p. 16)

In examples (3a) and (3c), there is a single switching point, English to BM and BM to English respectively; (3b) is more complex, showing a pattern of BM>Eng>BM>Eng. The influence of BM syntax is evident in the noun phrase *market VCD*, which follows the BM head-modifier constituent order. The utterance-final *you*, found in several colloquial South East Asian varieties of English, also shows a BM influence as BM has a range of discourse markers which serve to signal the end of a turn at speaking.

All three extracts show that discussion forum postings tend to resemble spoken conversational interaction rather than more formal and planned written language.

This study was conducted at a time when the language of the www was predominantly English. It is only in the past 15 years, since 2000, that the affordances of the www for other languages, including indigenous and minority languages, have become apparent (McLellan & Yeo, 2006). Online asynchronous forums are now located mainly in social media sites (discussed below).

Online News Media Reader Responses

The print media in West Malaysia publishes monolingual BM, English, Chinese and Tamil newspapers, but Sabah and Sarawak have newspapers that are bilingual, such as the *Utusan Borneo*, published in Sarawak in BM and Iban, and the trilingual *New Sabah Times*, which has sections in English, BM and Kadazandusun.

One major affordance of online editions of newspapers is reader response, where readers are invited to post their responses to reports, editorials and feature texts. These responses have the same interactional features as threaded online discussion forums, and one report can provoke a series of responses akin to a face-to-face conversation. They are moderated by the newspaper staff, and responses deemed inappropriate, offensive or potentially libellous are deleted.

Whilst Sabah newspaper websites do not offer this facility, it is available to readers of the *Utusan Borneo* and *The Borneo Post* using a software programme named Disqus™. A small corpus totalling 18 texts with 58 reader responses was collected from these newspapers between September 2013 and June 2014. These were analysed in terms of markedness, defined in this context as instances where the language choice of the reader response differs from that of the original posting. An unmarked response is one which uses the same language as the newspaper report. Table 7.6 gives basic information about this corpus.

TABLE 7.6 *Language choice in 58 reader response texts in The Borneo Post and Utusan Borneo, Sarawak*

	Number of responses	%
Unmarked	39	67.2
Marked	19	32.8

Almost one third of the reader responses show a language choice which differs from the corresponding news report. Text 4 is an example where the response text is code-mixed Malay and English, while the original *Borneo Post* report was in English.

Headline of news report: Include Dayaks in MEB—Masing
Date: 16 September 2013
Reader response text 1 (of 1)

4.   YB...macam mana mau buat 'road show' kalau 'road' nya tiada. Buat 'boat show' lah tauke...sambil2 tu buat 'miring' sekali...untuk menyejukan hati antu yang selalu halang org buat jalan ke kapit
    [*Free translation*: Yang Behormat ('The Honourable'—honorific for elected representatives), how can you do a 'road show' if there is no road. Why not do a 'boat show', boss?...and then a 'miring' (Iban traditional ceremony) as well, to freeze the souls of the ghosts which have always prevented people from making a road to Kapit]

This reader response is in main-language Malay, with three English noun-phrase insertions and one in Iban.

Example (5) shows a response in English to a report of a road accident in the Iban-language section of *Utusan Borneo*.

Headline of news report: Lelaki parai dalam kes bebadi jalai alun
                (Iban: 'Man injured in road accident case')
Date: 21 September 2013
Reader response text 1 (of 1)

5.   There are hundreds of fatal accident ramped against planted trees along Kidurong road since some decades ago. It would be safer for the road without big trees all along it even if the road is hot without shade. Yes there is a beauty of the scene but people's life is more important than that. Bintulu town planner should look seriously into this matter. I recommend flowers and small species type plant may be planted to beautify the road side. Do not blame the road users alone for careless driving. No one is expecting an accident.

This example shows a higher level of syntactic complexity and lexical density, hence it is more formal than example (4). Reader response texts can have variable levels of formality because of the asynchronous format of this online genre which permits readers to take time planning their texts before posting them.

As with the discussion forum texts, some of the reader response texts demonstrate language alternation between BM, Iban and English. Example (6) is one of 19 responses to a *Borneo Post* report. Of these responses, three show BM/English language alternation and another is in monolingual BM.

Headline of news report: See says difficult for Taib to retire
Date: 10 September 2013
Reader response text 4 (of 19)—extract
6.   And one thing that irks me most was when the teachers from the Peninsular Malaysia promotes us about the KLIA airport and all those modern infrastructure stuffs.
Perghh! Apa diaorang ingat kita Sarawakian masih tinggal kat hutan kah? Please lah beb, Sarawak dah jauh maju dah dari pemikiran diaorg.
And actually, we Sarawakians has a lot of young people who has tons of great potential on becoming a great teacher. But *shrugs* apa boleh buat, orang mahu hantar banyak cikgu Semenanjung ke Sarawak.
[*Free translation of BM in this text*: Do they think we Sarawakians still live in the jungle? Please, friend, Sarawak is far more developed than people think.... what can we do, they want to send many teachers from Peninsular Malaysia to Sarawak.]

The pattern of language alternation in example (6) is intersentential Eng>BM>Eng>BM. The style is less formal than the monolingual example (5) and is closer to the conversational discourse found in example (4). The language alternation is a contributing factor to the informality.

In instances where there is language alternation, or where the reader responses are in a different language to that of the original online news report, there is an assumption that readers share the same multilingual competences as the text producers and that they will have no problem understanding the response texts. The texts which show a measure of language alternation thus demonstrate how English coexists and functions as a resource for online text producers.

Blogs
Blogs are personal journals posted by individuals who avail themselves of the affordances of the WWW to share their thoughts and opinions with a potentially worldwide readership.

The Sabah and Sarawak (SASA) Superblog site (http://sasasuperblog.blogspot.com) is a network providing links to East Malaysian blogs. The homepage has links to 11 Sabah blogsites, with new postings uploaded in the month of November, and 12 Sarawak blogsites. Table 7.7 shows the languages of the blog postings.

TABLE 7.7   *Sabah and Sarawak blog postings in November 2014*

	BM	English
Sabah, 1–21 November 2014	6	5
Sarawak, 1–21 November 2014	7	5

SOURCE: HTTP://SASASUPERBLOG.BLOGSPOT.COM

These figures show near parity in the number of blog postings in BM and English. In the longer list of links to blog postings covering the past year, there are no blogs in any languages other than BM and English. Even those bloggers who present themselves as belonging to Borneo-indigenous communities, such as the Bidayuh (Sarawak) 'Lost Aborigine in his Home Country', post their texts in BM and English only. This can be analysed as a rational choice of language for attracting followers and getting messages across to as wide a readership as possible. Example (7) is an extract from this blog posted in February 2014:

7. Sarawak political party is weaken by fractions and the 'divide and rule strategy' by the Malayan sponsored political party. There is no way for political unity in Sarawak as they are engraved with different spirit and ideology of political struggle. The Dayak, the majority ethnic in Sarawak could not be united under one political struggle as ego and self-agenda overpassed the real struggle of the people.
    (Source: 'Lost Aborigine in his Home Country', http://tbsbidayuh .blogspot.com)

This text is further discussed below in relation to Gupta (2006).

Social Media (e.g. Facebook)
Social media, in particular social networking, has been the main online growth area worldwide over the past 10 years. With rapidly improving online connectivity in East Malaysia, Sabah and Sarawak netizens have made their presence felt in social media to such an extent that mainstream (East and West) Malaysian political leaders have at times called for restrictions and even for the banning or blocking of Facebook (Global Voices, Asia, 2014).

The examples in this section are from social media sites visible to all readers online and are limited to Facebook pages as other social media, such as Twitter and Instagram, tend to be protected, requiring users to log in with a username and a password.

The Facebook page of the KLF, which promotes the language and culture of Sabah's largest indigenous group, has status updates in Kadazandusun, BM and English. The Uvakkavo Facebook page is described as a 'community page for Borneo Kayans'. The Kayan are one of the Sarawak communities listed under the collective name Orang Ulu (see above). This page has its banner content in the Kayan language. The 'page info' is in English and Malay, and the wall postings (status updates) are in English, BM and Kayan, sometimes mixed in the same posting. The KLF and the Uvakkavo Facebook pages thus show the coexistence of a community language with two languages of wider communication.

The Bau subgroup of the Bidayuh community in Sarawak maintains a closed Facebook group called *Sinda Dayak Bidayuh Bau* (Bau Bidayuh Language). Status updates can only be viewed by members who have been accepted into the group. As of 31 August 2015, the total number of members was 9,638, a high proportion of the total Bau Bidayuh population of around 40,000. The introductory message (entitled 'About'), which is available for public viewing, is in Bau Bidayuh and reads as follows:

8. Sina Bidoyoh Bau de pakai otto adin mo bogo de bisapur/birawur duoh sina Kirieng duoh Biputis. Dati otto suba yak klakar pakai sina Bidayuh sa otto de juo' idoh komut tudu sinda kupuo.
Samah-samah otto bikutung pimande, bilajar sina bidayuh de bonar-bonar.
[*Free translation*: The Bau Bidayuh language that we use is often mixed and combined with Malay and English. So let us try to use Bidayuh as it is spoken in our villages.
So that we can maintain our unity and not be divided, let us study the Bidayuh language in depth.]

This message thus signals the creation of a space for interaction in one local variety of Bidayuh, with the subsidiary aim of encouraging group members to study the language while using it online. This Facebook group shows how a minority East Malaysian community can use the affordances of social media to create a space for the use and promotion of their language, which they regard as central to their identity, even though all members of the group are likely to be fluent in BM, Sarawak Malay and English as well as in Bau Bidayuh (McLellan, 2014; see Riget and Wang, this volume, for an insider's view of language use in the Bidayuh community).

Discussion: Questions Arising from the Findings

A number of questions arising from the findings presented here need to be addressed.

Question 1: Is the rise of EMD a threat to the survival of Sabah and Sarawak indigenous languages or is it an opportunity for these languages to be maintained and even to expand their currently restricted domains of use? The evidence presented here is inconclusive. EMD certainly offers scope for the maintenance of Borneo languages and for their expansion into new domains such as EMD. It is up to the digitally literate users of the languages to make the most of these opportunities. The optimistic answer is one of coexistence between the more and the less powerful languages in online contexts, as demonstrated in a number of the online texts discussed in this chapter.

Question 2: Is the predominance of English a result of the rubric of the websites (e.g. Facebook, where the interface and directions for what to include in each section are all in English)? There is no doubt that the rubrics play a role in pushing users towards using more English, but social media, like the whole www, is language neutral. As shown by the figures for language choice in websites worldwide (http://www.internetworldstats.com/stats7.htm), the earlier predominance of English is being increasingly challenged.

Question 3: Are the research data biased and unrepresentative because of the tendency for search engines to find English-language sites? The answer to this is the same as for the previous question: Yes, search engines such as Google™ and Yahoo™ tend to promote English-language sites, but this can be overcome by the use of smarter and more focused search strings.

Question 4: In view of the dominance of English noted in the above sections, which varieties of English occur most often in East Malaysian websites? Gupta (2006) addressed this issue using a similar methodology involving online searches for websites relating to Borneo and similar examples from online texts, although her study covers all of Borneo, not just East Malaysia. She found only minor deviations from Standard English which had little if any effect on the intelligibility of the texts. This can also be seen in the textual examples discussed in this chapter, especially example (7) from the blog 'Lost Aborigine in his Home Country', which clearly includes some non-standard English features. As Gupta (2006, pp. 9–12) rightly observed, many texts with similar non-standard features can also be found on websites based in countries where English is the first language.

Question 5: How can Sebba's notions of regulated and unregulated spaces be applied to East Malaysian EMD? As noted in the Conclusion section below, these notions fit very well and are useful descriptors for EMD in general and for multilingual EMD in particular.

Question 6: How relevant is the kueh lapis (layer cake) analogy to East Malaysian EMD? The relevance of this analogy may be limited since it is evident that not all the languages of East Malaysia are found online.

These questions are for readers' further reflection and consideration. The present author would not presume to offer more than the very brief answers given above.

Conclusion

This chapter has presented an initial analysis of some examples taken from small-scale textual corpora of EMD texts identified as originating from Sabah and Sarawak sources. One general pattern to emerge from the data sources discussed above is a greater freedom of language choice and a wider use of language alternation in social media sites (especially Facebook), which, in Sebba's (2009) terms, are 'unregulated spaces', as compared to the official and government websites, which are 'regulated spaces'. While government and government-linked organisations are constrained by Malaysian laws relating to language use, which normally require the use of BM, commercial, social media and private websites such as blogs and those developed by non-government organisations are not subject to such legal constraints.

The analysis in this chapter is necessarily limited to the textual end products as they appear online. Further research in this developing field could also focus on the processes by which such texts are compiled before they are uploaded and on the decisions made pertaining to language choice, such as for a classified advertisement text, where the text producer wishes to maximise impact and the sales of the products being offered.

The linguistic diversity of the East Malaysian states is not fully reflected in the websites surveyed for this chapter. By adopting a kueh lapis (layer cake) analogy, I have tried through the various examples discussed above to demonstrate that English in East Malaysian online discourse can be seen and analysed as but one layer of a complex multilingual situation. English does not exist in isolation in face-to-face interactions between Malaysians or in their online discourses.

Borneo cyberspace is currently dominated by BM and English, both of which can be labelled foreign languages in the Borneo context since the Sabah and Sarawak varieties of Malay differ considerably from the standardised BM.

Whether this situation will change with the advent of wider and cheaper online connectivity is a valid topic for further research.

References

Androutsopoulos, J. (2013). Code-switching in computer-mediated communication. In S. Herring, D. Stein, & T. Virtanen (Eds.), *Pragmatics of computer-mediated communication* (pp. 667–694). Berlin: De Gruyter Mouton.

Ariffin, O., & Teoh, B. S. (1994). Marginalization of language: The case of Iban in Sarawak. In P. Martin (Ed.), *Shifting patterns of language use in Borneo* (pp. 117–129). Williamsburg, VA: Borneo Research Council.

Crystal, D. (2001). *Language and the Internet*. Cambridge, England: Cambridge University Press.

———. (2011). *Internet linguistics: A student guide*. New York: Routledge.

Danet, B., & Herring, S. (Eds.) (2003). *The multilingual Internet: Language, culture, and communication in instant messaging, email and chat*. Special issue of the *Journal of Computer-Mediated Communication, 9*(1). Retrieved from http://jcmc.indiana.edu/vol9/issue1/.

———. (Eds.) (2007). *The multilingual Internet: Language, culture, and communication online*. New York: Oxford University Press.

Global Voices, Asia (2014, August 13). Malaysian government threatens to block Facebook over 'abuse' reports. Retrieved from http://www.globalvoicesonline.org/2014/08/13/malaysian-government-threatens-to-block-facebook-over-abuse-reports/.

Gupta, A. (2006). Standard English and Borneo. *Southeast Asia: A Multidisciplinary Journal, 6*(1), 79–94. Retrieved from http://www.anthea.id.au/papers/borneo005b.pdf.

Kaml Sadiq. (2005). When states prefer non-citizens over citizens: Conflict over illegal immigration into Malaysia. *International Studies Quarterly, 49*(1), 101–122.

King, J. (1994). A preliminary update to the language situation of Sabah. In P. Martin (Ed.), *Shifting patterns of language use in Borneo* (pp. 41–68). Williamsburg, VA: Borneo Research Council.

Kirkpatrick, A., & McLellan, J. (2011). World Englishes and/or English as a lingua franca. In J. P. Gee & M. Handford (Eds.), *The Routledge handbook of discourse analysis* (pp. 654–669). London: Routledge.

Lewis, P., Simons, G., & Fennig, C. (2014). *Ethnologue: Languages of the world* (17th ed.). Dallas, TX: SIL International. Online version: http://www.ethnologue.com.

McLellan, J. (2000). The language and discourse of the 'Minyu Sarawak Talk' discussion forum. In M. Leigh (Ed.), *Borneo 2000: Language, management and tourism* (pp. 11–20). Kuching, Malaysia: Institute of East Asian Studies, UNIMAS.

———. (2012). The view from below: Code-switching and the influence of 'substrate' languages in South East Asian Englishes. In E.-L. Low & Azirah Hashim (Eds.), *Englishes in South East Asia: Features, policy and language in use* (pp. 267–288). Amsterdam: John Benjamins.

———. (2013, August). Strategi menghidupkan semula bahasa-bahasa yang terjejas di Pulau Borneo: Suatu perbandingan antara Negara Brunei Darussalam dan Negeri Sarawak, Malaysia. Paper presented at the Forum on Borneo Language Diversity, Bandar Seri Begawan, Brunei Darussalam.

———. (2014). Strategies for revitalizing endangered Borneo languages: A comparison between Negara Brunei Darussalam and Sarawak, Malaysia. *Southeast Asia: A Multidisciplinary Journal, 14*, 14–22.

McLellan, J., & Campbell, Y. M. (2015). Bidayuh as a subject at pre-school and primary levels. Towards a greater role for a Borneo indigenous language in the Malaysian education system. In C. Volker & F. Anderson (Eds.), *Education in languages of lesser power: Asia-Pacific perspectives* (pp. 131–151). Amsterdam: John Benjamins.

McLellan, J., & Yeo, A. (2006, July). *Borneo languages in cyberspace: A proposal for revitalization of Borneo languages through development of online communities.* Paper presented at Borneo Research Council Conference, 'Borneo in the new century', Universiti Malaysia Sarawak, Kuching, Malaysia.

Noor Azam Haji Othman, & McLellan, J. (2014). Brunei English. Special issue on Englishes in Southeast Asia: Challenges and future directions. *World Englishes, 33*(4), 486–497.

Rensch, C. R. (2006). Studies in the early Bidayuh language: Proto Bidayuh and its relatives. In C. R. Rensch, C. M. Rensch, J. Noeb, & R. S. Ridu (Eds.), *The Bidayuh language: Yesterday, today and tomorrow,* (pp. 135–442). Kuching, Malaysia: Dayak Bidayuh National Association.

Sebba, M. (2009). Unregulated spaces: Exploring the potential of the linguistic margins. Retrieved from http://www.ling.lancs.ac.uk/staff/mark/unreg.pdf.

Stephen, J. (2006, July). *Language use in Kadazandusun-related websites: English, Malay or Kadazandusun language?* Paper presented at Borneo Research Council Conference 'Borneo in the new century', Universiti Malaysia Sarawak, Kuching, Malaysia.

Ting, S.-H. (2012). Variable impact of Malaysia's national language planning on non-Malay speakers in Sarawak. *Revista Brasileira de Linguística Aplicada, 12*(2). Retrieved from http://www.scielo.br/scielo.php?pid=S1984-63982012000200008&script=sci_arttext.

Topping, D. M. (1990). A dialect survey of the Land Dayaks of Sarawak. In J. Collins (Ed.), *Language and oral traditions in Borneo* (pp. 247–274). Williamsburg, VA: Borneo Research Council.

Appendix
Websites Discussed in this Chapter

Dayak Bidayuh National Association (DBNA)
http://dbna.org.my/

Jabatan Tanah dan Ukur Sabah
http://www.jtu.sabah.gov.my/homepage/

Kadazandusun Language Foundation (KLF) Facebook page
http://www.klf.com.my/index2.htm
https://www.facebook.com/klf6392g?fref=ts

Lembaga Pelabuhan Kuching
http://www.kpa.gov.my/

Lembaga Pelabuhan-Pelabuhan Sabah
http://www.lpps.sabah.gov.my/

Lost Aborigine in his Home Country blog
http://tbsbidayuh.blogspot.com

Portal Rasmi Jabatan Tanah dan Survei Sarawak,
http://www.landsurvey.sarawak.gov.my/modules/web/pages.php?lang=en&mod=weppage&sub=page&id=49&menu_id=0&sub_id=131

Sarawak Dayak Iban Association (SADIA) Facebook page
https://www.facebook.com/pages/Sarawak-Dayak-Iban-Association-Sadia-HQ/217438161654378

Sarawak Dayak Iban Association (SADIA) blog
http://sarawakdayakibanassoc.wordpress.com

SASA (Sabah and Sarawak superblog site)
http://sasasuperblog.blogspot.com/

See Hua Daily News
http://www.seehua.com

Sinda Dayak Bidayuh Bau Facebook Group
https://www.facebook.com/groups/bidayuhbau/?fref=ts

SMK Katibas
http://smkkatibas.weebly.com/index.html

SMK Sandakan
http://smksandakan.edu.my/

The Borneo Post
http://www.theborneopost.com/

The New Sabah Times
http://www.newsabahtimes.com.my/

Uvakkavo Kayan Facebook page
https://www.facebook.com/pages/Uvakkavo/160404570706246?fref=ts

Malaysian English and Language Policies

CHAPTER 8

Literacy Practices in English in Malaysian Educational Settings

Ambigapathy Pandian

Introduction

English is becoming a globally accepted language of communication and networking in the 21st century. This language plays a significant role in advancing knowledge and in developing international dialogues among different political positions and cultural understandings on international business, crisis management, climate change, children rights, migration and conflict resolution. The management of everyday life in what Kalantzis and Cope (2012) have termed the 'New Times' era requires engagement with new technologies and increasing interaction with culturally diverse people. Following these transformations, literacy policies and programmes need to respond to the changing domains of work, home, identities and citizenry.

In many parts of the world, English literacy has embraced the transformations and reshaped reading, writing, speaking and making meaning. The New London Group (1996) asserted that English language classrooms should present new ways of thinking and doing in literacy practices given the multimodal ways in which meanings are made in areas such as the www, video captioning, interactive multimedia, online games, desktop publishing, blogs and in-print texts in shopping malls.

Students of today are familiar with new media technologies that allow them to multitask: surfing the Internet and sharing text messages or photographs and playing digital games while listening to songs and creating their own multimedia texts. Currently, the use of multimedia has been successfully applied to many teaching and learning environments in many countries to enhance teaching settings and to cater for a wider variety of student learning styles (Birch & Gardiner, 2005; Sankey & St Hill, 2009; Spraguengh & Dahl, 2009). The increasing use of multimedia in teaching offers many opportunities to present multiple representations of content (text, video, audio, images, interactive elements) that respond more effectively to the different learning styles of diverse students.

Malaysia recognises the economic and social value of producing students who have good communication skills in English and who are able to participate productively in local and global multi-literacy activities (Ambigapathy, Pang, Shanthi, & Chee, 2013). Malaysia has made literacy a priority agenda, but the task of re-imaging and reshaping what it means to be literate and to produce students who can use literacy to conduct daily life activities in society and the economy has been a perplexing one. English literacy remains a thorny issue in the education field as it attracts competing attention in the planning and development of the language (Ambigapathy, Shanthi, & Ganeson, 2014; Singh, Kell, & Ambigapathy, 2002). Complaints about English literacy have intensified in the past few decades. There are many problems that confront English literacy students, teachers, researchers and policymakers. The causes of these problems run so deep, and intervention strategies, even though well intentioned, have produced very little change. This chapter first discusses the historical and political facets that have impinged upon the growth of English literacy practices. It then describes the emphasis in curricula approaches in English literacy and discusses the classroom realities that reveal that English literacy practices are fraught with problems and that Malaysia needs more evidence-based research and realistic structures and goals to advance literacy in the coming years.

English Literacy Agenda: Historical and Political Facets

In Malaysia, language policy and planning are often top-down processes where people of power and authority conduct discussions and make decisions within the context of politics (Dumanig, David, & Symaco, 2012; Normazidah, Koo, & Hazita, 2012; Gill, 2005).

The movements in the global literacy landscape have required Malaysia to deliberate on language planning and policymaking that address diverse living and knowledge experiences and yet keep the power relations among the different ruling groups in balance. While the agenda on English literacy has had to relate to the bigger picture of the creation and application of knowledge and skills to think critically about the world, the immense political force insisting on the need to sustain nationalism and multilingualism in multicultural Malaysia compels the 'journey of English literacy' to be a turbulent one (Ambigapathy, 2002, 2006).

As today's process of literacy changes, there are many aspects of English language learning that will have to undergo dramatic transformation, specifically when students are surrounded by information and opportunities that affect English language learning, namely, what they learn and how they learn (Cope & Kalantzis, 2009). Traditional classrooms advancing the transmission of disciplinary knowledge that suited traditional workplaces and the creation of a homogeneous people are becoming less appropriate in the present world. The old, conventional learning settings need to be displaced as emerging knowledge societies move towards new settings that dwell on new communication technologies, business prospects, cultural identities and global languages (Ambigapathy, Pang, Shanthi, & Chee, 2013).

All the developments stated above pose major challenges to the English literacy agenda. Teaching groups, parents, industry players and civil agencies have raised concerns that if Malaysian students do not have a command of the English language, they will not be able to participate in job productivity and in the global and local production of knowledge to solve problems in real life (Ambigapathy, Koo, & Kell, 2007).

However, the status of English literacy and the attitudes towards it are ambivalent due to the influence of nationalism, the dominance of the Malay language and competing global pressures from neighbouring countries (Hamid & Moni, 2011). Dumanig et al. (2012) and Azirah (2009) traced the development of English literacy from colonial days to the present day to indicate its frequent changeable leanings. During British colonial rule, Malaysia developed an education system encompassing English, Malay, Chinese and Tamil schools which sustained social and economic segregation among the ethnic groups. This led to difficulty in building social mobility and cohesiveness among the different ethnic groups as different forms of education were provided to these groups (Watson, 2011). Rising ethnic tensions disrupted economic, social and political progress in Malaysia, and the focus on nation building and the fostering of national unity were identified as critical policies requiring serious attention to ensure the growth of the country. Education and language policies that focused on unity were constructed, leading, in 1951, to the publication of the Barnes Report (cited in Wan Norhasniah, 2011) and the Fenn-Wu Report, which outlined various proposals regarding the choice of language used as the medium of instruction in schools (Azirah, 2009). The 1956 Razak Report proposed the establishment of two types of schools: national schools that would use Malay as the medium of instruction, and national-type schools, which could use English, Chinese or Tamil as their medium of instruction (Azirah, 2009).

Dumanig et al. (2012) asserted that upon attaining independence, Malay nationalists and intellectuals were worried about the underdevelopment of the Malay language and indigenous rights. They argue that the leaders of the country adopted a top-down path that would assure minority communities of a continued role for their languages and, at the same time, assure Malay nationalists of a greater role for the Malay language. The Malay language was seen as the language for national unity and nation building and a core element in the construction of the Malaysian identity. The English language and other vernacular languages took on a lower status in the literacy scenario. Still, multilingualism, according to Dumanig et al. (2012), was not a favoured arrangement. Discontented Malay nationalists were unhappy with the slow progress in the institutionalisation of Malay in the country and pushed for Malay supremacy in political domains and to secure Malay's position as the official language as well as the language of government administration and education (David & Govindasamy, 2003).

While confronting political and language struggles, in the 1990s, Malaysia also attracted many direct foreign investments through multinational companies and foreign companies which relied heavily on English as the medium of communication (Malakolunthu & Rengasamy, 2012; Puteh, 2010). The Malaysian state then implemented the Education Act 1996, which allowed for the use of English as the medium of instruction for technical areas in post-secondary courses, and the Private Higher Education Institute Act, which allowed for the use of English in courses provided through twinning with foreign universities.

Despite these initiatives, weak competency in English, especially among Malay students from public schools and public universities, was a major concern. Discontentment with the learning system in the Malaysian setting has raised numerous issues such as the role of education in the construction of national identity, the emphasis on an examination-oriented curriculum, the integration of information and communication skills, the place of the Malay language as the national language and the place of English as a global language, the teaching of science and mathematics in English and the increasing rate of unemployment among university graduates.

The government introduced English as the medium of instruction in science and mathematics in 2002 to ensure that Malay students did not lag behind non-Malay students, especially in seeking employment in the private sectors (Gill, 2005). The teaching of science and mathematics in English created a backlash from Malay nationalist groups and Malay intellectuals from public universities who read the change in the language of instruction to English as a threat to the Malays' identity as the superior ethnic group (Gill, 2005). Malay opposition to teaching science and mathematics in English has a nationalistic and historical basis. It is crucial to note that there was fervent criticism of the teaching of mathematics and science in English from Chinese school groups too. The Chinese opposition used reasoning based on the belief that their students had a better cognitive ability in their mother tongue than in English (Asmah, 2012).

Finally, the cabinet decided that the policy on science and mathematics teaching would be reversed from 2012; national schools reverted to the Malay language, while national-type schools switched back to mother-tongue languages.

The unsuccessful implementation of English as the medium of instruction for science and mathematics for schools eventually pressured the Malaysian Government to introduce a new language policy in 2010: 'To Uphold Bahasa Malaysia & to Strengthen the English Language' (Phan, Khoo, & Chng, 2013). Both languages are now seen as vital in producing human capital with the necessary knowledge, competency and skills to guide a knowledge-based economy.

In addition, the Malaysian Education Blueprint (2013–2025) was launched to promote the position of the Malay language not only as the national language but also as the main language of communication and knowledge and the language for nation building crucial to achieving the objectives of 1Malaysia (Ministry of Education, Malaysia, 2010, cited in Phan et al., 2013). The Blueprint also highlighted the critical need to strengthen proficiency in the English language to facilitate students to participate in the global language of communication and knowledge at both national and global level. The Malaysian Education Blueprint marked an important milestone in the development of English literacy in Malaysia as it connected learning with the need to keep pace with an increasingly competitive global economy and to balance the development of global citizenship with a strong national identity.

The discussion on the English literacy agenda and its historical and political facets and the precarious competing position it occupies in the Malaysian nationalistic educational setting will continue to attract controversy in the coming years. Given this delicate situation, any attempt to frame English literacy as an area of study in schools and institutions of higher education remains an extremely difficult task. The next section highlights the English literacy movements that have been witnessed in the primary, secondary and higher education systems in Malaysia and that have constantly been mired in controversy, particularly with regard to the changing dimensions of literacy and the process of learning.

Framing Malaysian English Literacy: Key Movements

English literacy is a difficult area to define as it encompasses many components, such as reading, writing, speaking, listening, grammar and literature (Limbrick & Aikman, 2005). Much of what formed early English literacy in Malaysia reflected the different ideologies that shaped literacy in Britain;

these ideologies influenced the development of English literacy in Malaysia in colonial days and continue to do so today. The rise of different Englishes (Singapore, United States, United Kingdom, Australia and Canada) made the development of English literacy in Malaysia a complex undertaking. As noted in the previous section, many of these views on shaping literacy policies may have been politically driven, and these views shifted as different contentious ideologies came into play in pre- and post-independence days. Numerous reports and government initiatives played a role in framing English literacy in Malaysia, including the 1956 Razak Report, the 1960 Rahman Talib Report, the 1967 Higher Education Committee Report, the Education Act (1961/1996), the National Language Act (1963/67, revised, 1971), the New Economic Policy period (1971–1990), the National Development Policy (1991–2000), the National Vision period (2001–2020), the Master Plan (2006–2010), the National Key Results Areas (2010–2012) and the Malaysian Education Blueprint (2013–2025).

It has been argued that the English syllabuses advanced in the Malaysian setting were largely foreign and reflected international movements taking place in Britain at that time (Rajaretnam & Nalliah, 1999). In general, the broad aim of English as a subject in the post-independence era drew a lot from earlier programmes on English language teaching (ELT) and learning which centred on developing practical literacy skills such as reading, writing, listening and speaking. It may be helpful to note at the outset of this discussion that the development of the English literacy area of the curriculum has been rather disjointed due to different ad hoc committees that were set up to develop the primary, lower secondary and upper secondary school syllabuses over the past few decades. The major movements in English literacy in Malaysia can be categorised into the following views of English:

- The structural approach to ELT in Malaysia
- Communicative language teaching
- The New Primary Schools Curriculum/Integrated Secondary Schools Curriculum[1]
- Communicative language teaching in the New Primary Schools Curriculum/ Integrated Secondary Schools Curriculum
- Supplementary ELT programmes—self-access learning (SAL)

---

1 This refers to the *Kurikulum Bersepadu Sekolah Rendah* (KBSR), which covers three areas (Communication, Man and his Environment and Self-development of the Individual) and the *Kurikulum Bersepadu Sekolah Menengah* (KBSM), which aims to enhance English language proficiency in order to meet students' needs for English in everyday life and for knowledge acquisition and future workplace requirements.

- Literature in ELT
- ELT in smart schools
- Government Transformation Programme (GTP): LINUS 2.0[2]

The Structural Approach to English Language Teaching in Malaysia

The syllabus items covered by the post-1970 English syllabus for primary and secondary schools placed emphasis on the learning of grammar and on oral exercises. The English syllabus for primary schools was based on a structural-situational approach in which much of the teaching focused on the learning of grammar. As noted by Abraham (1987), the structural approach offered a list of language structures and words as learning objectives. The teaching covered various language drills, while reading and writing followed the structural approach where sentences were often learnt in isolation rather than being linked to a specific situation. A teacher-centred approach dominated the classroom, where the mastering and rote learning of skills were stressed. This created some difficulty as students were compelled to learn a large number of skills, which were then tested via examinations. This approach produced students who were able to pass examinations and proceed to tertiary level education but were not proficient in using English to communicate their ideas or to accomplish purposeful tasks in an effective way. In other words, English literacy teaching gave more attention to the teaching of grammar, while the communicative aspects of language learning were neglected (Ambigapathy, 2002).

Communicative Language Teaching

The rapid development and industrialisation taking place in Malaysia called for English literacy teaching that could facilitate the preparation of manpower for the nation's workforce. The progressive industrial outlook of the country's growth and the rise of service sectors demanded a need for workers with communicative competencies. This led to the implementation of a communicative language teaching approach. Teachers had to reduce and simplify the grammar content in lessons and work towards creating situations for communication-based activities that were largely student centred and task oriented according to specific situations. Despite the introduction of this approach, there were problems with English literacy and communication proficiency, and the concerns about the declining standards of English persisted (Ambigapathy, 2002).

---

2 LINUS 2.0 is part of *Kurikulum Standard Sekolah Rendah* (KSSR) that comprises of content standards and learning standards which need to be achieved by a student in a specific period and level of schooling.

The New Primary Schools Curriculum/Integrated Secondary Schools Curriculum

Modernisation and industrialisation were crucial to nation building, and English literacy was integral to the shaping of students who had a command of English and the capacity to acquire skills that were job related. The ELT syllabus highlighted the importance of the three R's—the basic skills of reading, writing and arithmetic.

Apart from these objectives, ELT in the classroom gave attention to the spiritual, emotional, physical and intellectual development of students. The students' personal development was seen as critical, and the teaching strategies included efficient language learning through listening, speaking, reading and writing activities as well as the blending of moral and spiritual values in discussions and simulated real-life contexts (Ministry of Education, 1989). There was a clear push for intellectual development and higher order thinking skills such as analysing, evaluating, applying, and giving ideas and opinions, an aspect that was absent in previous ELT syllabuses. A more student-centred approach was developed so that students could engage in question-and-answer sessions with teachers. The Malaysian Ministry of Education noted that the Integrated Secondary Schools Curriculum syllabus allowed the integration of multiple dimensions of language content and situations which simulated real-life conditions, making language learning more realistic and practical.

Communicative Language Teaching in the New Primary Schools Curriculum/Integrated Secondary Schools Curriculum

The communicative component was an important part of English literacy in the KBSR/KBSM curriculum. While literacy policies had outlined productive directions for teaching English, studies by the Ministry of Education found that the reality at the classroom level was different from the original vision (Ambigapathy & Shanthi, 2013). The classroom went back to the chalk-and-talk drill and examination-oriented method. Classrooms focused on reading, comprehension, writing, grammar and vocabulary skills, which were all components of the Primary Schools Assessment Test conducted at the end of Primary Six, while listening and speaking skills, which were not part of the test, were neglected (Ministry of Education, 1989).

Classroom teaching relied heavily on past-year examination questions, worksheets, and exercise books. The communicative approach using fun-filled lessons based on songs, poems and language games, which had been clearly underlined in the New Primary Schools Curriculum/Integrated Secondary Schools Curriculum, was neglected. Teaching English in realistic and contextualised situations was left out, and class teachers opted for preparing students for examinations using revision books rather than working on language learning through creative approaches (Ambigapathy, 2002).

Supplementary ELT Programmes—Self-access Learning

Self-access learning (SAL) was another conception of the Curriculum Development Centre which aimed to promote students' sense of responsibility for their own learning. Underlying the concept of SAL was the view that every student had different needs, interests, attitudes and aptitudes and should be given the opportunities to be responsible for his or her own learning in different ways and at varied rates (Ministry of Education, 1989).

A range of organised learning materials and equipment, including resources such as journals, worksheets, cassette tapes and videotapes, were made available and accessible to pupils. Computer assisted language learning (CALL) programmes and games, radio cassette recorder sets and video recorders were provided so that students could work on their learning at their own pace and in their own time using organised learning materials and equipment (Ministry of Education, 1989). The materials were developed by teachers following the contents and skills stipulated in the prescribed curriculum.

Literature in English Language Teaching

Literature was included in English classrooms to inculcate the habit of reading among students. The Integrated Secondary Schools Curriculum English Language syllabus incorporated a reading skills component to give exposure to lots of interesting reading materials designed to increase students' general proficiency in the language and enhance their reading skills, critical thinking, and understanding of prose and poetry.

The Ministry of Education endorsed a working paper on the implementation of literature in the English language curriculum in March 1999. The literature programme was assessed by the Malaysian Certificate of Education in 2001 and the Lower Certificate of Education in 2002.

ELT in Smart Schools

The global economic scene in the late 20th century saw Malaysia forging towards Vision 2020[3] and moving from an industrial economy to a knowledge-based economy in line with new global developments and the advancement of technology, and a competent workforce skilful in the use of technological tools was seen as crucial to propel social and economic growth. Information

---

3 Vision 2020 is a plan launched by Mahathir to modernise the nation and to propel it towards becoming a fully developed country by year 2020.

communication technology, multimedia technology and worldwide networking through the Internet were seen as important areas that needed to be included in thinking about literacy in schools (Ministry of Education, 1989).

In January 1997, the Ministry of Education conceptualised the vision of the Malaysian Smart School. The Smart School Project is one of the seven flagship applications of the Multimedia Super Corridor. Smart schools continued with the syllabus structure used in the KBSM curriculum but implemented learning-to-learn skills, generic skills, interpersonal skills and thinking skills. English literacy took on reading, writing, speaking and listening components and integrated language (vocabulary, grammar and sound system), content (moral and spiritual values, patriotism, health and environment knowledge, etc.), texts types (information reports, speeches, dialogues, advertisements, brochures, etc.) and information technology (Internet, TV, radio, video, etc.). Creative and critical thinking were also added as important components. Other essential approaches, such as self-directed and individually paced learning, were continued, and it was envisioned that a more open and flexible curriculum would lead to a more student-centred approach to learning (Ambigapathy, 2002a).

Government Transformation Programme: LINUS 2.0

The 2004 School Certificate Examination Report on English Language 2 for Primary Year 6 (Ministry of Education, 2004) revealed that a majority of candidates had yet to master English writing skills and that the overall performance was far from satisfactory. The Malaysia Ministry of Education in its efforts to improve the Malaysian Education Curriculum, came up with the Malaysia Education Blueprint 2013–2025 (Ministry of Education, 2012), which introduced the New Standard Curriculum for primary and secondary schools and allotted additional time for ELT. The GTP and LINUS 2.0 are initiatives that aim to bring the transformation in English literacy envisioned in the Blueprint.

According to the Ministry of Education, the Malaysian education system has produced commendably strong proficiency in the Malay language among students, but the same cannot be said for English language proficiency as a very low percentage (28%) of students achieved a minimum credit in the 2011 Malaysian Certificate of Education (SPM) examination English paper (Ministry of Education, 2012). The declining English proficiency among school leavers and fresh graduates still remains a top concern among policymakers and educationists. LINUS 1.0, which has successfully improved proficiency in the Malay language, was identified as an appropriate model to enhance English literacy. LINUS 2.0 continues the work of LINUS 1.0 and consists of seven education initiatives, two of which are directly related to English: to ensure basic English literacy among Year 1–3 pupils and to enhance the quality of English language teachers.

The Standardised English Language Curriculum for Primary Schools (KSSR) is a new system introduced by the Ministry of Education in 2011 to prepare pupils with the knowledge, skills and values to confront the challenges of the 21st century. The new curriculum has been designed to go beyond the acquisition of communication skills and self-development. It further promotes strong character qualities and leadership skills and encourages pupils to embrace the use of science and technology, to develop values and to understand humanitarian issues and aesthetics. Although the KBSR also focuses on holistic learning, the current curriculum seeks to go beyond this approach. There has been a shift away from rote learning, where students simply followed instructions and were overly dependent on teachers. Using a modular-based system under KSSR, English literacy for the primary school encompasses listening, speaking, reading, grammar, reasoning, literature and language arts and aims to offer space for interactive activities that include drama, role play, debates, language games and songs to make the lessons more meaningful and facilitate the learning of the language. Students will be encouraged to think and reason and to make connections between their actions and social contexts as well as be active decision makers who are accountable for their actions. This curriculum will be followed by the Standardised English Language Curriculum for Secondary Schools (KSSM) in 2017.

English Literacy in Higher Education

Malaysia aims to be a prominent player in the international arena, specifically in the ASEAN, where the working language is English. ASEAN member countries today are at different stages of nation building and economic growth and aspire to become an integrated group of nations by 2015. English becomes important here as English proficiency is necessary for Malaysia to play a dynamic role in regional communication among neighbours in South East Asia. In this regard, the focus on English as a lingua franca (ELF) and a channel that facilitates participation is not only a quest of Malaysia but also of other member countries in the region.

In this regard, the place of higher education in Malaysia is critical as it is usually related to global contexts and activities. Higher education also requires English literacy to assist in academic matters, research and networking activities, to attract international students, to improve global rankings and to win global influence. English literacy is vital for students in institutions of higher education for gaining employment in the local and global economy. English will also open up opportunities for them to seek a wider learning experience, to exchange ideas and to be global competitors.

Research studies on English proficiency among higher education learners report that many undergraduate students have problems with note-taking skills and have limited critical ability to respond appropriately to an academic text. They also have difficulties with academic writing (Normazidah, Koo, & Hazita, 2012). Furthermore, many students have limited vocabulary knowledge and struggle with long sentences and reading comprehension (Normazidah et al., 2012).

Higher education in Malaysia needs to respond to the demands of globalisation, liberalisation and the advancement of ICT. Students have limited English literacy skills to cope with university education and to meet contemporary workplace requirements (Morshidi, Rozinah, Lee, & Ambigapathy, 2007). Indeed, Malaysian employers have consistently highlighted poor English literacy skills among fresh graduates as one of the top five issues confronting the Malaysian labour force.

The requirements and developments of higher education and the workplace have prompted the Malaysian Government to implement policies and strategies to enhance English language learning at primary and secondary school levels. Following the Malaysian Education Blueprint 2013–2025, the Minister of Education announced that from 2016, a compulsory pass in English language in SPM would be required to get a full SPM certificate and would be necessary for university admission. However, this decision has since been reversed, and the new dates for making English a compulsory subject have yet to be announced. The reversal in the policy, as will be discussed below, suggest difficulties in implementing big ideas when consultations with different groups are insufficient to understand classroom realities in schools.

The cultural, linguistic and technological diversity of both urban and rural learners demands that higher education institutions consider new approaches to providing high-quality English literacy teaching and learning for all students to rise to the challenges of everyday learning and living in the new century. Within the current Malaysian public higher education setting, there are different requirements for graduation with regard to the English language. Some universities state a compulsory pass in English language, while others do not require this. Some universities require students to take up at least two or more English language courses to polish their language skills in order to improve their academic performance and workplace readiness.

Getting Malaysians to master English is a priority for the government. Another programme has been devised to help undergraduates communicate in English and to prepare them to meet the requirements of the working world. Essentially, students will learn English according to three tiers: English for Employment, Intensive English and General English. The introduction of the three-tier system will address the different levels of preparedness, motivation and, more importantly, purpose for learning English among undergraduates. This initiative aspires to help students develop job search strategies and equip themselves with the necessary language skills.

The transformation of the education curriculum in the Malaysian Education Blueprint (2013–2025) focuses on the higher order thinking skills (HOTS) concept, which aims to produce knowledgeable students who are critical and creative in their thinking and can compete at the international level. HOTS are skills which equip students with the ability to apply, analyse, evaluate, and think creatively in and outside the classroom.

English Literacy at the Crossroads

The journey of English literacy in Malaysia has involved different views and approaches with some consideration of historical and political perspectives. Different aspirations and conceptualisations of literacy, what it means to be literate and how views of literacy are evolving in a period of considerable social and economic change in Malaysia present a complex situation for planning, taking action and implementing in actual learning settings. The representations, variations and adjustments operating at the school and higher education learning levels give rise to problematic realities. Many of the transformation programmes from primary to secondary school level have met with little success.

A study of literacy rates in the Malay and English languages and in mathematics among 5,300 secondary school students from Remove Class[4] to Form Five found out that the literacy rate was 71.20%, with a mean score of 72.08, for Malay and 27.20%, with a mean score of 29.31, for English, while the rate for

---

4 Students from vernacular schools who do not attain good grades in the Malay language in their Standard Six Examination are put in Remove Classes for a year before they move on to Form One. The purpose of this is to provide students from vernacular schools with a platform for improving and enhancing their language and communication skills before they proceed to Form One.

mathematics literacy was 36.80%, with a mean score of 36.50 (Fong, 2012). The dismal state of English literacy among secondary school students has drawn much attention from many groups concerned about language competency and students' preparedness to enter the workforce or seek higher education.

A report from the Ministry of Education on literacy performance for the years 2010 and 2011 revealed that the pass rate for Malay literacy was higher than that for English literacy, as shown in the table below.

TABLE 8.1 *Malaysian Certificate of Education examination (SPM) results for Malay, English and Mathematics*

Subject	Year	Urban		Rural		Overall % of passes
		No. of candidates	% of passes	No. of candidates	% of passes	
Malay	2010	211,892	91.0	192,243	91.4	91.2
	2011	198,476	91.4	207,829	91.0	91.2
English	2010	211,328	83.7	191,902	71.2	77.5
	2011	196,918	83.8	206,738	70.1	77.0
Maths (*)	2010	210,491	83.5	191,067	77.5	80.5
	2011	196,454	84.2	206,277	77.1	80.7

SOURCE: MALAYSIAN MINISTRY OF EDUCATION
(*) MATHS IS INCLUDED AS LITERACY ENCOMPASSES NUMERACY

Further, it was reported recently that an average of 20%, or close to 100,000 students, have failed English in the SPM in the past few years (The Star, 23 August 2015). The Malaysian University English Test (MUET), a test that measures achievement and communication skills in English language, has revealed that many students seeking admission to Malaysian public universities are only able to attain Band 2 or Band 3 (see Table 8.2). The statistics show that many students are only moderate or limited users of English. There are very few students who are able to attain Band 4 and above. In other words, there are very few competent users of English.

TABLE 8.2   STPM—MUET results (2012–2014)

March 2012 (34,196 candidates) Band 6—Very Good User   Band 5—Good User
March 2013 (40,378 candidates) Band 4—Competent User   Band 3—Modest User
March 2014 (38,299 candidates) Band 2—Limited User
                                Band 1—Extremely Limited User

Band	Listening [%]			Speaking [%]			Reading [%]			Writing [%]			Overall [%]		
	2012	2013	2014	2012	2013	2014	2012	2013	2014	2012	2013	2014	2012	2013	2014
6	1.71	0.06	0.10	0.30	0.06	0.18	0.62	0.07	0.19	0.00	0.00	0.01	0.01	0.00	0.01
5	10.56	2.41	2.47	1.99	0.93	1.06	6.11	2.92	3.85	0.28	0.09	0.37	1.03	0.16	0.42
4	18.28	13.85	12.89	12.74	8.27	8.52	17.41	16.04	13.92	2.78	1.41	4.10	10.74	4.10	7.65
3	15.06	16.76	19.53	39.58	34.70	33.15	31.86	37.45	27.06	18.52	8.36	33.35	32.34	26.64	30.58
2	24.12	29.51	38.94	34.44	41.93	42.23	33.59	35.50	36.30	58.86	37.10	53.57	42.34	46.76	47.77
1	30.27	37.41	26.06	10.95	14.12	14.85	10.41	8.02	18.67	19.56	53.03	8.60	13.54	22.35	13.57

SOURCE: MALAYSIAN MINISTRY OF EDUCATION

The attention on English literacy became critical when employers at private and public institutions revealed that local graduates are not able to speak and write English well. Employers have stressed that they need workers who are proficient in English speaking and writing, especially at a time where there are many global conversations and transactions (Archer, 2008). The following table depicts the different reading, listening, oral and writing skills in the Malay and English languages. As seen below, many graduates highlight that their skills in the Malay language are much better than their skills in the English language. Many graduates seem to have only average oral and writing skills in the English language and to face challenges in seeking successful employment (Ambigapathy et al., 2007).

TABLE 8.3 *Language skills of employed and unemployed graduates*

Learning Skills	Employed			Unemployed	
	Malay	English	Mandarin	Malay	English
Oral					
Good/Fluent	1356(93.1%)	572(39.4%)	253(47.6%)	602(98.5%)	160(26.2%)
Average	95(6.5%)	786(54.1%)	105(19.7%)	8(1.3%)	362(59.2%)
Poor/Not fluent	6(0.4%)	95(6.5%)	174(32.7%)	1(0.2%)	89%(14.6%)
Reading					
Good/Fluent	1399(96.3%)	961(66.3%)	205(39.9%)	606(99.2%)	366(59.9%)
Average	45(3.1%)	471(32.5%)	61(11.9%)	4(0.7%)	234(38.3%)
Poor/Not fluent	8(0.6%)	18(1.2%)	248(48.2%)	1(0.1%)	11(1.8%)
Listening					
Good/Fluent	1384(95.4%)	818(56.5%)	262(49.4%)	605(99.2%)	288(47.3%)
Average	59(4.1%)	601(41.5%)	104(19.6%)	4(0.7%)	302(49.6%)
Poor/Not Fluent	8(0.5%)	28(2%)	164(3.1%)	1(0.1%)	19(3.1%)
Writing					
Good/Fluent	1306(90.1%)	588(40.6%)	155(30.6%)	582(95.4%)	189(31.1%)
Average	134(9.2%)	746(51.5%)	86(17%)	26(4.3%)	361(59.5%)
Poor/Not fluent	10(0.7%)	114(7.9%)	265(52,4%)	2(0.3%)	57(9.4%)

One of Malaysia's educational challenges is improving the standard of English literacy. It is stressed here that the study of English among graduates in the higher education community cannot be detached from what happens at the school level. The findings of several studies have revealed that the realities operating at the school and university levels are highly complicated and problematic (Ambigapathy, 2004; Ambigapathy, 2003).

Some of the views of Malaysian teachers on the factors contributing to the low level of English literacy and English teaching include the limited number of required hours for teaching English and the intense emphasis on tests and public examinations that do not encourage effective learning in the English classroom. The studies also assert that teachers do not have enough training to teach English in the classroom and have difficulties related to teaching methods. They find it hard to develop activities for listening and speaking and for teaching correct grammar and writing (Ambigapathy, 2004; Ambigapathy, 2003). Interestingly, it is important to note here that there is a lack of competent English teachers. About 70,000 English language teachers sat the Cambridge Proficiency Test in 2013, and two thirds of them failed to reach a proficient level (Ministry of Education, 2012).

The views of teachers in many of the research studies in Malaysia express the frustrations that English teachers have with the complexities of the demand for higher standards, new assessments, integration of technology and the implementation of interdisciplinary projects. The teaching contexts in which teachers teach English involve rather big classes. Many teachers assert that they are overworked, overstressed and not motivated to engage in professional development. Indeed, many job candidates indicate the high levels of unemployment and that being a teacher was not their first option. It is recognised that there are many economic, social and infrastructural factors that need attention, but the research findings on the teacher and student dimensions suggest that there are many challenges in English classrooms in Malaysia and that any initiative for transformation will not occur unless teachers themselves feel the need for such a transformation (Ambigapathy, 2002).

In any sphere, programmes of change often encounter anxiety and ambiguity. Lack of evidence-based data that informs policy and reversals in programmes make the task of improving English literacy a problematic one. Another setback in the Malaysian Education Blueprint emerged when the Ministry of Education rescinded the decision to make English a compulsory pass subject in the SPM. Clearly this move brought mixed reactions. Teachers and practitioners on the ground have more time to prepare students, but the rescinding of the compulsory pass in English requirement in 2015 and the failure to set any new dates may mean that the move towards advancing English literacy proficiency will be delayed.

In this sense, decisions taken by high-level policymakers are important decisions and measures must be implemented on the basis of supporting data and consultations with all involved stakeholders. Leadership, as well as principals' and teachers' motivation, to advance English literacy practices; the availability of structures, resources and support for teachers and a sound understanding of enabling factors that contribute to effective classroom practices at both the macro and micro level are all essential.

To engage stakeholders in the transformation of English literacy in a fruitful manner, further attention must be given to action strategies at the micro level, specifically in the areas of curriculum and instruction, assessment and teaching (Cambridge Assessment, 2010).

Curriculum and Instruction

English literacy must not be treated as essentially a skills-based service subject. Curriculum works must address the gaps between the world of schools and higher education institutions and students' life worlds to successfully link literacy experiences to real-life decisions and problem solving. In this vein, policymakers, schools and institutions of higher learning need to secure commitment and support from many stakeholders. This is vital to establishing a clarity and consensus that will enable effective learning and engagement; for example, just increasing the proportion of time spent practising selected skills to raise the standards of English literacy will hardly be successful if the curriculum is limited. English literacy must also allow learners to explore the changing nature of society, communication, culture, creativity and critical thinking and the way they make sense of the surrounding world in fun and pleasurable ways. More importantly, schools must know how to implement curriculum goals by improving the creativity, breadth, relevance and engagement that they offer to students.

Many of the current generation of students in schools and institutions of higher learning are remarkably immersed in technology and think of ICT as an integral part of their social and learning life. As noted by the New London Group (1996), the evolving nature of literacy and the digital culture of students embraces not only texts but also still and moving images, graphics, sound, colour and space. Research in Malaysia has observed that children who manage media technologies in many ways, such as updating their Facebook status, taking photographs, uploading and downloading music and videos, using mobile phones to send and receive messages, and playing interactive media games, are coming to schools in which there are books, whiteboards and print materials in teacher-centred classrooms and where there is very little space for critical and creative media work (Shanthi, 2013).

Assessment

While it is important to gauge the English literacy standards among our students, it is also important to note that the accurate measurement of standards over time has serious limitations because of changes in context, curriculum, mode of assessment and views on what is relevant and important (Cambridge Assessment, 2010). It needs to be pointed out that in a pluralistic society like Malaysia, exercises in literacy assessments will reveal differences in outcomes for different groups of students, including the gender gap and students from different socioeconomic and ethnic backgrounds, leading researchers and scholars to ponder what it means to be 'differently literate' in such situations.

The mode of assessment set in internationally benchmarked English proficiency standards such as PISA and TIMSS[5] is another cause for concern as Malaysian students have not performed well in these assessments in the past. Care must be taken to ensure that the pressure to meet these assessment standards does not lead to teacher centeredness in classes, transmission-type teaching and technical skills that can be measured. In other words, principals and teachers should not be driven to be agents who deliver results rather than focusing on principles of learning. This in turn will create a paradox where strategies that are designed to improve standards of literacy can themselves be ones that undermine students' learning pleasure and outcomes in the classroom. Worse still, the culture of measuring academic achievement by the number of A's will breed a generation of educationists, parents and students who will be more concerned with academic results rather than with the joy of learning and individual improvement.

The Teacher Factor

Teachers are at the heart of schools, and there is a huge body of evidence that affirms that one of the most important factors in determining the effectiveness of a literacy programme is the quality of its teachers (Ambigapathy & Shanthi, 2010). Indeed, the success of any educational policy hinges on its implementation, as teachers play a critical role in accomplishing any transformation plans or shifts in instruction. Attention must be given to a wider range of teacher voices in framing policy decisions, improving teacher training and professional development and developing frameworks for instruction.

In the history of education reform, teachers have too often been an afterthought, and this is especially true in the case of teachers and English literacy. The views of teachers in many of the research studies in Malaysia express the frustrations English teachers have with the complexities of the demand for higher standards, new assessments, the integration of technology and the implementation of interdisciplinary projects. The teaching contexts in which teachers teach English involve rather big classes. Many teachers assert that they are overworked, overstressed and not motivated to engage in professional development (Ambigapathy & Shanthi, 2011). The selection of teachers is critical. Given the high levels of unemployment, teaching was not the first option for some teachers. Studies of the factors that affect the success of implementing change in schools and learning institutions have indicated several

---

5 PISA and TIMSS assessments provide data from internationally standardised tests that enable Malaysia to compare and monitor its performance with that of other countries.

factors, such as teachers' attitudes towards and beliefs about change, teachers' contextual pedagogic and technological knowledge and teachers' perception of leadership and how they are inspired by it, as well as the presence of monitoring and evaluation strategies that allow schools to assess the quality and impact of their work and changes over time (Ambigapathy, Shanthi, & Ganeson, 2014).

Nevertheless, there are many teachers who are always looking for ways and measures to improve the teaching and learning of English in order to keep learners interested and motivated. There are many studies that highlight the factors that lead to positive change in teaching practice, specifically the different forms of support that are most likely to encourage teachers to change their practice and the impact of changes in practice on student outcomes (Cambridge Assessment, 2010; Kalantzis & Cope, 2005).

In one study, the teachers revealed the opening of spaces and the development of opportunities for creative teaching and learning in schools (Ambigapathy & Shanthi, 2005). They noted that there was a lot of experimentation and risk-taking, which provoked mixed reactions from fellow teachers and some parents since several of the activities were not seen as 'helpful' in answering examination questions. Still, the teachers noted that students improved their reading, speaking, observation and writing skills. In addition, the students were also applying multimodal skills by using visuals, graphics, comics, symbols and YouTube videos in their projects. The teachers noted that there was a lot of peer discussion and sharing of knowledge among students as they also learned about diverse learning styles and the abilities of their friends in their teams as well as of other communities from different geographical locations and cultures in Malaysia (Ambigapathy & Shanthi, 2005; Kalantzis & Cope, 2005).

Conclusion

Malaysia is mindful of the priorities needed to improve the problematic nature of literacy practices, but excessive politicising of educational matters creates setbacks in the pathways to enhancing English literacy in Malaysia. We are at an important point of time that could lead to positive change in literacy practices in schools and other educational settings. Given the rapid movements in the new world settings, it is essential to respond quickly to the role of English literacy in this digital age. Different approaches and curriculum content and an assorted range of pedagogies and assessments mean that the agenda on English literacy will be a challenging one.

This discussion has attempted to stimulate conversations about English literacy by examining the current changes taking place in the world today and by presenting key facets that impinge upon planning and implementing initiatives in building possibilities for enhancing English literacy teaching and learning. The journey of English literacy has not been consistent, and unforeseen controversies and failures, as well as hopes and aspirations, will surface in response to the diverse demands of education and world realities. As Malaysia moves into the future, there must be a concerted effort to work towards programmes that promote meaningful participation, which in turn would support everyday living and problem solving. Policymakers in Malaysia recognise that local, state and national social, economic and cultural growth increasingly depends on the success of schools and higher learning institutions in raising the performance and language proficiency of students. The Malaysian Education Blueprint proposes key transformation strategies that will revamp the education system. In this regard, we can no longer stand as single-focus educators, researchers, administrators or curriculum experts in responding to new technologies and diversities surrounding us. The Blueprint offers useful viewpoints for thinking about the provision of education and English literacy in the coming years. It is important that the programmes in the Blueprint are conducted with inputs from different groups that deliberate on realistic contexts, organisational practices and underlying beliefs and support systems for teachers, administrators and students as well as on resources for practice development, monitoring and evaluation plans. Only then can we think of collaborating seriously on preparing young Malaysians to understand the challenges of the world about them and to consider options, alternatives and choices in life that can secure a brighter literate future for them in a new global era.

References

Abraham, D. (1987). *Planning and teaching: Practical suggestions for English in the classroom*. Petaling Jaya, Selangor: Penerbit Fajar Bakti.

Ambigapathy, P. (2002). English language teaching in Malaysia Today. *Asia-Pacific Journal of Education*, 22(2), 35–52. Retrieved from http:/www.tandfonline.com/

———. (2003). Designing an agenda on literacy: Focusing on Information Technology and language learning among teacher trainees in Malaysia. *International Journal of Learning*, 10, 2831–2840.

———. (2004). Breaking the silence—Voicing English language teachers in Malaysia, In M. E. Vethamani (Ed.), *Reading in TESL vol. 2: Essays in honour of Basil Wijasuriya* (pp. 27–48). Petaling Jaya: Sasbadi.

———. (2006). What works in the classroom? Promoting literacy practices in English. *3L The Southeast Asian Journal of English Language Studies, 11*, 15–39.

———. (2008). Literacies: Languages, mathematics and the sciences. In I. Bajunid (Ed.), *Malaysia from Traditional to Smart Schools* (pp. 197–219). Kuala Lumpur: Oxford Fajar.

Ambigapathy, P., Koo, Y. L., & Kell, P. (2007). *Innovation and intervention in ELT: Pathways and practices*. Serdang, Selangor: Universiti Putra Malaysia.

Ambigapathy, P., Liew, C. C. L., Tan, D. A. L., Jayagowri, M., Lee, B. C., & Toh, C. H. (2013). *New literacies: Reconstructing language and education*. Newcastle upon Tyne: Cambridge Scholars Publishing.

———. (2014). *Language teaching and learning: New dimensions and interventions*. Newcastle upon Tyne: Cambridge Scholars Publishing.

Ambigapathy, P., Pang, V., Shanthi, B. B., & Chee, V. P. W. (2013). *Multiliteracies in Education: Research & development perspectives with a focus on forms of literacy in English in schools in Malaysia*. Kota Kinabalu: Universiti Malaysia Sabah Press.

Ambigapathy, P., & Shanthi, B. B. (2005). Approaching learning by design as an agenda for Malaysian schools. In M. Kalantzis & B. Cope, B. (Eds.), *Learning by design* (pp. 285–313). Melbourne: Common Ground.

———. (2010). Driving the agenda of learning by design in science literacy in Malaysia. *E-Learning and Digital Media, 7*(3), 301–316.

———. (2011). Transforming literacy in Malaysian schools: Teachers, changes and the agenda on learning by design. *The International Journal of Learning, 17*(11), 63–86.

———. (2013). Ready for the workplace? English language and literacy skills among public university students in Malaysia. *Malaysian Journal of Languages and Linguistics, 2*, 56–71.

Ambigapathy, P., Shanthi, B. B., & Ganeson, M. J. (2014). Appropriating English language teaching in Malaysia. In P. Ambigapathy, C. C. L. Liew, D. A. L. Tan, M. Jayagowri, B. C. Lee, & C. H. Toh (Eds.), *Language teaching and learning: New dimensions and interventions*. Newcastle upon Tyne: Cambridge Scholars Publishing.

Ambigapathy, P., Suthagar, N., & Shanthi, B. (2007). Realities, relevance and responsibility in constructing workplace literacy: A focus on English language institutions of higher learning in Malaysia. In P. Kell & G. Vogl (Eds.), *Higher education in the Asia Pacific* (pp. 130–149). Newcastle upon Tyne: Cambridge Scholars Publishing.

Archer, W., & Davidson J. (2008). *Graduate employability: The views of employers*. Malaysia: The Council for Industry and Higher Education.

Asmah, Haji O. (2012). Pragmatics of maintaining English in Malaysia's education system. In E-L Low & H. Azirah (Eds.), *English in Southeast Asia: Features, policy and language in use* (pp. 155–174). Amsterdam/Philadelphia: John Benjamins.

Azirah, H. (2009). Not plain sailing: Malaysia's language choice in policy and education. *AILA Review, 22*(1), 36–51.

Birch, D., & Gardiner, M. (2005, December). *Students' perceptions of technology-based marketing courses*. Paper presented at the ANZMAC Conference Broadening the Boundaries, Fremantle, Western Australia.

Cambridge Assessment. (2010). *Exam standards: The big debate, report and recommendations*. Retrieved from www.cambridgeassessment.org.uk.

Cope, B., & Kalantzis, M. (2009). Multiliteracies: New literacies, new learning. *Pedagogies: An International Journal, 4*(3), 164–195.

David, M. K., & Govindasamy, S. (2003). Language education and nation building in multilingual Malaysia. In J. Bourne & E. Reid (Eds.), *Language education: World yearbook of education* 2003 (pp. 215–226). London: Kogan Page.

Dumanig, F. P., David, M. K., & Symaco, L. P. (2012). Competing roles of the national language and English in Malaysia and the Philippines: Planning, policy and use. *Journal of International and Comparative Education, 1*(2), 104–115.

Fong, P. C. (2012). Literacy among the secondary school students in Malaysia. *International Journal of Social Science and Humanity, 2*(6), 546–550.

Gill, S. K. (2005). Language policy in Malaysia: Reversing direction. *Language Policy, 4*, 241–260.

Goh, L. (2015, August 23). Will we ever be ready? *The Star*. Retrieved from http://www.thestar.com.my/Opinion/Columnists/commonsense/Profile/Articles/2015/08/23/Will-we-ever-be-ready-Setting-goals-without-a-realistic-structure-and-then-making-a-Uturn-make-the-d/.

Fenn-Wu Report. (1951). *Report of a mission invited by the Federation Government to study the problems of the education of Chinese in Malaya*. Kuala Lumpur: Government of Federation of Malaysia.

Hamid, A., & Moni, K. (2011). English in primary education in Malaysia: Policies, outcomes and stakeholders' lived experiences. *Current Issues in Language Planning, 12*(2), 147–166.

Hazita, A. (2009). English in Malaysia: A paradox in rural pluri-literacy practices. *Akademika, 76*, 27–41.

Kalantzis, M., & Cope, B. (2005). *Learning by design*. Melbourne: Common Ground.

——— (2012). *Literacies*. Cambridge: Cambridge University Press.

Koo, Y. L. (2008). *Language, culture and literacy: Meaning-making in global contexts*. Bangi: Penerbit Universiti Kebangsaan Malaysia.

Limbrick, L., & Aikman, M. (2005). *Literacy and English: A discussion document prepared for the Minister of Education*. Auckland: Faculty of Education, University of Auckland.

Malakolunthu, S., & Rengasamy, N. (2012). Education policies and practices to address cultural diversity in Malaysia: Issues and challenges. *Prospects, 42*(2), 147–159.

Meek, M. (1991). *On being literate*. London: Bodley Head.

Melor, M. Y., & Siti, S. (2014). Writing needs and strategies of FELDA primary ESL pupils. *Journal of Education and Human Development, 3*(2), 1017–1035.

Ministry of Education, Malaysia. (1951). *Barnes report*. Kuala Lumpur: Government Press.

———. (1989). *Compendium: A handbook for ELT Teachers*. 1/89. Kuala Lumpur: Malaysian Ministry of Education.

———. (2004). *The Development of Education. National Report of Malaysia. 31 July 2004*. Kuala Lumpur: Malaysian Ministry of Education.

———. (2010). *To uphold Bahasa Malaysia & to strengthen the English language*. Retrieved from http://www.moe.gov.my/mbmmbi/moe_mbmmbi_03.htm.

———. (2012). *Preliminary report. Malaysia education blueprint 2013–2025*. Retrieved from http://www.moe.gov.my/userfiles/file/PPP/Preliminary-BlueprintEng.

Morgan, W. (1997). *Critical literacy in the classroom: The art of the possible*. London: Routledge.

Morshidi, S., Rozinah, J., Lee, N. H. L., & Pandian, A. (2007). Findings and discussion. In S. Morshidi, J. Rozinah, & N. H. L. Lee (Eds.), *The effectiveness of academic programmes at higher education institutions towards lifelong learning* (pp. 35–64). Penang: USM Press.

Myhill, D. (2011). The future of English: One subject, many voices. *English Drama Media, 20*, 23.

New London Group. (1996). A pedagogy of multiliteracies: Designing social futures. *Harvard Educational Review, 66*(1), 60–92.

Normazidah, C. M., Koo, Y. L., & Hazita, A. (2012). Exploring English language learning and teaching in Malaysia. *GEMA Online Journal of Language Studies, 12*(1), 35–51.

Phan L. H., Khoo, J., & Chng, B. (2013). Nation building: English as an international language, medium of instruction, and language debate: Malaysia and possible ways forward. *Journal of International and Comparative Education, 2*(2), 58–71.

Puteh, A. (2010). The language medium policy in Malaysia: A plural society model? *Review of European Studies, 2*(2), 192–200.

Rajaretnam, T., & Nalliah, M. (1999). *The history of English language teaching in Malaysia*. Shah Alam, Selangor: Biroteks.

Sankey, M., & St. Hill, R. (2009). The ethics of designing for multimodality: Empowering nontraditional learners. In U. Demiray & R. Sharma (Eds.), *Ethical practices and implications in distance education* (pp. 126–155). London: Ideas Group International.

Shanthi, B. B. (2013). Media literacy in the life worlds of Malaysian children. *Global Studies of Childhood, 3*(1), 72–85.

Singh, M., Kell, P., & Pandian, A. (2002). *Appropriating English: Innovation in the global business of English language teaching*. New York: Peter Lang.

Spraguengh, E. W., & Dahl, D. W. (2009). Learning to click: An evaluation of the personal response system clicker technology in introductory marketing courses. *Journal of Marketing Education, 32*(1), 93–103.

Thang, S. M., Ting, S. L., & Nurjanah, M. J. (2011). Attitudes and motivation of Malaysian secondary students towards learning English as a second language: A case study. *The Southeast Asian Journal of English Language Studies, 17*, 40–54.

Wan Norhasniah, W. H. (2011). An analysis on ethnic relation between the Malay and Chinese communities in Malaysia from civilizational perspective: Language and education's experiences. *International Journal of Humanities and Social Science, 19*(1), 225–235.

Watson, K. (2011). Education and language policies in South East Asian countries. In C. Brock & L. P. Symaco (Eds.), *Education in South East Asia* (pp. 283–304). Oxford: Symposium Books.

CHAPTER 9

Impact of the English Language on University Policy in Malaysia and Japan

Sachihiko Kondo

Introduction

In this chapter, the individual policymaking attempts of Malaysian and Japanese tertiary education will be outlined and analysed with particular focus on the mediums of instruction. Both countries have endeavoured to transform their local tertiary education institutions into more global-market ready ones, or, more precisely, into 'education hubs'. Within an education hub, scholars and policymakers aim to effectively increase a country's attractiveness and influence throughout a region. A hub is intended to recruit, train and retain a skilled workforce; to further economic development; to shift a country towards a knowledge- and service-based economy; and to build strategic and influential alliances which attract international students. According to Knight (2012), hubs may be categorised as student, skilled worker or research/innovation hubs. In the following sections, we examine the policies of Malaysia, which has utilised its colonial linguistic legacy to reform its educational institutions into 'transit points' for international students. The analysis will also be applied to Japanese attempts to attract international students, through which Japanese universities can overcome their own Galapagos syndrome by using the English language comprehensively in their faculties. Throughout the chapter, the discussion will be extended to the future educational policies of non-English speaking countries under the predominant status of English in academia (Crystal, 2003).

World University Ranking

World university ranking is a largely symbolic phenomenon in the 21st century, in which branding and marketing have become dominant principles in every aspect of our lives, be they cultural or academic. It reflects increasing student mobility across borders. The OECD (Organisation for Economic Co-operation and Development, 2014) reported that the number of students enrolled outside their country of citizenship has risen dramatically, from 0.8 million worldwide in 1975 to 4.5 million in 2012, a more than fivefold increase. Except for a few universities, almost all higher education institutions are rooted in particular towns, regions or countries, and they are often given toponomastic names or named after their founders. Historically, they have supported many local students and some non-local students, including international ones. Under these circumstances, tertiary education was essentially domestic, and there was no need for international comparisons among universities located in different countries, at least until the end of the 20th century.

The history of university ranking schemes or their adequacy as a criteria for cross-border comparison is beyond the focus of this discussion. However, we cannot ignore the fact that world ranking is one of the paramount concerns in university management today. As a piece of evidence, on 16 September 2014, Professor Awg Bulgiba, Mahmud, Deputy Vice Chancellor of the University of Malaya (UM) and Chairman of the UM Ranking Committee, made the following announcement:

> Dear colleagues,
> UM'S PERFORMANCE IN THE WORLD UNIVERSITY RANKINGS 2014
>
> On behalf of the University of Malaya, I am pleased to announce that UM has has [sic] been ranked 151st in the QS World University Rankings 2014. This is an improvement on its 2013 rank of 167.
> UM was also ranked 32nd in the QS Asian University Rankings 2014, a slight improvement from its previous rank of 33rd in 2013. In addition, UM is the only university in Malaysia to be ranked in the 301–400 Band by the Academic World Ranking University (AWRU), a slight improvement over its 401–500 Band in 2013.
> As Chairman of the UM Rankings Committee, I would like to thank EVERYONE for their commitment and support thus far.
> I look forward to your continued support in this matter. (University of Malaya, 2014).

Let us look at an example from Japan. At the Center for Research and Development of Higher Education of the University of Tokyo, the top university in Japan, researchers work on the critical analysis of the various forms of university ranking, with a particular interest in revealing their backgrounds and methodologies. They have proposed improvements to the ranking technologies and implement these improvements in their own university (University of Tokyo, 2014).

Comprehensive universities, such as the UM or the University of Tokyo, have diverse missions, namely competitive tertiary education and cutting-edge research, but university ranking is likely to be more helpful for educational marketing than for research marketing. One could argue that a major part of a university's performance is evaluated on the basis of research excellence. Several of the quantifiable criteria, such as number of citations, patents or awards won by researchers, indicate the competitiveness of a university's research. On the other hand, most aspects of the educational outcome are difficult to quantify because they are often expressed through individual feelings of satisfaction. With the exception of some statistics such as teacher-student ratio or the number of students who successfully obtain a national licence (such as medical or legal professionals), it is not easy to quantify the quality of university education; the success rate for degrees can be another indicator.

The concern described above leads us to further discuss who the stakeholders of the world university rankings are. There is no need to go into detail on the individualistic nature of quality research. Let us remember that the Nobel Prize, except in the field of peace, is awarded to individuals, not to institutional activities. There is no need for an institutional ranking for research stakeholders, who are likely to contact particular individual professors rather than anonymous professors in a particular institution if they need to do so. In contrast, in education, there is a global university marketplace for the many customers of educational services. In many cases, rankings give these customers, university applicants and their parents, a form of guidance in the chaotic education marketplace. As previously noted, most universities are local institutions rooted in their respective locations with highly individualistic sociocultural settings and therefore are essentially not comparable. However, education consumers often mistakenly think it is possible to compare things that cannot be compared, and the world rankings satisfy their somewhat illogical expectations (Hazelkorn et al., 2014). Furthermore, the excellence of home universities is a likely indicator of the extent to which home countries and their administrations are successfully going to transform their societies into knowledge-based ones. Other important stakeholders are politicians and bureaucrats, who are accountable for their budgeting decisions.

In the global higher education marketplace, instructional languages play an important role in marketing strategies. Malaysia and Japan are countries whose official language is not English. Although they have distinct perspectives, expectations and historical settings, both countries have aimed to establish an English-oriented educational system in order to adapt to the global marketplace. Let us examine the efforts made by these countries in terms of motivations, background and outcomes.

Malaysian Tertiary Education in the Late 20th and Early 21st Centuries

In two of the following sections, the problematic nature of Malaysian university restructuring since the 1980s will be examined. Malaysia's restructuring policy, aimed at creating a 'student transit point' (Sugimoto, 2005), has put too much emphasis on the educational aspect, especially its medium of instruction. To quote Selvaratnam (1989), an expert in East Asian tertiary education:

> The historical origins and growth of universities in Malaysia can be seen in four specific stages. First, the implantation and development of institutions of higher education in Malaysia and Singapore before Malaysia's independence in 1957; second, the establishment of the University of Malaya in Kuala Lumpur in 1961; third, the establishment and growth of three new national universities and an International Islamic University after 1969; and, finally, the upgrading of the colonial modeled Agricultural and Technical Colleges in 1971 and 1972 to full university status (p. 188).

Whereas Selvaratnam outlined post-war Malaysian education up to the 1970s, it must be noted that until the 1980s, Malaysia had only six universities and two colleges, which educated only 2.07% of the corresponding age group. This capacity obviously failed to meet the increasing social demand for higher education. In the period 1981 to 1985, Malaysia was number one in the world for sending its own students abroad, mainly to the United Kingdom, the United States, Canada and Australia (Sugimoto, 2005). This trend continued through the 1990s, although in that decade, China also began to send a huge number of students to tertiary education institutions worldwide.

One could regard 20th century Malaysian tertiary education as an internationally dependent education system (Altbach, 1989). In 1995, the Malaysian government reported that nearly 20% of Malaysian students studied abroad, costing the country an estimated 800 million USD (Blessinger & Sengupta, 2012). The Malaysian government was then forced to consider the serious side effects of internationally dependent education; some of those who had a foreign tertiary education were rather reluctant to return to Malaysia, instead preferring to find jobs in their study destinations. Added to this, the Asian monetary crisis in the late 1990s hit the Malaysian economy and Malaysia started seriously considering the effects of money and brain drains. As Sugimoto (2005) suggested, the implementation of the full-cost fee policy for non-UK resident students by the Thatcher administration was, to a certain extent, another reason for the Mahathir government to revise Malaysia's educational dependence on the United Kingdom. Due to the factors mentioned above, the government turned a passive higher education policy (an internationally dependent one) into a more aggressive one.

As early as the 1980s, private providers of higher education in Malaysia started inviting foreign universities to offer training programmes and to open franchises to offer diplomas, certificates and qualifications up to bachelor's level. Reinforcing this trend, the Education Act of 1996, which ended strict control over the private sector's and foreign universities' ability to confer full degrees, opened the door much wider for private and foreign institutions. It was the fanfare of the new century for Malaysian tertiary education policy. In 1986, only 50 private institutions offered tertiary education services in Malaysia. Twenty years later, in 2005, there were 539 private tertiary education institutions in Malaysia, several of which offered their programmes in cooperation with foreign institutions: for example, 2+1 (or sometimes 3+0) programs, in which students study 2 years in Malaysia and 1 year in another country to obtain their certificates (Akiba, 2013; Tham, 2013). What is more, there are currently nine branches of foreign universities (the University of Reading is likely to open a new campus at Johor Bahru in 2015, thus becoming the 10th foreign university branch campus in Malaysia), 18 university colleges, one virtual university, and one Open University in Malaysia. In particular, concerning the UK-Malaysia relationship, at least 70 institutions of higher education from the UK have some kind of collaborative arrangement with Malaysian private institutions (Aftersch, 2015a; Blessinger & Sengupta, 2012).

The author suggests that a symbolic example of 21st century Malaysian higher education is the foundation of the Nottingham University Malaysia Campus in 2000 near the capital city Kuala Lumpur. In addition to being a business school for professionals, it offers bachelor's degrees in the arts and social sciences, engineering and science and, most importantly, foundation courses (pre-college course) for those who do not have sufficient proficiency in English or academic skills for UK universities. This gives us an idea of how Malaysia has become a 'franchisee' of branded universities, and their brand impact makes Malaysia a competitive regional hub for higher education in South East Asia.

The policy revision implemented by Malaysia not only retains Malaysian students at home but also attracts more international students. Sugimura (2010, 2013) noted that in 1999, as few as 3,500 international students studied in Malaysia, but by 2002, the number had increased to 29,000, and in 2008, roughly 69,000 international students were studying in Malaysia. Thus, with regard to the education hub concept (Knight, 2012), Malaysia has successfully taken on the student hub option. Note that brand universities and

IMPACT OF THE ENGLISH LANGUAGE ON UNIVERSITY POLICY   177

newly established private colleges, whose medium of instruction is English, attract many non-Malaysian students, and these students are contributing to Malaysia's economy (Akiba, 2013; Agatsuma, 2014). Akiba (2013) also pointed out that in the post-9/11 period (following the synchronised terrorist attacks in 2001 in the United States), due to international political tensions, Malaysia has become a popular study destination for young Muslims to pursue their degrees in English. One may wonder, however, if the definition of 'franchise' may extend to the idea of colonisation or recolonisation. Today, Malaysian universities seem to successfully participate in the globalised marketplace, which is evidently administered by the former coloniser and its kin.

Malaysian Universities as Educational Transit Points

In the post-independence period, the new Malaysian government defined Bahasa Malaysia as the national language to be used in public education, including tertiary education institutions. From the point of view of a newly independent state, it was quite natural to put emphasis upon the indigenous language and culture to counteract colonial influences (Foo & Richards, 2004; Anderson, 1983; Nair-Venugopal, 2013). However, English has been continuously used, especially in urban areas, among the multilingual and multi-ethnic communities of Malaysia, whatever the varieties of its form may be.

According to a ranking of English proficiency among non-native English speaking countries (EF Education, 2014), Malaysia is ranked 11th worldwide, top of the Asia countries and just above its own former colonial brother, Singapore (12th); Korea is ranked 24th and Japan 26th. It can be argued that it is contradictory to proceed with a discussion concerning English proficiency ranking when the author expressed a negative view about university ranking at the beginning of this chapter. The author fully understands this possible contradiction but would like to clarify that Malaysia has a good reputation for English fluency among its general public. With this reputation, Malaysia could maximise the effect of the Education Act of 1996. The official language at the Nottingham Malaysia campus (and other branch campuses of foreign institutions) and in the 2+1 programmes is English, which is the very medium of instruction the Malaysian government once tried to avoid in their home institutions under the ethno- and culture-centred bumiputraism.

Drawing from Sugimura (2010, 2013), Malaysia's student hub functions as an educational transit point, a preliminary destination for students who will eventually go on to English-speaking countries such as the United States, the

United Kingdom, Canada and Australia to get their intended higher degrees. The influx of foreign students enrolling in Malaysia has transformed the country into one of the strongest emergent contenders in the international student mobility market. The process of becoming a regional educational transit point has also attracted criticism. First of all, even if many foreign students are attracted to Malaysia, they are just consumers of educational goods; there is little chance they will be a part of Malaysian society after their graduation. Secondly, newly established universities or colleges emphasise the educational aspects of tertiary education but often contribute insufficiently to Malaysian industry due to their poor research commitments (Sugimura, 2010, 2013). With a few exceptions, such as Newcastle University Medicine Malaysia, which admitted 60 local undergraduate students in 2011 (Aftersch, 2015b), even today, the ethos and the administrative focus of Malaysian branches of non-Malaysian higher education institutions are centred on language (academic English), liberal arts and social science education, with less emphasis on science and engineering research (Sugimura, 2010, 2012, 2013; Sugimoto, 2005). Crystal (2003) claimed that English has already established its status as the global language. Finally, although there is a large market for those who need to study English or to study something in English, due to the globalised nature of that language, Malaysian higher education institutions cannot be exceedingly optimistic regarding their business prospects as learning English or in English are not unique to Malaysia.

With respect to the tertiary education marketplace, in the last couple of decades, Malaysian institutions seem to be winning the game and admitting more international students. Strategically, Malaysia has transformed its institutions into educational transit points which are functioning as training centres for academic English or as pre-university schools for non-native English students. Although these policies have successfully turned Malaysia from an importer of higher education services into an exporter of such services, they have practically parasitised the framework of foreign tertiary education. When at transit airports, jet setters rarely purchase expensive products: they are more likely to buy small souvenirs or just beverages; they are also more likely to shop more actively or sign sizeable contracts at their final destinations.

Successful Indigenisation of Education and Research at Japanese Universities

With regard to Japanese tertiary education institutions, it cannot be emphasised enough that there is a specific dilemma between the advantages and disadvantages of the 'indigenisation' by which collaborative education and research links create an academically self-sustained framework which forms a knowledge/innovation hub (Knight, 2012) within this highly developed island country.

In 1884, the Japanese Ministry of Education stated that in Japanese universities, the Japanese language was the preferable medium of instruction. The reason for this was partly because the academic hegemony of English was not as fully established at that time as it is today and there was the heavy burden of learning several languages, such as French, German or English, alongside new and complex scientific knowledge (Nakayama, 1989). Since then, in Japanese higher education institutions, foreign educational contents have been translated into the majority's mother tongue. In this light, it appears that Japanese universities have opened up wider educational opportunities by removing language barriers, at least within their own territory. Today, at most Japanese universities, including the flagship universities, the instructional language is Japanese. In the post-war period, when Japan enjoyed rapid economic growth, linguistically localised and mass-produced tertiary education supplied a sufficient number of qualified human resources to the demanding industrial sectors. One may find that since 1884, Japanese policymakers have allowed their own higher education institutions to employ an 'indigenising' policy for their educational content that has been considered quite successful, as will be seen in the next paragraph.

There is one further advantage of this kind of university indigenisation in Japan: the reinforcement of research. Once a sufficient amount of educational and research content has been translated into the local language, the entire system becomes self-sustaining: the indigenised academic knowledge helps to educate people more and supports the research level of the universities, especially at flagship universities. In other words, the quantity of education and research has helped maintain the quality of research. Since the first Japanese Nobel Prize laureate (Physics) in 1949, Professor Yukawa Hideki, there have been, as of 2015, 21 Japanese laureates: 18 scientists, two novelists and one politician (Peace Prize). Among non-Western countries, Japan is the country that has been awarded the most Nobel Prize distinctions. In fact, two of the Japanese-born Nobel Prize laureates, Professor Nambu (Physics in 2008) and Professor Nakamura (Physics in 2014), had already become naturalised citizens of the United States, but both of them earned their degrees from universities in Japan. We understand that it is debatable whether the number of Nobel Prize winners indicates the research quality of the corresponding country. However, it certainly reflects, the author believes, the reputation of a nation's academic excellence; thus, the author is in a position to claim that the Japanese-style research and educational indigenisation has been successful, at least until the end of the 20th century.

One of the pleasant events involving successful research indigenisation is the case of Professor Masukawa Toshihide, who, in 2008, received the Nobel Prize in Physics for his distinctive contributions in theoretical physics, sharing the award with two other Japanese physicists. He delivered his memorial lecture in Stockholm in his mother tongue, Japanese. The only English phrase in his lecture was, at the very beginning, 'I'm sorry, I can't speak English'. He then continued his lecture in Japanese with an English interpreter ('Masukawa's first overseas journey', 2008). In one interview, Professor Masukawa remarked that he had spent more time studying mathematics and science subjects in his school days and that he had hated English because of his poor pronunciation ('What causes a solar eclipse?', 2008). The example of Professor Masukawa suggests that if one can have sufficient academic support in one's mother tongue, such as good text books, excellent lectures, supportive tutorials and, probably most importantly, helpful colleagues, it is possible to conduct leading research. He is an example of the competitiveness of the Japanese indigenised research culture. To analyse the university culture of this island country, however, it may be useful to examine other aspects of Japan, especially from the viewpoint of its linguistic isolation, often referred to as the Galapagos syndrome.

Are Japanese Universities Galapagos Islands?

The Galapagos Islands are the place where Charles Darwin got the inspiration for his epoch-making theory of evolution, *On the Origin of Species by Means of Natural Selection, or the Preservation of Favoured Races in the Struggle for Life*, published in 1859. Darwin found several unique species that were beautifully adapted to the environment of these geographically isolated islands. His findings also suggested that over-optimisation might cause problems for the survival of uniquely evolved species if the given environment was to change or if these natural life forms were forced to survive, for various reasons, in unfriendly environments.

Galapagos syndrome is a popular term in Japan, originally used to describe the Japanese cell phone industry. Mobile phones in Japan had been confined to satisfying the culture of demanding Japanese consumers, and, to a certain extent, the industry ignored international market trends and realities. Japanese mobile phone manufacturers, world-leading competitors from the late 1990s to the early 2000s, competed against each other in the domestic market, offering distinctive products, services and gimmicks primarily for Japanese customers. For instance, in that period, Japanese handset makers and wireless telephone operators introduced a number of world-leading innovations such as camera phones, mobile internet (i-mode),¹ mobile payment (FeliCa Wallet; micropayment technology of handsets and IC cards developed by SONY Co. Ltd.; SONY, 2015), mobile TV, 3G broadband services and so forth. In so doing, several of the functions of Japanese cell phones were only usable in Japan and could not be extended to countries outside Japan. There was a dogma among the management staff of top industries that if they could successfully sell their products in the Japanese market, then world customers who admired the latest technologies would buy these products too. In other words, they did not optimise their products to adapt to the international market; instead, they expected world customers and the world market to adapt their lifestyles, business styles or infrastructures to the latest Japanese technologies (Fasol, 2013).

It is no wonder that despite their excellent performance internally, the Japanese-made mobile phone lost its world market share in the competition against products from Korea, Taiwan, China and the United States. The finishing blow was the smart phone technology developed by Apple, which offered a customisable global platform for phone users and network operators worldwide. Today in Japan, 20th-century type mobile phones are often referred to as the Galapagos type (Gala-kei) in order to distinguish them from smart phones. As Uenishi and Matsushima (2013) suggested, the Galapagos syndrome was caused by organisational institutionalism, and the term is used to describe Japan's unique culture of technology that has not expanded beyond the islands in the Far East.

Recall our earlier discussion on the indigenisation of education and research in Japanese universities. As a matter of fact, we cannot ignore the globalised nature of science and technological innovations in which English has become the lingua franca (or global language) among intellectuals. In the words of Crystal (2003), 'In the 1950s, the case for English as a world language would be more than plausible. Fifty years on, and the case is virtually unassailable' (p. 71). Under these circumstances, Professor Masukawa, aged 68 when he obtained his first passport to travel abroad and deliver a speech in his native language at the Nobel lecture, is truly a rare species, even from the point of view of today's average Japanese academics.

Unlike the case of Masukawa, there are several unfortunate examples of the geographical and linguistic isolation of Japan. For instance, it could be useful here to cite the Nobel Prize awards in 1996. In that year, the Nobel Prize in Chemistry was awarded to Sir Harold Walter Kroto, a British chemist, for his

---

1   The letter 'i' stands for interactive, information and Internet, a registered trademark for a mobile internet service developed by NTT DoCoMo, the leading mobile network operator in Japan.

discovery of the 'Fullerene C_{60} molecule structure', which had been published in 1985 in *Nature* magazine. Later it was revealed that in 1970, 15 years prior to Kroto's discovery, Professor Osawa Eiji had theoretically predicted the structure of Fullerene C_{60} quite precisely when at Kyoto University. Until 1996, neither Sir Harold Kroto, *Nature*'s editors, nor the Nobel Foundation were aware of Osawa's pioneering contribution because his prediction was published in an academic journal in Japan, in Japanese (Swinbanks, 1996). Together with some other examples, this negative event has certainly motivated Japanese researchers to publish in English. In the world of natural science and technology, in order to make their work visible among colleagues worldwide, researchers must be proficient in English.

Japanese is the single official language of Japan, and the presence of linguistic minorities continues to be very small. At the same time, as the cases of Professor Masukawa and Professor Osawa illustrate, Japan is one of the few non-English-speaking countries that has conducted excellent doctoral education and world-leading research in its own language. This indigenised knowledge/innovation hub (Knight, 2012) has attracted a number of international students (Japan Student Support Organisation (hereinafter, JASSO), 2014).

In January 2008, former Prime Minister Fukuda Yasuo revealed his plan to invite 300,000 international students annually to Japan by 2020. At that time, there were 123,829 international students across the nation. The figure 300,000 was chosen to maintain the Japanese higher education system's share of the international student mobility market. Among other relevant factors, post-secondary education was facing oversupply as a result of the younger population's demographic decline. Thus, competitiveness, or attractiveness, in the international student market has become crucial for tertiary education institutions in Japan, both to attract talented postgraduate students to sustain research capacities and to compensate for the shrinking market of domestic students, mainly at the undergraduate level (Yonezawa, 2009).

Two years after Fukuda set this target, in 2010, the number peaked at 141,774 as of 1 May. At that time, 92.5% of the international students in Japan came from Asia and 60% of the total international student population came from the People's Republic of China. However, the earthquake in March 2011 drastically turned the tide. The old customers of Japanese higher education in previous decades, namely Chinese and Korean students (and their families), became reluctant to study in Japan (JASSO, 2014).

One may have already noticed that a considerable number of international students study the Japanese language before they enter universities or postgraduate schools in Japan. In most Japanese universities, the medium of instruction is Japanese, and so many international students attend Japanese language institutions in preparation for their academic activities and entrance examinations in Japan. Mainly regarding postgraduate studies, Yonezawa (2007) noted the following:

> Because of language barriers and the country's location, Japanese graduate education at flagship universities is facing difficulty in attracting top-level international students and academic staff. The Japanese language largely dominates daily academic and social life in every field. Whereas publication in English is on the rise in fields such as engineering and the natural sciences, manuscripts in the social sciences (except for economics) continue to be largely published in Japanese. It is quite unusual for a faculty meeting to be held in English or even bilingually. (p. 488)

International students and academics who expect lectures by or discussions with, for example, Professor Masukawa or Professor Osawa must study Japanese first. Accordingly, the successful indigenisation of research and education in Japan has come to be interpreted negatively. In general, the research output of Japanese flagship universities is still high, and some of these institutions are on an equal footing with other world-class universities in this respect. However, despite their relatively high reputation, as shown in various international rankings, Japanese flagship universities face challenges in maintaining or improving their international status. With respect to education, Japan has already failed to be considered a predominant study destination for its Asian neighbours, especially in the post-3/11 period (following the earthquake and a series of nuclear power plant malfunctions in March 2011).

Research-wise, it is unfortunate for Japan that a beautifully adapted academic 'Galapagos finch' (such as Professor Osawa) could not successfully pick a medal-shaped 'fruit' with a portrait of a bearded gentleman. Education-wise, the Galapagos metaphor can be well applied to current Japanese universities for a few reasons. Firstly, they are beautifully adapted to the given environment of their culturally and linguistically isolated 'islands', and they have been very productive under this self-sustaining environment. Secondly, they have shown vulnerabilities and inflexibility when adapting to unexpected changes in the environment involving globalisation. Furthermore, and most importantly, universities not only produce research output: they also produce graduates. Under the rules of the survival of the fittest and natural selection, if home-grown students from 'indigenised universities' are only adapted to limited environments (Seargent, 2009), it will hardly be possible for them to survive in the competitive globalised society (McVeigh, 2002).

University Internationalisation Initiatives in Japan: Bridging from Islands to the Rest of the World

When Fukuda declared the 300,000 international students plan, his cabinet also proposed an idea to support core universities in the process of the internationalisation of the entire Japanese higher education system (also known as 'Global 30' or G30) by providing a prioritised allocation of grants for 5 years. In July 2013, the Ministry of Education, Culture, Sports, Science and Technology (MEXT) announced the selected 13 universities, which were expected to build and improve on a system whereby international students can study and engage in research. It was revealed that among the variety of conditions for the G30 project proposal, what MEXT desired the most was the implementation of English-medium bachelor's degree courses alongside or integrated with conventional Japanese-medium courses. Apart from some exceptions in liberal arts colleges, this was almost the first systematic attempt, especially in comprehensive research-oriented flagship universities, to implement courses in which students obtained a BA or BSc certificate without the requirement of Japanese proficiency (Eto, 2014).

In the author's university, some graduate schools had already opened courses entirely taught in English; the decline in Japanese applicants in their disciplines or subjects may have motivated professors to choose English as their medium of instruction. In contrast, in the case of the newly implemented English bachelor courses, there were no incentives for Japanese home-grown professors because the university was successfully recruiting top ranked high-school graduates from the regional market. The prestigious institutional medal of being a 'G30 member university' was the only compelling force.

As one of those who was involved in the G30 project, today, the author may conclude that the project has not been as successful as originally expected in terms of the internationalisation of Japanese universities. One of the disappointments is that many G30 students are not proficient in Japanese, and Japanese firms are often reluctant to put them on their payrolls. These graduates are not adaptable to the Japanese business environment despite recent discussions of modern business styles in Japan, including the daily usage of English in the office. If the universities expect too much from Japanese companies and their human resource management policies, their attitude would not be so different from that of Japanese cell phone manufacturers. Seen from this perspective, by creating a number of English-medium bachelor degree courses in the 13 top-ranked Japanese universities, the project was just one of the first attempts to bridge the gap between education in these isolated, self-sustaining islands and the rest of the world.

In September 2014, MEXT selected 37 universities (13 Type A and 24 Type B) for the Top Global University Project, which provides prioritised support for world-class universities that can lead the internationalisation of all Japanese universities. The Type A (Top Type) category is for world-class universities that have the potential to be ranked in the top 100 in any of the world university rankings. The Type B (Global Traction Type) category is for innovative universities that can lead the internationalisation of Japanese society through their continuous improvement. Note that within the Type A Top Global Universities, as many as nine universities, including the author's university, are former members of the G30 consortium (MEXT, 2014).

Having worked on both the G30 and Top Global University Type A proposals at his university, the author has come to realise that the G30 put emphasis on the international competitiveness of education and the Top Global University Project puts emphasis on research activities. In order to be ranked in the top 100 worldwide, research excellence must be an institution's paramount concern. In addition, what applicant universities must have planned are some numerical targets with regard to, for example, the ratio between home-grown staff and those educated in foreign institutions; the number of international students; the number of local students who experience international education; internationalised new admission systems; lectures conducted in English; English-medium courses and programmes; systematic instalment of the GPA system, which originated in the United States; lectures with a numbering system and so forth. The requests made by MEXT go even further, requiring Top Global Universities to prepare accommodation in which local and international students can interact and collaborate well in order to nurture Japanese students to be more globally competitive.

It is too early to evaluate the outcome of the Top Global University Project. However, as discussed previously, MEXT continues to regard the creation of lectures and courses in English as the top priority for university reform in Japan. Concerning the global education marketplace, the Japanese government believes that institutional adaptation to English will be the key factor for their survival, whereas it is still uncertain how long English will sustain its status as the global language. Learning the bitter lessons of the case of Professor Osawa, the Japanese government has come to put much more emphasis on universal access to their education and research rather than elaborating on their own uniqueness within their isolated islands.

Conclusion

Returning to the starting point of this chapter, university rankings, one may draw some conclusions about globalisation from the efforts o Malaysian and Japanese tertiary education institutions, especially with regard to mediums of instruction. The basic idea of 'ranking' is that commodities and services are replaceable. In the modern marketplace of tertiary education, the English language has been considered the lingua franca of academia. This has forced non-native English countries to revise their academic frameworks to match the global educational marketplace.

First of all, in order to adapt to the marketplace, Malaysia seems to be taking an extreme approach: transforming their tertiary education institutions into transit points for non-Malaysian students and/or becoming a franchisee of brand universities. It is salient that Malaysia has now successfully industrialised its higher education, thereby maximising its own colonial linguistic legacy, but is still struggling to elevate its research reputation worldwide. If Malaysian universities continue in this direction, Malaysian tertiary education may come to be viewed as just a subsidiary of the higher education institutions (and systems) of the market leaders.

Secondly, Japanese universities, under the pressure of bankruptcies due to current demographic shifts, have endeavoured to participate in the global education marketplace, departing from their self-sustained and comfortable home market. Recently, the language barrier has been one of the greatest concerns. Since the beginning of the 21st century, Japanese policymakers have tried to abandon the 'isolation policy' in university education and change its professors' mindsets. Their efforts, through which more international students have been attracted to study in Japan, may help to educate home students to become a global-business-ready workforce (Seargent, 2009).

The author has come to understand that neither Malaysia nor Japan are game changers; rather, they are just two of the players in a game facilitated and coordinated by a few market-dominant countries. Whatever their market performances, it is hardly possible for them to change, or to win, the game. In the English-language dominant academic marketplace, their educational services might be considered as replaceable commodities, whereas a handful of core market leaders could firmly retain their dominant status. In this regard, healthy scepticism is needed by Malaysians and Japanese when they seriously consider the globalisation of their universities under the predominant status of the English language.

Here, we might refer to Knight (2012) once again: Universities, including the comprehensive flagship ones, are global institutions which study universal disciplines and are ranked within the global educational marketplace. They are also, conversely, local institutions which academically serve local communities as irreplaceable student, skilled worker or research/innovation hubs. These hubs are expected to increase a country's attractiveness in its region, and they may require, in turn, a rich diversity of culture and language, which may add value and attract more individuals. In addition, diversity might encourage more innovation. Concerning this, tertiary education policymakers in Malaysia are likely to have an advantage over those in Japan because of their multi-ethnic, multicultural and multilingual social backgrounds and experiences.

References

Aftersch. (2015a). *Types of institution*. Retrieved from http://afterschool.my/institution/.

———. (2015b). *Newcastle University Medicine Malaysia (NuMED)*. Retrieved from http://afterschool.my/institution/newcastle-university-medicine-malaysia-numed/.

Agatsuma, T. (2014). Marēsia ni okeru transu-nashonaru no kōtō-kyōiku no tenkai: Ōsutoraria daigaku bunkō jirei o chūshin to shite [Development of transnational higher education in Malaysia: Case study on off-shore campus of Australian university]. In H. Sugimoto (Ed.), *Transu-nashonaru kōtō-kyōiku no kokusai hikaku: Ryūgaku gainen no tenkan* [*International comparisons of transnational higher educations: Ideological transformations for student mobility*]. (pp. 224–240). Tokyo: Toshindo.

Akiba, H. (2013, Jan). Marēsia no kyōiku-jijyō: Ryūgakusei ukeire taikoku o mezasite [International education in Malaysia: Aiming to be the great host country of international students]. *Web-Magazine Ryūgaku Kōryū*. Retrieved from http://www.jasso.go.jp/about/documents/akibahiroko.pdf.

Altbach, P. (1989). Twisted roots: The western impact on Asian higher education. In P. G. Altbach & V. Selvaratnam (Eds.), *From dependence to autonomy* (pp. 1–21). Dordrecht: Kluwer Academic Publishers.

Anderson, B. (1983). *Imagined communities. Reflections on the origin and spread of nationalism*. London: Verso.

Blessinger, P., & Sengupta, E. (2012, July 2). Is Malaysia the regional leader in international higher education? *The Guardian*. Retrieved from http://www.theguardian.com/higher-education-network/blog/2012/jul/02/higher-education-in-malaysia.

Crystal, D. (2003). *English as a global language* (2nd ed.). Cambridge: Cambridge University Press.

EF Education. (2014). *English proficiency index* (4th ed.). Retrieved from http://media.ef.com/__/~/media/centralefcom/epi/v4/downloads/full-reports/ef-epi-2014-english.pdf.

Eto, K. (2014, May). Siretuka suru sekai no ryūgakusei kakutoku kyōsō to waga kuni no ryūgakusei seisaku [Intensifying international student recruitment and our nation's policy]. *Web-Magazine Ryūgaku Kōryū*. Retrieved from http://www.jasso.go.jp/about/documents/201405etokazuhiro.pdf.

Fasol, G. (2013). Japan's Galapagos effect (Galapagos syndrome). *Eurotechnology Japan*. Retrieved from http://www.eurotechnology.com/2013/08/05/galapagos-2/.

Foo, B., & Richards, C. (2004). English in Malaysia. *RELC Journal, 35*, 229–240.

Hazelkorn, E., Loukkla, T., & Zhang, T. (2014). *Rankings in institutional strategies and processes: Impact or illusion?* Brussels: European University Association.

JASSO. (2014). Result of an annual survey of international students in Japan 2013. Retrieved from http://www.jasso.go.jp/statistics/intl_student/documents/data13_e.pdf.

Knight, J. (2012). International education hubs: Collaboration for competitiveness and sustainability. *New Directions for Higher Education, 168*, 83–96.

Masukawa's first overseas journey: 'I was invited' to attend a Novel Price Award ceremony. (2008, December 5). *Asahi Shimbun*, Evening Edition, p. 14.

McVeigh, B. J. (2002). *Japanese higher education as myth*. Armonk: M. E. Sharpe.

MEXT (2014). *Selection for the FY 2014 Top Global University Project*. Retrieved from http://www.mext.go.jp/b_menu/houdou/26/09/__icsFiles/afieldfile/2014/10/07/1352218_02.pdf.

Nair-Venugopal, S. (2013). Linguistic ideology and practice: Language, literacy and communication in a localized workplace context in relation to the globalized. *Linguistics and Education, 24*, 454–465.

Nakayama, S. (1989). Independence and choice: Western impact on Japanese higher education. In P. G. Altbach & V. Selvaratnam (Eds.), *From dependence to autonomy* (pp. 97–114). Dordrecht: Kluwer Academic Publishers.

OECD. (2014). *Education at a glance 2014: OECD indicators*. Retrieved from http://www.oecd.org/edu/Education-at-a-Glance-2014.pdf

Seargent, P. (2009). *The idea of English in Japan: Ideology and the evolution of a global language*. Bristol: Multilingual Matters.

Selvaratnam, V. (1989). Change amidst continuity: University development in Malaysia. In P. G. Altbach & V. Selvaratnam (Eds.), *From dependence to autonomy* (pp. 187–205). Dordrecht: Kluwer Academic Publishers.

SONY. (2015). *FeliCa: Contactless IC card technology*. Retrieved from http://www.sony.net/Products/felica/about/index.html.

Sugimoto, H. (2005). *Marēsia ni okeru kokusai kyōiku kankei: kyōiku eno gurōbaru inpakuto* [Malaysian education from an international perspective: Globalization impact on education]. Tokyo: Toshindo.

Sugimura, M. (2010). *Kōtō-kyōiku no kokusai tenkai ni okeru toranjitto pointo: Marēsia no kotōkyōiku senryaku* [Transit point within international development of higher education: Higher education strategy of Malaysia]. *College Management, 160*, 34–37.

———. (2012). *Kōtō-kyōiku seisaku ni okeru gakusei-idō: 'kyōiku-habu' no sōshutu to tabunka-shakai no henyō* [International students' movements and higher education policies: Formation of education hubs and change of multicultural societies. *Asia and Pacific Studies Review, 37*, 3–16.

———. (2013). Marēsia: Kousai gakusei idō no tranjitto pointo [Malaysia: Transit point of international student mobility]. In Y. Kitamura & M. Sugimura (Eds.), *Gekidō suru ajia no daigaku kaikaku: Gurōbaru jinzai o ikusei suru tameni* [Asian university reform in turbulence: Fostering global human resources] (pp. 99–114). Tokyo: Sophia University Press.

Swinbanks, D. (1996). Japanese pioneer recalls 'prescient paper.' *Nature, 383*, 562.

Tham, S. Y. (2013). Internationalizing higher education in Malaysia: Government policies and university's response. *Journal of Studies in International Education, 17*(5), 648–662.

Uenishi, S. & Matsushima, N. (2013). *Organizational field comprising competitive relationships: The case of the 'Galapagos syndrome' in the Japanese mobile phone industry*. Discussion Paper Series Kobe University. Retrieved from http://www.b.kobe-u.ac.jp/paper/2013_19.pdf.

University of Malaya. (2014). *UM's performance in the world university ranking 2014*. Retrieved from http://engine.um.edu.my/about/displayevent.php?category=activity&id=256.

University of Tokyo (2014). Basic Research Division of Center for Research and Development of Higher Education. *University rankings and evaluation*. Retrieved from http://www.he.u-tokyo.ac.jp/en/research/ranking-and-benchmarking/.

'What causes a solar eclipse?', I asked my father on our way to/from a public bath: Masukawa at Nobel Lecture. (2008, December 9). *Asahi Shimbun*, Morning Edition, p. 30.

Yonezawa, A. (2007). Japanese higher education at a crossroads. *Higher Education, 54*, 483–499.

———. (2009). The internationalization of Japanese higher education: Policy debates and realities. *Nagoya University Higher Education Review, 9*, 199–219.

Afterword

∴

CHAPTER 10

A Prognosis for the Future

David Deterding and Toshiko Yamaguchi

The eight main chapters have emphasised the significance of the English language for contemporary Malaysia in four domains (linguistic features, language attitudes, English in online discourse, and English and language policies). When we try to envision the future of English in the country, our perception is that it will build on a composite of various interlocking factors and conditions.

In this final chapter, we present a brief prognosis of the future of English in Malaysia in terms of two major aspects, namely the growth of the population of English speakers, and documentation of the English in use. Let us begin with the first of these.

We assume that the number of speakers of English will increase in the coming years, partly because, as Saw predicts (2015, Chapter 11), the population in Malaysia will steadily grow over the next 30 years. This represents a sharp contrast to contemporary Japan, where the population has been declining aggressively (*The Star*, 28 February 2016). In Malaysia, economic considerations will attract Malaysians, particularly the young, to urban areas, where there is significantly more need to use English. Importantly, however, it is not certain that migration from rural to urban areas will result directly in the establishment of an indigenous variety of the English language.

Recall that Standard BE is promoted for English-language education by the Malaysian Ministry of Education's blueprint (Saraceni, 2015, p. 173), but the question remains: How many Malaysians actually speak and write something close to Standard BE? Quirk claimed (1990, p. 5) that unlike native varieties of English, postcolonial varieties such as ME may remain inherently unstable. However, other scholars, such as Kirkpatrick (2007) and Saraceni (2015), have noted that BE was historically also subject to substantial influences from other languages, particularly French and Norse. So, are New Englishes any different in this respect from so-called native varieties of English?

Whether or not ME is actually any different from BE with respect to influences from other languages, it is certainly true, as has been shown by the studies in this book, that it exhibits a wide range of emergent ESL features. These features reflect the personal involvement of speakers and hearers in the use of the language, resulting in local flavours of pronunciation, the irregular usage of grammar and lexis and the frequent adoption of simplified expressions.

While we anticipate that there will be more speakers of English in the future, the acceptance of ME as a distinct variety of English is not guaranteed solely by demographics. So what will ensure the emergence of a distinct variety of English in Malaysia? This concerns the second aspect of our prognosis.

Although English is neither the national nor the official language of Malaysia, we predict that the pronunciation, grammar and lexis of ME will continue to develop as long as it is in active use in Malaysian society. It is clear that this development will proceed according to the basic role of language, that is, facilitating communication between speakers and hearers, which has been regarded as 'the essence of language' by prominent scholars (Jespersen, 1992 [1924], p. 17, among others). Why do Malaysians pluralise uncountable nouns (*furnitures* or *equipments*)? Some people would claim that this is an error as the speakers may not know that the standard forms of *furniture* and *equipment* are mass nouns. However, an alternative answer is that this usage has a communicative function in that the speakers add a plural -s to enable hearers to infer that the referent for the noun is inherently plural. In this respect, the use of *furnitures* is actually communicatively helpful (Seidlhofer, 2011), and it should not be regarded as an error. We predict that this new form will become increasingly accepted in a wide range of different Englishes, even though, at present in Malaysia, the acceptance of this new form may vary depending on different social or educational dimensions. In addition, the frequency of words, phrases or constructions may also contribute to the process of the development: When a particular form with a particular meaning, whether grammatical or ungrammatical in standard grammar and/or acceptable or unacceptable in a society, is used frequently, this will be the one favoured by people owing to the high frequency of its use. This paralinguistic scenario is likely to add to the indigenous establishment of an English language. In the long run, local variations must reach a level of stability. While such stability always accompanies individual choices, those choices should be explained by some underlying patterns. In other words, a local variety of English should arrive at a stage at which it is manifested as a social entity shared by its speakers and has a system of its own (cf. Itkonen, 2003, p. 13).

In order to consolidate the future of English in Malaysia, then, we should, as the first step, have a good grasp of the language in its synchronic state; that is to say, Malaysia should strive to document exactly how people use the language. Describing how the language is used may well include consideration of the speaker's cognitive, functional and sociocultural strategies while using it, and these considerations will be central to this documentation.

For the last 30 years, the term *intelligibility* has been a key concept in judging the communicative sustainability of World Englishes or English as a lingua franca. Without forgetting Rajagopalan's (2010) elegant criticism of this term, documentation, as suggested above, may provide solid resources for conceptualising ME while, at the same time, its educated variety will remain highly intelligible in an international setting, and this will ultimately lead to the point at which we may discover and demonstrate a system unique to ME. This documentation is bound to require time, effort and coordination. Unlike Japan, where English has never obtained a historical presence and will probably remain a foreign language, Malaysia can take pride in undertaking this important and challenging task.

References

Itkonen, E. (2003). *What is language? A study in the philosophy of linguistics*. Åbo: Åbo Akademis tryckeri.

Jespersen, O. (1992 [1924]). *The philosophy of grammar*. Chicago/London: The University of Chicago Press.

Kirkpatrick, A. (2007). *World Englishes: Implications for international communication and English language teaching*. Cambridge: Cambridge University Press.

Quirk, R. (1990). Language varieties and standard language. *English Today, 21*, 3–10.

Rajagopalan, K. (2010). The soft ideological underbelly of the notion of intelligibility in discussions about 'World Englishes'. *Applied Linguistics, 31*(3), 465–470.

Saraceni, M. (2015). *World Englishes: A critical analysis*. London/New York: Bloomsbury.

Saw, S.-H. (2015). *The population of Malaysia* (2nd ed.). Singapore: Institute of Southeast Asian Studies Publishing.

Seidlhofer, B. (2011). *Understanding English as a lingua franca*. Oxford: Oxford University Press.

Index

abstract nouns   37
Academic World Ranking University (AWRU)   173
academic writing   158
accommodation strategies   15
acoustic analysis   65
acoustic quality   17, 45, 61, 66
acrolect   13–14, 25, 130
advertisements   18, 130–131, 133, 141, 156
aesthetics   157
Alice in Wonderland   46, 51
American English   11, 16, 56, 58, 70
amplitude   65–66, 71–74, 78–79
Anglican school   104
Anglicans   103
animism   103
Apple   180
Arabic   89–90
arithmetic   154
articles   13, 31, 39
articulatory strengthening   45, 56–57, 60
ASEAN   13, 81, 157
assessment   54, 90, 163–166
assimilation   57
attitudes   18, 68, 88–99, 107–108, 111–112
Australia   8, 98, 152, 175, 178
Australian English   11, 58
Austronesian   103, 128–129

Bahasa Malaysia (BM)   7, 10–11, 16, 89, 106, 108, 111, 125–126, 130–139, 141, 151, 177
bahasah penjajah   14
Bajau   5, 93, 127
balanced bilinguals   92
basilect   13–14
Bau Bidayuh   139
Bau District   104–105
Bau-Jagoi   103
beaver dams   60
Bidayuh   5–6, 18, 102–122, 128–129, 133, 138–139
Bintulu   136
Bisaya   102
blogs   125, 133, 137–138, 140, 147
Borneo   3, 103, 125–126, 131–133, 135–141

brain drain   175
British   ix, 6, 104–105, 106, 149
British-cum-local identity   59
British English (BE)   9, 16, 65–85, 193
British National Corpus   15
Brooke regime   103–104
Brunei   3, 17, 127
Buddhist temples   95
bumiputera   4–6, 90, 127

cable television   115
Cambridge Proficiency Test   163
Canada   152, 175, 178
Cantonese   6, 38, 40, 97
Caribbean English   25
Catholic schools   104
Catholics   103–104
cardinal numbers   31, 36–39
chalk-and-talk   154
China   98, 175, 181, 182
Chinese dialects   6, 38, 89–90
Chinese grammar   38
Chinese language   11, 17, 25, 27, 34–42, 89–99, 115, 130–132, 135
Chinese people   4–8, 89–99, 105, 110, 128, 131, 150
Christians   103
churches   95, 103
citation forms   67
classified advertisement (CA)   130–133, 141
classifier languages   26, 34–36, 38–39, 41
classifiers   17, 26, 34–41
cocoa crop   102
code-mixing   18, 90, 125, 131–132, 134, 136
codification   17, 58
collective facts out there   62
Colombo Plan   105
Common European Framework of Reference   81
communication   8, 15, 46, 58, 60–61, 67–69, 79–81, 89–90, 114, 126, 133, 139, 147–153, 156–157, 159–160, 164, 194
communicative language teaching   152–154
communicative strategies   15
complaints   9–10, 16, 148

compound nouns   17, 67, 69, 71–79
comprehensibility   68–69, 80–82
Computer assisted language learning (CALL)   155
consonant clusters   13, 15
contact situation   12, 15
count nouns   13, 17, 26–42
covert prestige   97, 99
contact situation   12, 15
creativity   155–156, 159, 164, 166
critical thinking   155–156, 164
curriculum   6, 10, 80, 108, 148–167
Curriculum Development Centre   155

Darwin, Charles   180
Dayak Bidayuh National Association   133
Dayaks   89, 93, 99, 102, 133, 136
debates (interactive activity)   157
dental fricatives   12, 45, 48–50, 56–57, 60–62
determiners   28, 30–33, 35, 38, 39
dialectal diversity   129
diaspora   133
dictionaries   58
diglossia   90
diphthongs   12
discussion forums   125, 133, 135
Dragon School   105
drama (interactive activity)   157
drop-out rate   110
duration (phonetics)   66, 69, 71–73, 78–79
durian   102
Dusun   5
Dynamic Model   9, 10, 15, 16–18, 58, 61

East Malaysia   3, 4, 5, 99, 105–106, 125, 129, 133, 138, 140, 141
East Malaysian   4, 5, 125, 129, 130, 137, 139, 140, 141
Education Act   105, 150, 152, 176–177
education hub   172, 176
educational transit point   177–178
electronically-mediated discourse (EMD)   126–141
emergent status of ME   18
endonormative stabilisation   16, 58
English as a lingua franca (ELF)   13, 67–68, 157, 181, 194–195
English as a second language (ESL)   15, 59, 69, 70, 193

English as an international language   110
English textbooks   15
ethnic segregation   6
Ethnologue   89, 127
examinations   80–81, 108, 150, 153–154, 155, 162, 166, 183
exonormative stabilisation   59
Expanding Circle   26, 41, 68

Facebook   125, 133, 138–141, 164
familiarity   68
fatigue   68
Federated Malay States   6
Federation of Malaya   7
Federation of Malaysia   105
films   109, 112–113, 120, 121
final consonant clusters   13
Foochow   128
foreign language   ix, 8, 25, 61, 97, 109, 120, 141, 195
French   70, 179, 193
Fukuda Yasuo, Prime Minister   182, 184
functional-cognitive approach   60
fundamental frequency (F0)   65, 69, 72, 75–79

Galapagos syndrome   18, 172, 180–181, 183
game   147, 164, 178, 186
gatekeepers   126
general ordinals   39
generalisation   26, 33
generalising patterns   39
German   93, 179
Global 30 (G30)   184
global ranking   157
Google   130, 140
Government Transformation Programme   153, 156–157
grammar   9, 12–18, 25, 35, 42, 151, 153, 154, 156, 157, 163, 193–194

Hakka   97, 128
heritage language   6, 128
Higher Education Committee Report   152
higher order thinking skills (HOTS)   154, 159
Hindu temple   95
Hokkien   6, 38, 40, 97, 128
home language   46, 107–108, 115
homophones   60
human communication   61

INDEX

Iban   4–6, 102, 105, 128–129, 131–132, 134, 136
identity   6, 15, 16–19, 59, 79, 89, 91, 139, 150–151
inanimate nouns   36–37
indefinite articles   31, 39
Indian languages   6, 89
Indian people   4–7, 110
indigenisation   178–180, 181, 183
indigenous speech community (IDG)   58–59
individual variation   46, 49, 51, 55, 61–62
Indonesia   3, 4, 127
Inflation   60
initial consonant clusters   15
initial position hypothesis   49
Inner Circle   12, 14, 26, 48, 58, 62
Instagram   139
intelligibility   15, 66–70, 79–82, 133, 140, 194
International Islamic University   175
Internet   115, 125–144, 147, 156
interviews   107, 114
intonation   65–66, 68–69
irregularity   46, 59
Islam   89
isolation policy   186
Italian   70, 91, 92

Japan   18, 68, 172–187, 193, 195
Japanese language   93, 179, 182–183
Japanese Ministry of Education   179
Japanese occupation   104
Japanese speakers   61
Java   3
Johor Bahru   176

Kadazan   92
Kadazandusun   125, 127, 132–133, 135, 139
Kadazandusun Language Foundation (KLF)   133, 139, 144
Kajang   102
kamupung tanpa wayar   129
Kayan   102, 139
Kelabit   102
Kelantan   92
Kenyah   102
kindergarten   113
Klang Valley   71
Kolej Tun Abdul Razak   105
Korea   68, 177, 181, 182
Kota Kinabalu   131

Kuala Lumpur   7, 46, 90, 92, 95, 100–101, 102, 175, 176
Kuching   91, 102–105, 107, 130–131
Kuching Port Authority   130
kueh lapis (layer cake)   126, 141
Kyoto University   182

Land and Survey Department   130
language alternation   125, 129, 132–134, 136–137, 141
language contact   41, 59
language games (interactive activity)   154–155, 157
language maintenance   129, 140
language planning   126, 148
language policy   7, 108, 130, 148, 151
language shift   27, 41, 114, 126, 129
law courts   106
lectal variation   12–14
lexical borrowing   15
lexical stress   65–67, 69, 70, 75, 78–82, 85
lingua franca   8, 11, 13, 67–68, 80, 82, 99, 114, 126–128, 157, 181, 186, 194–195
Lingua Franca Core (LFC)   80
linguistic isolation   180–181
linguistic landscape   ix, 90–91, 95
linguistic pluralism   9
linguopalatal contact   56
LINUS (Literacy and Numeracy Screening) 2.0   153, 156–157
literacy   10, 147–167
literature in English Language Teaching   153, 155
longhouses   102
loudness   65
Lun Bawang   102
Lundu   102, 105

Mahathir Mohamad, Dr   8, 155, 175
Malay language   6, 17, 25, 34–42, 89–99, 103, 106–108, 115, 126–127, 135–136, 149–150
Malay people   89–99, 102, 128, 150
Malaysian Certificate of Education (SPM)   10, 155, 156, 158, 160
Malaysian Education Blueprint (2013–2015)   81, 110, 151–152, 158–159, 163, 167
Malaysian English Newspaper (MEN) Corpus   26

200   INDEX

Malaysian University English Test (MUET) 160
Malaysianisation 7
Mandarin 6, 11, 38, 40, 89–92, 97–98, 128, 162
Manglish 13, 16
map of Malaysia 3
markedness 135
mass nouns 13, 17, 34, 194
Masukawa Toshihide, Professor 180–183
matched guise test 18, 91, 94–95, 97–100
mathematics and science 16, 106, 150, 180
medium of instruction 6–8, 10–11, 105–109, 111–113, 115, 149–150, 172–187
Melanau 5, 102, 128–129
mesolect 13–14
Ministry of Education, Culture, Sports, Science and Technology (MEXT) 184–185
Ministry of Education, Malaysia 10, 80–81, 110–111, 151, 154–157, 160, 163, 193
Miri 102, 132
miscommunication 15
mission schools 104–105, 111, 115
mixing 16, 18
models of pronunciation 68
monophthongs 12, 15
motivation 7, 107, 109–110, 114, 117, 119, 133, 159, 163, 174
multilingualism 126, 148, 150
multilingual 3, 25
multimedia in teaching 147
Multimedia Super Corridor 156
multinational companies 150
multitasking 147
Murut 5, 127

nation building 106, 149–151, 154, 157
National Development Policy 152
National Language Act 105, 152
national schools 6–8, 11, 106, 109, 149, 151
national-type schools 6–7, 92, 149, 151
nationalism 7, 18, 89, 148–149
nativisation 10, 12, 14–17, 25, 39, 45–46, 58–59, 61
Negri Sembilan 6, 11–12, 14
New English/New Englishes 9, 11–14, 45–46, 48, 58–59, 61, 193
New London Group 147, 164
New Primary Schools Curriculum 152, 154

New Sabah Times 131–132, 135
New Standard Curriculum 156
New Straits Times 27, 30–33
new [t] 17, 45–46, 48–54, 56–57, 59–61
new varieties of English 79
Newcastle University Medicine Malaysia 178
newspapers 9, 14, 16, 27, 125, 130–133, 135
niche 60–61
Nigeria 68
Nobel Prize 174, 179–181
nominal classification 26–28, 33–35, 37–38, 40–41
non-count nouns 26–28, 30–40, 194
Norse 193
North Wind and the Sun 46, 50
Nottingham University Malaysia Campus 176
nucleus 71
numerals 35, 38, 40

off-shore campuses 8, 18
official language 7, 89, 97–99, 105–106, 150, 174, 177, 194
official language of Japan 182
oil palm 102
online discourse 125–142
Open University in Malaysia 176
Orang Asli 89, 111
Orang Ulu 102, 128–129, 139
Osawa Eiji, Professor 182–183, 185
Outer Circle 9, 14, 26, 39, 41, 58, 68
overgeneralisation 26
overt prestige 97, 99

Padawan District 105
paddy planting 102
Pahang 6
partition 29
past tense marker 13
Penan 102
Perak 6
Philippines 3, 127
Pinyin 92, 101
pitch 65, 66, 67, 71–72, 78
places of worship 95
plural morphology 30, 38
policy 16, 18, 104–108, 110, 130, 148, 151–152, 158, 163, 165, 175–176, 179, 186

policymakers   8, 148, 156, 163–164, 167, 172, 179, 186–187
political correctness   93
population   3, 4–6, 11, 92, 101, 102, 104, 107, 127–129, 182, 193
Population and Housing Census   127
postcolonial English   19, 58
postcolonial   9, 193
Praat   46, 71
prestige   59, 90–91, 94–99
primary schools   6, 80, 90, 104–106, 108, 151–155, 156–159
Private Higher Education Institute Act   150
proficiency   67, 81–82, 106, 111, 113, 127–128, 151, 153, 156–157, 162–163, 167, 177
prognosis for the future of ME   193–195
prominence   65–66, 67, 69, 71
pronunciation   9, 11, 13–17, 45, 48–49, 52, 54, 56, 59–62, 65, 67–70, 75, 79–82, 180, 193–194
pronunciation teaching   68–69

questionnaires   71–72, 78, 90–91, 93, 107, 109, 111, 114, 117–122
Quop area   104

Rahman Talib Report   152
Rajah Brooke   103
rambutan   102
Rara Bakati   103
Razak Report   149, 152
readers' responses   125, 134–137
reading comprehension   80, 158
reduced vowels   14, 67
reduplication   35, 39
regional hub   18, 176
regularisation   13, 26, 41
regulated spaces   126, 140–141
religion   90, 95, 103
research excellence   174
rhythm   65, 68–69
rhythmic   70
risk taking   166
role play (interactive activity)   157
roofing language (*Dachsprache*)   97
Royal Commission of Inquiry   127
rubber crop   102

Sabah   3, 5, 99, 105–106, 125–128, 130–132, 135, 137–141
Sabah and Sarawak Superblog   137, 144
Sabah Land and Survey Department   130
Sabah Ports Authority   130
Sabah Malay   127
Salako   103
Sandakan   130
Sarawak   3–5, 18, 91, 99, 102–122, 125–126, 128–133, 135, 137–141
Sarawak Dayak Iban Association (SADIA)   133
Sarawak Land and Survey Department   130
Sarawak Malay   115, 128, 139
scaffolding   82
science and mathematics   150–151
second language   8, 12, 14, 46, 41, 47, 58, 89, 99
second language acquisition   9, 11, 27, 61
Second World War   105
secondary schools   6, 15, 80–81, 105–107, 109–111, 130, 151–160, 182
See Hua Daily News   131, 144
segmental features   65–85
Sekolah Menengah Kebangsaan (SMK) Katibas   130, 144
Sekolah Menengah Kebangsaan (SMK) Sandakan   130, 144
Selangor   6
self-access learning (SAL)   152, 155
Serian   102, 104–105
settler speech community (STL)   58–59, 61
Seventh Day Adventists   103–105
Sikh temple   95
simplification   12–13, 15, 25–26, 39, 41
simplified expressions   193
Singapore   3, 9, 25, 48, 66, 68, 91, 98–99, 152, 175, 177
Singapore Colloquial English   98
Singapore English (SE)   15, 98
Singgai   104
Singlish   9
Sinhalese   34
smart phone   181
Smart School Project   156
SMK (National Secondary School)   105, 144
social media   115, 125, 133, 135, 138–141
solidarity   96–99

songs   113, 115, 147
songs (interactive activity)   154, 157
Sony   181
Spanish   55, 93, 126
spectrum   50, 71–72
sporadic changes   55–56
standard BE   193
Standard English   9, 14, 25–28, 30, 32, 33, 38
    40–41, 60, 140, 157, 193
Standard Malay   89–90, 94, 97, 128
Standard Malaysian English   14
standard pronunciation   60
standards of English   16, 18, 114, 153
Stockholm   180
stress   13, 65–71, 75–76, 78–82, 85
structural approach   152–153
structural nativisation   59
student transit point   175
substrate influence   26, 39
substrate languages   26, 41
Sumatra   3
suprasegmental features   68–70, 80, 82
Swahili   34
syllabification   71
syntactic variation   26–27, 29, 33, 38, 41

Ta'ee   104
tags   13
Taiwan   181
Tamil   6, 11, 25, 31, 46, 47, 89, 90, 135, 149
teachers   7–8, 10, 14–15, 80–81, 104, 106, 111,
    137, 148, 153–155, 157, 162–167, 174
textbook   75
TH sounds   14, 17, 45–62
Thailand   3
The Borneo Post   131–132, 135, 137
The Star   11, 27, 30–33, 160
third language   47
threatened languages   128
Three Circles   9

three R's   154
Top Global University Project   185
tourism   89
tuition   113
twinning   150
Twitter   138

uncountable nouns – see noncount nouns
United Kingdom (UK)   8, 98, 152, 175–176, 178
United States   98, 152, 175, 179, 185
universities   7, 8, 18, 71, 150, 158, 160, 162,
    172–186
University of Malaya (UM)   8, 90–91, 173, 175
University of Reading   176
University of Tokyo   173–174
unregulated spaces   126, 140–141
Utusan Borneo   131–132, 135

videos   109, 120, 126, 147, 164, 166
Vietnam   3
Vision 2020   8, 155
vocabulary   70, 82, 154, 156, 158
voice projection   70
voiceless stops   45, 57
VOT (voice onset time)   45, 49–53
vowels   14, 55, 65, 67

websites   125–144
West Malaysia   3, 5, 105–106, 125, 126, 130,
    135, 138
White Rajahs   104
Wikipedia   92, 98, 100–101, 127–128
worksheets   154
World Englishes   17, 68, 133, 194
world university ranking   172–174, 185
World Wide Web (www)   126, 135, 137, 140,
    147

Yahoo   140
YouTube   166

Printed in the United States
By Bookmasters